NO PITY

NO PITY

People with Disabilities Forging a New Civil Rights Movement

Joseph P. Shapiro

TIMES BOOKS

RANDOM HOUSE

*For my parents,
Gertrude and Harold Shapiro,
and for Suzanne*

Library of Congress Cataloging-in-Publication Data

Shapiro, Joseph P.
    *No pity : people with disabilities forging a new civil rights movement /
Joseph P. Shapiro.—1st ed.*
        p.   cm.
    Includes index.
    ISBN 0-8129-1964-5
    *1. Handicapped—Civil rights—United States. 2. Discrimination
against the handicapped—United States—History. 3. Handicapped—
Government policy—United States—History. I. Title.*
HV1553.S52   1993
323.3—dc20   92-34751

Manufactured in the United States of America
9 8 7 6 5 4 3 2

First Edition

BOOK DESIGN BY OVER/CC DESIGN

Acknowledgments

Above all, my most profound thanks go to the hundreds of people with disabilities who have generously and patiently told me about their lives and how the gap between the way they view themselves and the way others insist on seeing them creates barriers to their full inclusion in American life. Since 1988, when I first began writing about disability rights issues, their openness and eagerness to tell their stories and history facilitated my role as an observer of their movement.

I cannot adequately express my appreciation to everyone who helped me understand disability issues and assisted my reporting. Beyond those I have featured in these pages, I need to thank many others, including Liz Savage, Judy Heumann, Colleen Wieck, Paul Longmore, Evan Kemp, Mark Johnson, Lex Frieden, Temple Grandin, Bridgetta Bourne, Jean Stewart, Michela Perrone, Dr. Henry Betts, Mark Lewis, Ginny Thornburg, Laura Cooper, Anne Marie Pecht, Bob Williams, Karen Franklin, Marylou Breslin, Maria Ledger, Tom Hlavacek, Nancy Hansen-Bennett, George Covington, Bob Rosenberg, Barbara Blease, Connie Martinez, Sandra Jensen, Tom Hopkins, Beverly Evans, Rosalie Winard, Andi Farbman, and Bob Perske. I feel particularly indebted to members of the vibrant and growing disability press, journalists who have covered the issues of disabled people long before those of us in the mainstream press thought their issues to be of importance. Among those are Mary Johnson of *The Disability Rag,* Cyndi Jones and Bill Stothers of *Mainstream,* Lucy Gwin of *This Brain Has a Mouth,* Mary Jane Owen of Disability Focus, Victoria Medgyesi of *Fourth Wave,* columnist Dianne Piastro and Joan Headley of *Rehabilitation Gazette.*

One of the joys of writing this book was the opportunity to renew my friendship with Jim, described in the tenth chapter. Our friendship has taught me much about what it means for a person to be labeled and segregated, as well as a little bit about the dilemmas and battles that parents, family and friends face when they advocate for someone with a developmental disability. I thank Jim for agreeing to let me tell his story (and for the two notebooks he gave me after I told him I was writing a book). Most of all, I enjoyed being able to help Jim accomplish some of his goals and could not have done so without tremendous help from those who also befriended Jim and who led me through the often mind-boggling social service system, particularly Marijo McBride, Colleen Wieck, again, and Steven Schmit. Jim's family—his sisters and brothers and his marvelous aunt Evelyn—were caring and helping. I am also indebted to Kay Hendrikson, David Hancox, Anita Schermer, Luther Grandquist, Alex Henry, Jan Menke, Deb Lenway, Corinne Fowler, Larry Reiss, Dan McCarthy, Kathy Dohmeier, Deb Holtz, Nancy Gurney, Joyce Syverson, Jill Bengs, Irving Martin, John Norman, Sue Abderholden, Angela and Rick Amado, Nancy Gertz-Larson, Roger Strand, the staff at Robert E. Miller

Homes, and Scott County. Jim is fortunate to live in a house with capable, caring staff, led by Bob and Char Vollbrecht and Karen Behm, and to have good neighbors like Jim and Diane Bergquist.

Many friends and coworkers helped and encouraged me during the writing of this book. Among them are Lee Rainie, Merrill McLoughlin, Mike Ruby, Don Baer, Jerry Buckley, Peter Bernstein, Roger Rosenblatt, Abigail Trafford, Gordon Witkin, Jeff Katz, Leslee Bliss Kukie, Amy Saltzman, Al Sanoff, Ellen Goldstein, Meg Roggensack, Mike Janik, Elliot Staffin, Janet Bass, Stacy Ettinger, Marjorie Shapiro, Ben Griffin, Peggy Argus, Scott Argus, Eleanor Greenfield, Orr Kelly, and Susan Vavrick. I benefited by being able to at times rely upon the immensely talented and resourceful library staff at *U.S. News & World Report.*

Neither this book nor my interest in exploring disability issues would have been possible without the assistance of the Alicia Patterson Foundation. Long before disability issues were fashionable, Peggy Engel understood the importance of the issue and I am particularly grateful for her encouragement. I thank members of the foundation's board for their confidence, especially Joe Albright and Alice Arlen. And in taking this from reporting to publication, many thanks go to my agent, Gail Ross, for her energy and skill and to my talented editors at Times Books, Betsy Rapoport and Peter Smith. Thanks go to them and their colleagues for their painstaking attention to this book and their many fine suggestions.

I enjoyed sharing my discoveries for this book with Suzanne Greenfield. She provided support and strength and—as she read every word—always wise and thoughtful suggestions.

Contents

NO PITY

Introduction
You Just Don't Understand

Nondisabled Americans do not understand disabled ones.

That was clear at the memorial service for Timothy Cook, when longtime friends got up to pay him heartfelt tribute. "He never seemed disabled to me," said one. "He was the least disabled person I ever met," pronounced another. It was the highest praise these nondisabled friends could think to give a disabled attorney who, at thirty-eight years old, had won landmark disability rights cases, including one to force public transit systems to equip their buses with wheelchair lifts. But more than a few heads in the crowded chapel bowed with an uneasy embarrassment at the supposed compliment. It was as if someone had tried to compliment a black man by saying, "You're the least black person I ever met," as false as telling a Jew, "I never think of you as Jewish," as clumsy as seeking to flatter a woman with "You don't act like a woman."

Here in this memorial chapel was a small clash between the reality of disabled people and the understanding of their lives by others. It was the type of collision that disabled people experience daily. Yet any discordancy went unnoticed even to the well-meaning friends of a disability rights fighter like Cook. To be fair to the praise givers, their sincere words were among the highest accolade that Americans routinely give those with disabilities. In fairness, too, most disabled people gladly would have accepted the compliment some fifteen years before, the time when the speakers' friendships with Cook had begun. But most people with disabilities now think differently. It is not that disabled people are overly sensitive. But as a result of an ongoing revolution in self-perception, they (often along with their families) no longer see their physical or mental limitations as a source of shame or as something to overcome in order to inspire others. Today they proclaim that it is okay, even good, to be disabled. Cook's childhood polio forced him to wear heavy corrective shoes, and he walked with difficulty. But taking pride in his disability was for Cook a celebration of the differences among people and gave him a respectful understanding that all share the same basic desires to be full participants in society.

Never has the world of disabled people changed so fast. Rapid advances in technology, new civil rights protections, a generation of better-educated disabled students out of "mainstreamed" classrooms, a new group consciousness, and political activism mean more disabled people are seeking jobs and greater daily participation in American life. But prejudice, society's low expectations, and an antiquated welfare and social service system frustrate these burgeoning attempts at independence. As a result, the new aspirations of people with disabilities have gone unnoticed and misunderstood by mainstream America. This book attempts to explain, to nondisabled people as well as to many disabled ones, how the world and self-perceptions of disabled people are changing. It looks at the rise of what is called the disability rights movement—the new thinking by disabled people that there is no pity or tragedy in disability, and that it is society's myths, fears, and stereotypes that most make being disabled difficult.

There are hundreds of different disabilities. Some are congenital; most come later in life. Some are progressive, like muscular dystrophy, cystic fibrosis, and some forms of vision and hearing loss. Others, like seizure conditions, are episodic. Multiple sclerosis is episodic and progressive. Some conditions are static, like the loss of a limb. Still others, like cancer and occasionally paralysis, can even go away. Some disabilities are "hidden," like epilepsy or diabetes. Disability law also applies to people with perceived disabilities such as obesity or stuttering, which are not disabling but create prejudice and discrimination. Each disability comes in differing degrees of severity. Hearing aids can amplify sounds for most deaf and hard-of-hearing people but do nothing for others. Some people with autism spend their lives in institutions; others graduate from Ivy League schools or reach the top of their professions.

Medicine once promised to wipe out disability by finding cures. Instead, doctors only spurred a disability population explosion by keeping people alive longer. In World War I, only four hundred men survived with wounds that paralyzed them from the waist down, and 90 percent of them died before they reached home. But in World War II, two thousand paraplegic soldiers survived, and over 85 percent of them were still alive in the late 1960s. The development of antibiotic drugs and new medical procedures improved the odds. As recently as the 1950s, death remained likely in the very early stages of a spinal cord injury as a result of respiratory, bladder, and other health complications. Now doctors neutralize those problems, and paraplegics and quadriplegics can live long, healthy lives.

Similarly, after World War II, the development of chemotherapy from wartime gas experiments allowed many people to survive cancer. Insulin allowed others to live with diabetes. And in the 1980s, hospital trauma centers modeled after Vietnam War helicopter evacuation units began saving people with severe head injuries from auto accidents and other traumas. In the mid-1970s, 90 percent of people with severe head injuries died; today 90 percent live. Premature babies born at twenty-three or twenty-four weeks old, instead of the usual forty weeks, live now, too. The world's smallest baby, weighing 9.9 ounces, was saved by doctors in Chicago in 1989. In the early 1980s, it was a rarity for extremely low birth-weight infants to survive. Today, almost 50 percent weighing as little as one pound, two ounces, to one pound, ten ounces, survive, and the majority will have some disabling neurological condition.

The graying of America, too, expands the ranks of the disabled. One-third of disabled Americans are sixty-five or older. Today, 32 million Americans, or about 13 percent of the population, are over age sixty-five; by the year 2020 the older population is expected to hit 51 million people, or 17 percent. This will bring about an increase in potentially disabling chronic conditions such as cardiovascular disease and rheumatoid arthritis, as well as cancer. But older people have avoided affiliation with the disability rights movement. They have grown up with prejudices about a disabled life being a sad and worthless one. Many fear the same stigma will be used to take away their independence. The concerns of disabled and older people overlap—both seek to maximize independence and stay out of institutions—and the two could become forceful allies. But the shame of disability will have to ease first.

There are some 35 million to 43 million disabled Americans, depending on who does the counting and what disabilities are included. In 1991 the Institute of Medicine, using federal health survey data, came up with a total of 35 million—one of every seven Americans—who have a disability that interferes with daily activities like work or keeping a household. "Disability ranks as the nation's largest public health problem, affecting not only individuals with disabling conditions and their immediate families, but also society at large," the report concludes.

During debate on the Americans with Disabilities Act, lawmakers, President Bush, advocates, and members of the media freely used the higher figure of 43 million. That number came from other federal data. But even this figure did not include people with learning disabilities, some mental illness, those with AIDS, or people who are HIV positive and have other conditions covered under the civil rights legislation. Researchers cannot agree on the size of the disability population because they have no consensus on what constitutes disability, notes Mitchell LaPlante of the Disability Statistics Program. Most researchers like LaPlante use activity limitation as the definition. Many disability rights advocates, however, include health conditions that may not be limiting but still stigmatize or cause discrimination, like having had cancer. Some even looser estimates that include any disease or chronic health condition count 120 million or more disabled Americans. Some 31 million Americans, for example, have arthritis, but it limits the activities of only 7 million.

There are some 30 million African-Americans. So, even at the lowest estimate, disabled people could be considered the nation's largest minority. Not all disabled people, however, see themselves as part of a minority group. Many even deny they are disabled, to avoid the taint accompanying that label.

Disability, however, is the one minority that anyone can join at any time, as a result of a sudden automobile accident, a fall down a flight of stairs, cancer, or disease. Fewer than 15 percent of disabled Americans were born with their disabilities. "Disability knows no socioeconomic boundaries," notes Patrisha Wright, the Washington lobbyist for the Disability Rights Education and Defense Fund. "You can become disabled from your mother's poor nutrition or from falling off your polo pony."

And since disability catches up with most of us in old age, it is a minority that we all, if we live long enough, join. "It doesn't matter if your name is Kennedy or Rockefeller, or Smith or Jones, your family's been touched," says Wright.

My own look at disability culture began with a simple phone call in 1988, the type that reporters get daily, from a public relations woman. Would I write about a man whom her group, the National Multiple Sclerosis Society, had flown to New York to honor as their Man of the Year? They had put him up in a hotel across the street from the club where he was to be feted. But getting across the street had been bizarrely difficult. There were no curb cuts at the end of the block, making his hotel a remote island in the middle of Manhattan. Taxicabs could not pick up the man's heavy battery-powered wheelchair. Buses lacked wheelchair lifts. So the MS Society had hired a van with a special hydraulic lift simply to transport this man across the street. It was an interesting story, but not something that I could write for my weekly newsmagazine. I was looking, I explained, for something with broad national significance, something important that was happening in the lives of all disabled people throughout the country. The persistent PR woman, Arney Rosenblat, called back. There was something gathering momentum around the country called the disability rights movement, she said. That very week in Washington, members of an obscure government council were meeting to complete their version of the Americans with Disabilities Act, a bill to give disabled people the civil rights protection that had already been extended to blacks, women, and ethnic minorities.

A few days later, I sat in a conference room in a modern marble-and-glass Washington hotel where two dozen men and women had come together to finish writing the bill. In Washington, drafting legislation is an everyday occurrence. And this bill was being written by an utterly anonymous presidentially appointed council. However laudable their goal, the members were putting together dreamy, pie-in-the-sky legislation. Lobbyists for business groups were already lined up to crush it. Congress and the White House would pay it no more than passing attention.

Yet I was drawn in by the impassioned talk in the room. Disabled people were a vast minority group, it was being argued, oppressed by discrimination. Some of the obvious disabilities were represented on the council: spinal cord injuries, hearing loss, neuromuscular diseases like muscular dystrophy, polio, and visual impairments.

Even more enticing to me was that this civil rights legislation was being drafted by thirteen politically conservative members of an unnoted federal council, all of whom had been appointed by President Ronald Reagan. The Reagan Administration had always seemed hostile to civil rights causes. Now, members of the National Council on the Handicapped, out of step with the president who had chosen them, were drafting a sweeping civil rights bill.

Still, while this was interesting, I was not sure that I saw a story. I left the hotel. The U.S. Capitol rose majestically a few blocks to the south. Outside the hotel lobby, I stood in a line for a taxi. Behind me came a young man in a suit, pushing the wheels of his bright orange wheelchair. There were two cabs at the curb. The doorman signaled for the first cab in line, which drove up the circular drive to pick me up. The second taxi, a station wagon, started moving too. But then the driver jerked the vehicle in an abrupt U-turn and sped off down the avenue toward the Capitol. As I got into my cab, I glanced back at the man in the wheelchair, now waiting to see if another taxi would come along. His face showed no anger, no emotion at all, as if getting passed up by cabdrivers was an everyday occurrence. I was reminded of the MS Society's Man of the Year, unable to cross the street in one of the world's most modern cities, stranded without transportation. The cabdriver had spotted the

man's wheelchair. He did not want to be bothered helping to
fold the man's chair and lift it into the back of the station wagon.
If not for cabs, how would this man get back to his office or to
his home? Few buses in Washington had wheelchair lifts. The
subway system was accessible, assuming the elevator at his stop
was working. But the subway reached only some parts of the
city. Access to transportation, then, would circumscribe where
the man lived and where he worked, or if he even worked at all.
If people like him were precluded from working, then they
would depend on welfare. If a society expected its disabled
people not to work and instead need public assistance, would it
even try to give them a decent education? Back at my office, I
began writing my first story about disability as a rights issue.

My next epiphanic encounter with the disability rights
movement would come just a few weeks later, in March of 1988,
when students at Gallaudet University, the nation's only four-
year liberal arts school for the deaf, demanded the selection of
the first deaf president in the school's 124-year history. When
the one hearing candidate was chosen instead, outraged students
protested, closing down the school. It was hypocritical, students
told me, for a school that boasted of readying deaf students for
the world to think a deaf educator unfit to lead them. Once
again, I was intrigued, this time by the moral certainty of these
students rebelling against the paternalistic attitudes of school
officials.

From these beginnings, I set out to understand the new
point of view of disabled Americans. In the five years since, I
have conducted over two thousand interviews with several hundred people. In the course of that work, I took a one-year
sabbatical, on a fellowship from the Alicia Patterson Foundation,
specifically to study the disability rights movement. As a journalist covering social policy issues for *U.S. News & World Report*,
I found that there was a disability angle to any subject I covered,
from access to health care to aging, from abortion to prenatal
care, from education to work, from welfare to civil rights.

I also discovered a unique movement that had much to teach other social and civil rights movements. The disability movement is a mosaic movement for the 1990s. Diversity is its central characteristic. No one leader or organization can claim to speak for all disabled people. It is accepted, as a matter of course, that members of the disability cause will hold shades of belief and not hew to an overriding orthodoxy. All social crusades are made up of people with complex and varying opinions. But today the black civil rights and feminist movements, in particular, are perceived as struggling with such diversity of thought and weakened by challenges to traditional thinking. The result is to diminish our appreciation of the enormous change each cause has brought about. Without one highly visible leader, the disability movement has gone largely unnoticed by nondisabled people. But by its acceptance of differences, the campaign for disability rights has forged a powerful coalition of millions of people with disabilities, their families, and those that work with them. People with disabilities have been a hidden, misunderstood minority, often routinely deprived of the basic life choices that even the most disadvantaged among us take for granted. In the last twenty to thirty years, little noticed alongside the civil rights struggles of African-Americans, women, gays and lesbians, and other minorities, another movement has slowly taken shape to demand for disabled people the fundamental rights that have already been granted to all other Americans. It has led to the emergence of a group consciousness, even the start of a disability culture, which did not exist nationally even as recently as the late 1970s.

This book is in part a chronicle of the formation of this movement and the issues and identities that define it. At the same time, I hope to help draw attention to the political and social issues that have yet to be resolved. There is potent and widespread support for the movement's accomplishments and goals among disabled people, their families, and friends, and even many of the charity and professional groups that are so often the target of the movement's anger, but the struggle is far from over.

CHAPTER 1

TINY TIMS, SUPERCRIPS, AND THE END OF PITY

The poster child is a surefire tug at our hearts. The children picked to represent charity fund-raising drives are brave, determined, and inspirational, the most innocent victims of the cruelest whims of life and health. Yet they smile through their "unlucky" fates—a condition that weakens muscles or cuts life expectancy to a brutish handful of years, a birth "defect" or childhood trauma. No other symbol of disability is more beloved by Americans than the cute and courageous poster child—or more loathed by people with disabilities themselves.

"Pity oppresses," complains Cyndi Jones, who publishes and edits *Mainstream,* a national disability magazine. No other symbols of disability play up pity more, Jones says, than charity telethons and their poster children. Jones should know; she is a former poster child herself.

Jones remembers feeling like Cinderella when, at age five,

she was chosen as the March of Dimes poster girl in St. Louis. It was 1956. A photographer flew in from New York and outfitted her in fine, frilly party dresses. She was kissed by the mayor. Her image—smiling gamely and holding on to her crutches—was painted on a huge billboard in the heart of downtown. She was a television celebrity, too, having appeared on the January telethon. There, she touched hearts—and opened wallets—across St. Louis when she dropped her heavy aluminum crutches at a producer's instruction and walked a few wobbly and terrifying steps before falling with a clumsy thud to the stage. It was good drama for a telethon, although the young girl had cried at the thought of having to abandon her crutches, knowing she would not get very far.

The Cinderella spell was broken for good a few months later in Jones's first-grade classroom when her teacher handed out a flyer urging parents to sign up their children for a polio vaccination. PARALYTIC POLIO IS INCREASING AGAIN, declared the headline across the top of the page. VACCINATE YOUR FAMILY NOW AGAINST POLIO. Underneath were two photos. One was of a young brother and sister, holding hands and joyfully skipping through a field. Over their picture was stamped: THIS. Next to them was a picture of Jones, leaning grimly on her braces, hair curled, decked out in one of her new party dresses. The caption over Jones's picture said: NOT THIS. Jones slid down in her seat, embarrassed, hurt, feeling "invalid," she recalls, and holding back tears. She hoped none of her classmates would recognize her but knew every one of them would. She now understood with a bitter clarity. It had all been a lie; she was not special—she and her polio were feared.

That Jones and most other disabled people have come to find the poster child an oppressive symbol reflects the fact that a disability rights movement is radically reshaping the world of people with disabilities. The 35 million to 43 million disabled Americans have come to take a growing pride in being identified as disabled. And, like blacks, women, and gays before them, they are challenging the way America looks at them.

Rejected is society's deeply held thinking of tin cups and Tiny Tim—the idea that disabled people are childlike, dependent, and in need of charity or pity. People with disabilities are demanding rights, not medical cures. To Jones, there is nothing tragic about the childhood polio that resulted in her needing a wheelchair or a three-wheeled, motorized scooter to get around. Disability becomes a tragedy only when she and her husband, Bill Stothers, who also uses a wheelchair, cannot get into a restaurant or are kicked out of a movie theater because the manager decides their scooter and wheelchair make them a "fire hazard," as happened near their home in San Diego.

But what if a miracle cure were developed overnight? Wouldn't Jones eagerly swallow a magic pill that would wipe away the lingering paralysis of her polio and let her walk again? She answers quickly: No. "It's the same thing as asking a black person would he change the color of his skin," says Jones. That is not to deny that being disabled is difficult. Some people with disabilities have persistent pain or chronic poor health. Many can expect shortened life expectancies and loss of independence over time. For Jones, as with other polio survivors, there is the fear that her muscles will deteriorate with age and that, in addition to lacking mobility, she will lose the ability to care for herself. Yet, as Jones sees it, "The main thing disabled people need to do is to claim their disability, to feel okay about it. Even if you don't like the way society treats you as a disabled person, it's part of your experience, it's part of how you come to be who you are."

And that is why the poster child image oppresses. "The poster child says it's not okay to be disabled," argues Jones. "It plays on fear. It says this could happen to you, your child, or your grandchild. But it says, if you just donate some money, the disabled children will go away."

The early poster child campaigns of the mid-1940s and

1950s did "evoke images of cure," says Marilynn Phillips, a Morgan State University professor of folklore who has studied images of poster children. There were never poster adults. Disability was barely tolerable—and only to be pitied—when it struck cute and innocent children. It was unmentionable in adults. The poster child was pictured often on the lap or in the arms of a protective adult, who, the ad copy suggested, could help restore the child's health by donating to the charity. "It was a secular religion. If you sent your money, your dimes, you got miracles. You got cures," says Phillips, who, like Jones, is another regenerate poster child.

"Then something funny happened: not everybody was cured," says Phillips. Dr. Jonas Salk invented his polio vaccine, and the fear of polio subsided. But the vaccine did not cure Jones, Phillips, or the other children and adults who already had the virus. "It was promised we'd be fixed and we weren't," says Phillips. "So something had to be wrong with us," not with the unrealistic expectation that they would be cured. Disabled children became an affront to the country's postwar faith in "technology and progress—the good old American way," contends Phillips. Starting in the mid-1950s, she says, there was a new image in the charity poster child campaigns: the valiant "crippled" child on crutches, trying to walk.

Now, says Phillips, disabled children were "damaged goods" who had to "try harder" to prove themselves worthy of charity and society's respect. If science could not cure disabled people, then society would expect them to cure themselves. It would take hard work, determination, and pluck. "It was the Horatio Alger cripple story," says Phillips. The worthy cripple was expected to overcome his or her disability. "You were expected to be jumping up stairs, even if you used a wheelchair. You were expected to be doing anything you had to do, even if it meant collapsing at the end of the day."

It was not just those with polio but all disabled people who were expected to overcome in this way. For those with polio, however, this expectation proved to be a bitter irony. The "best" polio patients were those who tried hardest to beat their paralysis by building up other, working muscles. They walked on heavy braces and crutches, although it was exhausting. Those who used a wheelchair because it was easier were reproached as lazy. But in the 1980s, medical specialists began reporting studies of postpolio syndrome, the atrophy of a polio survivor's working muscles as he or she aged. Those who had walked on crutches now had to settle for using wheelchairs. Those who had maneuvered push wheelchairs now traded them in for battery-powered ones. The irony was that the "best" patients, those who had exerted themselves the hardest, later seemed to watch their remaining muscles be eaten away the fastest. Doctors had not advised such early exertion out of any medical certainty that walking was physiologically superior to using a wheelchair, says Phillips. They had done so because sociologically it was expected.

The belief that a disability could be overcome led to the rise of the other ruling image of disability: the inspirational disabled person. It is another model deeply moving to most nondisabled Americans and widely regarded as oppressive by most disabled ones. The disability rights movement discards the notion that people with disabilities should be courageous or heroic superachievers, since most disabled people are trying simply to lead normal lives, not inspire anyone. Many disabled people even use a derisive nickname for such people: "supercrips."

The "supercrip" is the flip side of the pitiable poster child. It is just as hurtful, Jones argues, because it implies that a disabled person is presumed deserving of pity—instead of respect—until he or she proves capable of overcoming a physical or mental limitation through extraordinary feats. Today, these "supercrips" remain among our most glorified disabled role models, lavishly lauded in the press and on television. Such uncommon achievers have included Mark Wellman, a paraplegic park ranger who won widespread press coverage for climbing granite peaks in Yosemite National Park, and Terry Fox, a cancer survivor whose run across Canada on an artificial leg became television movie fare. (In an arch cartoon by John Callahan, himself a quadriplegic, two heads mounted on skid carts at a street corner beg with tin cups. The first head says to the second, who is identical except that he is wearing an eyepatch, "People like you are a real inspiration to me!") While prodigious achievement is praiseworthy in anyone, disabled or not, it does not reflect the day-to-day reality of most disabled people, who struggle constantly with smaller challenges, such as finding a bus with a wheelchair lift to go downtown or fighting beliefs that people with disabilities cannot work, be educated, or enjoy life as well as anyone else.

CALLAHAN
©1988

"People like you are a real inspiration to me!"

Even disabled achievers who do not seek such veneration often have it thrust upon them by an adoring public and press. Baseball pitcher Jim Abbott was cheered sincerely but with a

paternalistic fervor during his rookie season. Because he was
born without fingers on his right hand, Abbott has an unconventional way of pitching. He throws with his complete hand,
cradling his pitcher's glove on the other. He had taught himself
how to move the glove onto his left hand in one swift motion
as he completed his pitching delivery. He can catch the ball in
his right hand, then whip off the glove, pick out the ball, and
throw it with his complete hand. *USA Today* led its sports page
with a breathless account of Abbott's first spring training game
in March 1989. ABBOTT SHINES IN ARIZONA read the headline
atop the story that reported that the pitcher had "flourished,"
struck out slugger Jose Canseco, and even "made a smooth pivot
to nail" a runner at second base. A more restrained accounting
from the Associated Press in the same day's *New York Times*
carried the headline ABBOTT STRUGGLES IN DEBUT and reported
a very different game. The "smooth pivot" was actually a
botched play, in which Abbott "allowed a run when he was slow
trying to turn a double play." He may have struck out Canseco,
but he "struggled" with wildness in the two innings he pitched,
during which he gave up a run and walked three batters.

Despite the reverential treatment Abbott got for a mediocre
performance, he was not seeking worship. Like most other disabled people, he wanted only to make it in his profession on
equal terms with everyone else. Abbott knew that his manager,
in search of a pennant, was not going to allow sentimentality to
determine his starting pitching rotation. Abbott did make the
California Angels that year and went on to prove himself one of
the more talented pitchers in professional baseball. Because he
made nothing special of his disability, his unorthodox playing
style soon became secondary to his earned run average.

While Abbott's acceptance on his own terms may be what
disabled people hope for, the poster child and "supercrip" images remain the most significant obstacle to normal interaction
between nondisabled and disabled people. Disability rights ac-

tivist Marylou Breslin can tell a story of how her own reality clashed with stereotypes and prejudice about disability. Awaiting her flight at the airport, the executive director of the Berkeley-based Disability Rights Education and Defense Fund (DREDF) was sitting in her battery-powered wheelchair, in her dressed-for-success businesswoman's outfit, sipping from a cup of coffee. A woman walked by, also wearing a business suit, and plunked a quarter into the plastic cup Breslin held in her hand. The coin sent the coffee flying, staining Breslin's blouse, and the well-meaning woman, embarrassed, hurried on.

Most disabled people can tell similar stories, like National Public Radio's John Hockenberry. He had been the network's prolific West Coast correspondent. But Hockenberry's bosses and colleagues had never met him until one day, a few years after he had begun filing his reports, he showed up at NPR's Washington headquarters. His appearance was jolting. Hockenberry is a paraplegic. Only a few in the newsroom knew this. How, his fellow correspondents wondered, had a man in a wheelchair managed to cover political races or the exploding Mt. Saint Helens volcano? Then they realized, in a disturbing wave of self-recognition, that had they known of his disability, Hockenberry almost certainly never would have been given such challenging assignments. It would have been assumed that he was not able to cover them.

Our society automatically underestimates the capabilities of people with disabilities, observing what I call the Hockenberry Rule. Or, put differently, a disability, of itself, is never as disabling as it first seems. The only thing that could have kept Hockenberry from being an accomplished reporter would have been the paternalistic assumptions of his colleagues.

According to the thinking of the disability rights movement, it is not so much the disabled individual who needs to change, but society. It may be the automatic assumption that a man in a wheelchair cannot get around to do his job. Or that a woman in a wheelchair holding a cup of coffee—even if she is a smartly dressed attorney with a briefcase—is a beggar in need of charity. It may be an employer's refusal to hire a cancer survivor or someone with epilepsy, or a larger societal failure to build offices, houses, hotels, and stores accessible to people in wheelchairs. Says disability rights activist Judy Heumann, "Disability only becomes a tragedy for me when society fails to provide the things we need to lead our lives—job opportunities or barrier-free buildings, for example. It is not a tragedy to me that I'm living in a wheelchair."

For the first time, people with disabilities are defining themselves. They are saying their existence is all right. Mary Johnson, the editor of *The Disability Rag,* the irreverent magazine of the disability rights movement, says the best analogy may be with gay rights. Like homosexuals in the early 1970s, many disabled people are rejecting the "stigma" that there is something sad or to be ashamed of in their condition. They are taking pride in their identity as disabled people, parading it instead of closeting it.

This simple but iconoclastic thinking—that a disability, of itself, is not tragic or pitiable—is at the core of the new disability rights movement. Using it, disabled people have quickly begun to attack discrimination wherever they find it, deriving unexpected power by playing off the very stereotypes they seek to destroy. Consider the case of Evan Kemp, Jr., one of the advisers credited with convincing President George Bush to make disability civil rights a priority of his administration.

Kemp, one might say, was the original Jerry's Kid. His parents, along with parents of other children with muscular dystrophy and related conditions, founded the Muscular Dystrophy Association. In 1947, Kemp, then twelve, had come down with an illness that, for years, confounded doctors. It was initially thought to be amyotrophic lateral sclerosis, better known as Lou Gehrig's disease. A doctor told him to his face that he would die before reaching his fourteenth birthday. When he did not die, doctors decided that he had Duchenne muscular dystrophy and likely would not live beyond his teens. Not until Kemp was twenty-eight was his illness diagnosed properly as Kugelberg-Welander syndrome. The rare muscle-weakening disease related to polio is one of the forty conditions supported by the muscular dystrophy telethon. In 1959, Kemp's mother and other parents put together the first telethon on a television station in Cleveland, where the Kemps lived. Their idea was to use the new medium of television to broadcast a variety show where entertainers and celebrities would ask viewers to donate money for muscular dystrophy medical research. In 1966, Jerry Lewis took over the national telethon, which he would perfect as an extravaganza of Las Vegas glitz and schmaltz. To date, Lewis's Labor Day telethon has raised over $1 billion, and other charities have begun their own telethons. Without question, Lewis's tireless fund-raising built MDA into an organization that would support important scientific work. But Kemp felt that such telethons fostered the stereotype that muscular dystrophy was a tragedy, its "victims" childlike and perpetually sick, and that these misconceptions hurt disabled people more than the condition itself. Kemp, a quadriplegic who uses a wheelchair, would encounter such attitudes often. In 1991, as chairman of the federal Equal Employment Opportunity Commission, he had flown to Jacksonville, Florida, to make a speech. City officials sent an ambulance, instead of a van, to pick him up. Kemp refused to ride in it, since he was not sick. Instead, he flew back to Washington.

A long history of such slights helped put clout behind Kemp's 1981 attack on the Muscular Dystrophy Association's annual Labor Day telethon. On the opinion page of *The New York Times,* Kemp complained that the telethon encouraged prejudices about disabled people. "By arousing the public's fear of the handicap itself, the telethon makes viewers more afraid of handicapped people," wrote Kemp. "Playing to pity may raise money, but it also raises walls of fear between the public and us." Further, by focusing on innocent children, the telethon, he said, "seems to proclaim that the only socially acceptable status for disabled people is their early childhood. The handicapped child is appealing and huggable—the adolescent or mature adult is a cripple to be avoided." Kemp objected that the telethon focused on the tragedy of a small number of children who died from muscular dystrophy, when in reality a far greater number of adults, like himself, led normal lives with neuromuscular conditions. Finally, he charged, "the telethon's critical stress on the need to find cures supports the damaging and common prejudice that handicapped people are 'sick.' As sick people, it follows that we should allow others to take care of all our needs until a cure is found." For one of the few times in its history the telethon collected less money than the year before, the result perhaps of both recession and Kemp's complaint. It would take another decade before large numbers of disabled people would echo Kemp's complaint about the telethon's "pity approach." In large part this was because a broad disability rights mind-set would not flower until the passage of the Americans with Disabilities Act in 1990 and its enactment into law in 1992. It vexed MDA officials that the disability movement's anger was cresting at the moment of some of MDA's most spectacular research success. Most stunning was the finding announced in 1992 of the precise DNA location of the gene that caused myotonic dystrophy. Yet, once again, these breakthroughs were not cures so much as prevention measures. And to the new disability rights movement prevention had ominous overtones. Many activists fear that with the growth of such predictive tests, pregnant women will be expected or coerced to abort fetuses when there is an indication of disability. Others worry that if genetic engineering can one day wipe out an illness, a person who already has that disability will be seen as a freak or devalued as a preventable mistake.

As disabled people asserted their demands for dignity, Jerry Lewis seemed to intensify his mawkish pandering. In a 1990 magazine article, the comedian wrote of imagining himself as one of Jerry's Kids. It would be, he mused, the life of "half a person," stuck in a wheelchair ("that steel imprisonment") to watch the "other cripples" play while wishing he could "play basketball like normal, healthy, vital and energetic people." (To a reporter in Chicago, Lewis used the word "mongoloid," a particularly odious and obsolete term for retardation that seemed jolting coming from the mouth of a self-styled champion of disabled people.) Yet in his magazine article, Lewis also spoke of the need for accessible homes, restaurants, planes, and hotels, making his writing a strange stew of the worst pity stereotypes mixed with a dash of disability rights thinking. The telethon is now a similarly odd concoction. It features a handful of tales of successful children in school or adults at work—a nod to the evolving sensitivities of disabled people and their families—but remains fixed on the fear of disease, the misery of disability, and unfortunate Jerry's Kids doomed to early death. That the children on the telethon were picked for their smiling and cheery personalities makes their impending tragedy all the more pitiable.

But pity opens hearts, and that raises a quandary for charities like MDA: Do they listen to the complaints of critics like Kemp and sacrifice what is considered their best money-making pitch? One Los Angeles columnist, impressed by the $80 million raised in 1991, thought Lewis's critics ungrateful and misguided. He wrote, "Let's ask this last question of the marchers who would like to see Lewis drummed out of the telethon: Just who is going to keep this cash machine going?"

Other charities, however, have junked the pity approach in their telethons. The National Easter Seal Society and United

Cerebral Palsy Associations have turned their shows into vehicles for rights advocacy. The numbers on the tote board climbed steadily, from $23 million in 1985 for Easter Seals to $42 million in 1992, disproving old ideas that a telethon had to make hearts bleed. "Our mission is to enhance the independence of people with disabilities," explains Easter Seals president James E. Williams, Jr., "and that can't be done on the backs of the people we serve by using pity." The charity replaced its poster child with a "representative" child and adult. Those chosen are shown as successfully integrated in their schools, jobs, and communities. "One of the biggest problems facing disabled people is stereotypes. If you portray people as objects of pity, in a mass medium like a telethon which has sixty million viewers, then it only reinforces those stereotypes," says Williams.

Many disabled people, like Kemp, point to the Easter Seals and UCP telethons as acceptable models. But for others, like Marilynn Phillips, "There are no good plantations and there are no good telethons." Indeed, other telethons, even when they avoid pity language, still tend to divide the world between the lucky and unlucky, between us and them. Even the best still play maudlin violin music softly underneath the profiles of adults. There is always an implied and frightening threat that all of us are vulnerable to the same misfortune.

From Image to Action

It is not only those paralyzed by polio and related conditions who have begun to reject our society's image of and expectations for them. Patrisha Wright, president of the Disability Rights Education and Defense Fund, believes that "All disabled people share one common experience—discrimination." Statistics show that disabled people agree. Seventy-four percent of disabled Americans say they share a "common identity" with other disabled people, and 45 percent argue they are "a minority group in the same sense as are blacks and Hispanics," according to a 1985 poll by Louis Harris and Associates. These numbers, reflecting a militant disabled population, may surprise a society that still assumes disabled people will be grateful for charity and eager to be made whole again. If anything, disabled people are far more likely today to view themselves as part of an oppressed minority. Since 1985, the Gallaudet student protests and passage of the Americans with Disabilities Act have broadened the sense of group identity and a commitment to overcoming prejudice.

Often the discrimination is crude bigotry, such as that of a private New Jersey zoo owner who refused to admit children with retardation to the Monkey House, claiming they scared his chimpanzees. It may be intolerance that permitted a New Jersey restaurant owner to ask a woman with cerebral palsy to leave because her different appearance was disturbing other diners. Resentment may have led an airline employee in New York to throw a sixty-six-year-old double amputee on a baggage dolly— "like a sack of potatoes," his daughter complained—rather than help him into a wheelchair and aid him in boarding a jetliner. Others may feel that disabled people are somewhat less than human and therefore fair game for victimization, as when a gang of New Jersey high school athletes allegedly raped a mildly retarded classmate with a baseball bat in 1989. Because of the girl's retardation, a judge later relaxed the rape shield law that existed to protect the privacy of rape survivors. She became twice victimized as the 1992 trial focused on her sexual behavior— including whether she had once delighted in seeing boys naked in a locker room—as much as on the actions of the boys accused of raping her. In a similar case, three volunteer ambulance rescuers allegedly pummeled to death a homeless man with retardation in the back of their ambulance because he annoyed them, as if, in a prosecutor's words, he were "a punching bag."

In other cases, however, the discrimination at issue is more subtle because it is based on the paternalistic assumption that disabled people are not entitled to make their own decisions and lead the lives they choose. One such case was that of Tiffany Callo, a woman with cerebral palsy, who in 1988 fought, unsuccessfully, for custody of her two young sons. California welfare officials asserted that she was too physically disabled to care for them. The state was willing to pay the bill for expensive foster care rather than fund several hours a day of in-home child care to support Callo. Basic rights of parenthood were denied that would have been unquestioned for a nondisabled person. Being a successful parent, after all, has less to do with one's ability to move around than with the love and nurturing that Callo's supporters said she brought to her family. "So what if it takes longer to change a diaper?" asks Callo. "That's where disabled parents do their bonding. It's quality time."

Also troubling was the case of Sharon Kowalski, seriously disabled from a head injury in an automobile accident, who was refused her wish to leave a nursing home to live with her former roommate, Karen Thompson. A court questioned whether she had the judgment to make such a decision. The head injury had impaired some of her mental ability, particularly her short-term memory. Yet Kowalski remained capable of making a choice. She still had wishes, emotions, and knowledge. When I visited Kowalski and Thompson, the tenderness between them was clear. They held hands, and Kowalski smiled broadly as Thompson recounted how the two had recently gone fishing from a boat on the Mississippi River. Kowalski, animated and happy, was clear about wanting to leave the suburban Minneapolis nursing home and move into the new home Thompson had built to be wheelchair accessible. Kowalski spoke briefly, slowly typing out her answers on a small computer with a voice synthesizer that Thompson had bought for her. Mainly, she communicated with smiles and sounds.

It was a scene far different from the one painted by St. Louis

County District Judge Robert Campbell. The judge conceded
that Kowalski, when asked where she chose to live, "has consistently said, 'St. Cloud with Karen.' " But Campbell decided
Kowalski was no longer capable of making choices for herself
and ruled that she needed the continued protection of a nursing
home. The issues were difficult and compounded by Kowalski's
homosexuality. Kowalski's parents denied their daughter could
be a lesbian and claimed she was being exploited by Thompson
to raise money for lesbian causes. (Actually, Thompson had been
a closeted lesbian until Kowalski's accident forced her to go
public.) Campbell noted that another woman now lived with
Thompson and feared this could hurt Kowalski emotionally,
though Kowalski already knew about the other woman from her
occasional trips to Thompson's home. Even if Kowalski regretted her decision, she could always choose to return to a nursing
home or live elsewhere. No nondisabled woman would be denied
her free choice to live with her lesbian lover. The judge's failure
to honor Kowalski's clearly stated wishes was part of the "infan-
tilizing of people with disabilities," complained the late disability rights attorney Timothy Cook. "We're treated like
eternal children." After seven years of court battles, Thompson
finally won guardianship of Kowalski in late 1991.

But the biggest problems of discrimination are more everyday and more entrenched, such as employment bias. Only one-
third of disabled people hold jobs. Two-thirds of the rest say
they can work and would like to work, according to the 1985
Harris poll (the most recent available on the subject), but they
are prevented from doing so because, among other reasons, they
face discrimination in hiring or lack transportation. They "want
to work and can work," instead of being forced to accept welfare,
says Sandra Swift Parrino of the National Council on Disability.
Although she says a disability may limit the type of work a
person can do, more often companies simply do not want to hire
or accommodate physically disabled workers. Those who do not

work collect federal disability and welfare checks, costing nearly
$60 billion a year. When other costs, such as medical treatment
and rehabilitation and lost productivity, are included, it is estimated that the cost of disability to the nation runs $170 billion
a year. "It doesn't make sense to maintain people in a dependency state when those people want to be productive, tax-paying
citizens," argues Jay Rochlin, former director of the President's
Committee on Employment of People with Disabilities.

Rarely does a company say outright that it will not hire a
disabled person. Paul Steven Miller is a dwarf—he prefers to
describe himself as being of "short stature"—who graduated
near the top of his Harvard Law School class in 1986. While his
classmates quickly snared prestigious jobs, he was rejected by
each of the more than forty law firms where he interviewed.
Finally, an attorney in a Philadelphia firm explained that, although the partners were impressed by his credentials, they
feared their clients might see Miller in the office hallway "and
think we're running some sort of circus freak show." Miller now
handles disability discrimination cases for the Los Angeles–
based Western Law Center for Disability Rights.

Even when disabled people have jobs, they earn far less than
their coworkers and are far less likely to be promoted. According
to a study by Syracuse University economist William Johnson,
this is the result of employers' prejudices and their underestimation of disabled workers—not because of limits on the work that
disabled employees can do. Even after Johnson factored in things
such as the possibility of a disabled person's lack of experience
or lowered productivity, disabled men, he found, still make 15
percent less than nondisabled coworkers. For women, there is a
30 percent difference. A 1989 Census Bureau survey supported
Johnson's findings and concluded that the gap between the
earnings of disabled workers and their nondisabled coworkers is
growing. A disabled worker in 1987 made only 64 percent of
what his nondisabled colleagues earned. In 1980, it was 77
percent.

In part, this discrepancy reflects employers' fears about hiring someone with a disability, which remain strongly rooted despite recent prohibitions against discrimination in hiring disabled people. Edward Yelin, a professor of health policy at the University of California, San Francisco, adds that "persons with disabilities, like those from minority races, constitute a contingent labor force." When industries retrench, these contingent workers are the first to lose their jobs. When there is growth, they are the last to be hired.

The workplace is a haywire world for disabled people in other ways as well. For one thing, a job may mean the loss of essential health insurance and Social Security benefits. Historian Paul Longmore is one example. In 1988, he burned a copy of his biography of George Washington outside the Social Security offices in Los Angeles to protest the threat to his benefits. Longmore received a $575 monthly Social Security check and $20,000 a year from state Medicaid that paid for his ventilator and the in-home attendant who helped him live on his own instead of in a nursing home. That money allowed him to get his doctorate in American history and eventually write the biography. But the Social Security law was drawn up at a time when it was assumed that people like Longmore would never work but would always need government assistance. For Longmore to make even minimal income—Social Security disability income recipients are not allowed to have resources of more than $2,000—would be taken as a sign that he was no longer disabled and no longer in need of aid. Since Longmore expected to make about $10,000 in royalties from the book over several years, he would lose all of his benefits yet still be in need of them. It simply did not pay for him to work and be a taxpayer. Since the mid-1980s, Congress has responded to complaints by Longmore and others and rewritten some of these catch-22 rules. One new program lets disabled people on Medicaid—and denied insurance under company health plans because of their preexisting conditions—pay the Medicaid premiums and hold on to their public health insurance. But work disincentives remain.

Disabling Images

Like any other emerging minority group, disabled people have become sensitized to depictions of disability in popular culture, religion, and history. There they find constant descriptions of a disabled person's proper role as either an object of pity or a source of inspiration. These images are internalized by disabled and nondisabled people alike and build social stereotypes, create artificial limitations, and contribute to the discrimination and minority status hated by most disabled people.

In the Old Testament, being blind, lame, deaf, crippled, sick, or diseased is a sign of having done something to incur God's disfavor. Disability is brought on by sin. In the New Testament, people with disabilities are cursed or possessed by evil. Today, many of these traditional views remain in the church. There are evangelical preachers who claim the power to heal those with the proper faith, and the more commonplace Sunday school stories cast the disabled as pitiable. Many churches now make an effort to reach out to people with disabilities, such as the United Methodist General Conference, which revised its hymnal to delete "dumb," "lame," and other references offensive to people with disabilities. Other churches and synagogues, notes Ginny Thornburgh of the National Organization on Disability, welcome disabled worshipers by installing wheelchair ramps, buying large-print hymnals, or providing sign-language interpreters.

Portrayals in literature and popular culture, too, shape our images of disability. Often a disabled character is depicted as helpless and childish, like Tiny Tim in Charles Dickens's "A Christmas Carol," and in need of cure or care from a nondisabled person. But it was more common in classical literature (as it often is today) for an author to exaggerate a disability as an emblem of a character's "sinister, evil or morally flawed" nature, according to Kean College special education professor Arthur Shapiro. William Shakespeare, Shapiro notes, gave Richard III a hunchback, even though the real king had no such disability, to make more ominous and obvious his ability to murder ruthlessly. Shakespeare's king speaks of being "deform'd, unfinished, sent before my time," of dogs barking at him because they were frightened by his looks, and feeling "determined to prove a villain" because of his anger over his disability. Another such villain is Herman Melville's Captain Ahab, who has lost a leg to Moby Dick and his mind in a madly obsessive pursuit of revenge.

These images undergird some of society's deepest fears and prejudices about people with disabilities, says Shapiro in an article co-written with Howard Margolis. "Lenny, the mentally retarded character in Steinbeck's *Of Mice and Men* who killed living things—including a young woman—because he was unaware of his own strength, is an image that may very well be involved in the minds of those who oppose group homes for the developmentally disabled," they write. And journalist Paul Glastris speaks of the blow to his own self-image at finding himself, at fourteen, living in a Shriners Hospital for Crippled Children, being fitted for a prosthetic arm and discovering a mural of the limbless and evil Captain Hook menacing the pretty and good Wendy and Peter Pan.

The modern successor to these diabolical characters is a staple of horror movies. Freddy Krueger, the villain of the *Nightmare on Elm Street* films, was turned into a hateful, sadistic killer because of his disfigurement, caused by a fire that left him more monster than human being. Every movie season has its examples of such fiendish disabled people, from the coldhearted banker in a wheelchair in the 1946 film *It's a Wonderful Life* to Jack Nicholson's demented Joker, disfigured by a fall into a vat of acid, in 1989's hit *Batman,* and Danny DeVito's embittered Penguin, abandoned by his parents when he was born with flippers instead of arms in the 1992 sequel *Batman Returns.*

The precursor of the modern horror movie was the freak show. Scholars of disability history debate whether the carnival sideshows amounted to a crass exploitation of people with disabilities or their glorification. Between the 1860s and early 1900s, disabled people were seen as marvels of nature, not as frightening freaks, argues Robert Bogdan, a Syracuse University professor of special education. The well-appointed Victorian home would have a photo album filled with pictures not only of family members, statesmen, generals, and authors, but of Henry "Zip the Pinhead" Johnson; General Tom Thumb, "the perfect man in miniature"; Chang and Eng, the Siamese twins; or other sideshow attractions. Bogdan argues that with the professionalization of medicine, scientists, and then the public, stopped celebrating these "human oddities," and the freak shows died out. Doctors in the new twentieth century decreed that these freaks were no longer "benign curiosities" but "pathological" and "diseased," Bogdan argues. They became, he says, " 'sick' and to be pitied." Other scholars, including historian David Gerber, claim that the willingness of dwarfs and others to be put on display only shows the extreme extent of their victimization and that other forces, like movies, brought about the end of the freak show. One of the first horror films was the 1932 movie *Freaks,* in which the circus sideshow attractions extract a bitter and bloody revenge on a beautiful aerial artist and her lover, the strongman.

Just as disabled people have begun protesting the power of pictures on a charity telethon, they are objecting, too, to the way they are portrayed in popular culture and the media. Language has been one of the first battlegrounds. Disabled people resent words that suggest they are sick, pitiful, childlike, dependent, or objects of admiration—words that, in effect, convey the imag-

ery of poster children and supercrips. "Invalid" is out, as is
"afflicted with" and "patient," unless the person is really in a
sickbed, or common adjectives such as "brave" and "courageous," since most disabled people are not seeking to be models
of inspiration.

"Disabled" has become the usage of choice, replacing "handicapped" in recent years and becoming the first word to emerge
by consensus from within the disability community itself. More
acceptable still is "person with a disability" (or "who is deaf,"
"who has mental retardation," etc.), since it emphasizes the
individual before the condition. One of the most common at-
tacks on the disability movement is to mock the politically
correct terms often used to describe disability. Yet it is almost
always nondisabled people—relying on the stereotype that a
disabled person should be an inspiration overcoming some challenge—who use prettifying euphemisms. Virtually no disabled
person uses these cute phrases. Concoctions like "the vertically
challenged" are silly and scoffed at. The "differently abled," the
"handi-capable," or the "physically and mentally challenged"
are almost universally dismissed as too gimmicky and too inclusive. "Physically challenged doesn't distinguish me from a
woman climbing Mt. Everest, something certainly I'll never
do," says Nancy Mairs, an essayist and poet with multiple sclerosis. "It blurs the distinction between our lives." Only by using
direct terminology, she argues, will people think about what it
means to be disabled and the accommodations she needs, such
as wheelchair-accessible buildings or grab bars in bathrooms.

Dianne Piastro, who writes the syndicated column "Living
with a Disability," complains that such terms suggest that disability is somehow shameful and needs to be concealed in a
vague generality. "It's denying our reality instead of saying that
our reality, of being disabled, is okay," says Piastro. Mary Johnson, editor of *The Disability Rag,* complains that such euphemis-
tic terms come from nondisabled "do-gooders" who "wouldn't

understand disability culture if we ran over their toes with a wheelchair." These words have "no soul" and "no power," says Johnson. "They're like vanilla custard."

Is there a word with the requisite soul power? There was a surprise when Johnson's magazine surveyed its readers. Newly in vogue among some physically disabled people is the very word that is the ultimate in offensiveness to others: "cripple." "It's like a raised gnarled fist," says Cheryl Wade, a Berkeley, California, performance artist, who likes "crippled" because it is a blunt and accurate description of her body, which has been twisted by rheumatoid arthritis. "Crips," "gimps," and "blinks" have long been for the exclusive, internal use by people of those disabilities. (Terms for nondisabled people include "walkies" and "a.b.s" for able-bodied and "TABs" for the "temporarily able-bodied," a you'll-get-yours-yet reminder that disability hits most of us in old age if not before.)

"Cripple" will not become safe for general usage right away, but its newfound popularity shows that the stigma of disability is being rejected and replaced with a pride in being identified as disabled. Mairs, another who prefers "cripple," compares the change to the civil rights movement's replacement of "Negro" with "black." In reclaiming "cripple," disabled people are taking the thing in their identity that scares the outside world the most and making it a cause to revel in with militant self-pride. That disabled people are reappropriating words to redefine themselves and thinking about "the power of negative language," says Brandeis University sociology professor Irving Kenneth Zola, is a sign of a new and thriving group identity.

Language is not the only arena in which disabled people have begun to appreciate the power of imagery to make or smash stereotypes. With the disability rights movement's emergence, movies and television in the late 1980s and early 1990s began to adopt more positive and realistic portrayals of disabled characters. Disability, after all, can make for compelling drama. Deaf actress Marlee Matlin won an Oscar in 1986 for her passionate portrayal—and lyrical use of sign language—of a deaf student who falls in love with her hearing teacher in *Children of a Lesser God.* In 1989, Dustin Hoffman won an Academy Award for his representation of an autistic savant in *Rainman.* Actor Daniel Day Lewis won the same trophy the following year for his characterization of Irish writer and artist Christy Brown, who had cerebral palsy, in *My Left Foot.* In 1991, Robert DeNiro won other film honors as a man in a postencephalitic trance in the movie *Awakenings,* based on the autobiographical account of neurologist Oliver Sacks's experiments in reaching a ward of patients who had become disabled during the "sleeping sickness" epidemic of 1916 through 1927.

Television, which still loves sugary disability tales for its made-for-television movies, has nonetheless developed positive characters, particularly in longer-running series. In 1989 Chris Burke became the first television star with mental retardation. He plays Corky, the mildly retarded son who goes to mainstreamed high school classes in "Life Goes On." Marlee Matlin depicts a deaf attorney in "Reasonable Doubts." And nondisabled actor Larry Drake plays Benny Stulwicz, the office clerk with mental retardation in "L.A. Law." Such is the power of television that a corporate personnel director called a local retardation agency to inquire if they had any "Bennys" for hire.

The most consistently positive portrayals have come, perhaps surprisingly, from advertising. Few depictions have shattered myths of dependency and inability more quickly than the DuPont television commercial featuring Vietnam veteran Bill Denby, with two prosthetic legs, playing a spirited game of basketball on an urban blacktop. Similarly, a Budweiser commercial of a wheelchair marathoner with his fit and stunning blonde lover helped tear down widespread assumptions that to be paralyzed is to be sexually dysfunctional. Kmart, Toyota, McDonald's, Levi's, Xerox, IBM, AT&T, and many others have included disabled people in print and television ads, mixing them in with nondisabled people, to give the positive image that they are just like anyone else.

That advertising would play such a corrective role bespeaks the power of the disability rights movement: disabled people have emerged as a consumer group. They are mighty in part because of the millions of dollars they spend. As more disabled people move into competitive jobs, they have more money to spend. Another source of strength is simply their large numbers. The Minneapolis-based Target department store chain put its first model with mental retardation, a young girl with Down syndrome, in a Sunday newspaper advertising insert in 1990. "That ad hit doorsteps at six A.M. Sunday and a half hour later my phone was ringing," recalls George Hite, the company's vice-president for marketing. "It was the mother of a girl with Down syndrome thanking me for having a kid with Down syndrome in our ad. 'It's so important to my daughter's self-image,' she said." That ad, one small picture among dozens in the circular, generated over two thousand letters of thanks to stunned Target executives.

There is a new militancy, too, as people with disabilities have come to recognize the strength of their numbers. Their anger is often directed, in protests and economic boycotts, at stereotypical depictions in movies and television. Members of the San Francisco–based National Stuttering Project picketed outside movie theaters showing *A Fish Called Wanda* in 1988, and eventually got a letter from the film's producer explaining that a character who stutters in the film because of his repressed anger was not to be taken as a portrayal of all people who stutter. The National Stuttering Project argued that its members are hurt by widespread assumptions that people stutter because of shyness or some emotional disorder when in fact they are no different psychologically from anyone else, and stuttering may be more related to physiological or genetic conditions.

Similarly, in 1991, members of the National Federation of the Blind protested outside of ABC network offices around the country in complaint of a Mr. Magoo–like character in the slapstick sitcom "Good and Evil." The blind character destroys a chemistry laboratory by clumsily wielding his long white cane and then woos a fur coat on a coatrack, mistaking it for a woman. After four major companies pulled their advertisements, the network announced after only five episodes that the show was canceled.

Some might dismiss such objections as a case of disabled people having no sense of humor or being overly sensitive and politically correct. "If we were at a point where blindness was not regarded as a negative and if we had truly achieved equal opportunity, then we could laugh and say this is not a realistic portrayal of a blind person," says federation official James Gashel. But for people with visual handicaps who face discrimination in everyday life and a 70 percent rate of unemployment, contends Gashel, such depictions are dangerous. They confirm, he says, every debilitating myth and stereotype that "people hold to some degree to be true about blind people—that you won't know what room you're in until somebody tells you; you won't know a man from a woman unless you touch them; you'll break things, you'll stumble over things; you cannot perform in your profession competently; and that you can't measure up in competing with sighted people."

Gashel's unemployment figures for blind people are illustrated by the folly of the State Department in refusing to hire Avraham Rabby, who passed the Foreign Service exam three times with near-perfect scores, spoke four languages, and was impeccably educated. But Foreign Service officials argued that he needed to be able to see another person's "body language" in order to handle negotiations. Most ridiculous, complained the Equal Employment Opportunity Commission in 1987, was that the State Department recruited disabled people like Rabby but then refused to hire them. After four years of fighting, Rabby was accepted into the diplomatic corps in 1991.

Fear, disabled people understand, is the strongest feeling they elicit from nondisabled people. Fear underlies compassion for the poster child and celebration of the supercrip. After a spinal cord tumor left him a paraplegic, anthropologist Robert F. Murphy studied his condition through an ethnographer's eyes. Disabled people "contravene all the values of youth, virility, activity and physical beauty that Americans cherish," he wrote in *The Body Silent.* "We are subverters of the American Ideal, just as the poor are betrayers of the American Dream," argues Murphy. "The disabled serve as constant, visible reminders to the able-bodied that the society they live in is a counterfeit paradise, that they too are vulnerable. We represent a fearsome possibility." So society shields itself from this "fearsome possibility" by distancing disabled people and treating them as social inferiors.

When people insist on seeing him as either a supercrip, a poster child, or an affront, says historian Paul Longmore, he knows he represents their worst nightmare. Longmore walks slowly because his body was bent by childhood polio, and he must use a ventilator at night. A stranger once approached him on the street and said, "If I were you, I'd kill myself." Usually, people express such sentiments indirectly in overblown admiration or pitying sympathy. In this case, the stranger's tone made it clear that the sight of a man with a severe disability was an offense, implying that Longmore ought to take his advice.

The force of fear was evident in 1991 when Los Angeles television news anchor Bree Walker Lampley got pregnant. Call-in radio show host Jane Norris of KFI dedicated two hours to the proposition that Walker Lampley was being morally irresponsible by bringing a disabled child into the world. Walker Lampley has a condition called ectrodactyly, a partial fusing of the bones in the fingers and toes. It is a relatively minor disability. The unconventional appearance of her hands did not impede her professionally. Her condition did not even prevent her from typing out news stories on a computer. Nor did it stop her from being a good mother. Her daughter by a previous marriage also had inherited ectrodactyly.   -

Whose business, then, was it that her child had a 50 percent chance of inheriting the same condition? "Face facts here, having that sort of deformity is a strike against you in life. People judge you by your appearance," said talk-show host Norris, making clear her own position. "By the shape of your hands, and the shape of your body and the shape of your face. They just do. They make value judgments about you. Whether it's right or whether it's wrong, it just is. And there are so many options available—adoption, surrogate parenting. . . . It would be difficult to bring myself to morally cast my child forever to disfigured hands."

All the prejudices that disabled people say stem from the poster child and inspirational cripple images were on display in Norris's ugly call-in show. There was pity for a life of imagined misery. "It's a horribly cruel thing to have the baby, knowing it's going to be deformed," said one caller, Valerie from Mission Viejo. "If I were a child and I was going to grow up knowing that my parents had me anyway, I think I would truly hate them all their lives no matter how good they were to me." There was the idea, too, that a disabled person commands respect only to the extent that he or she can be an object of inspiration. "I want to know what her motive is for having this child," demanded Lisa of Costa Mesa. "What's to guarantee that this child will be as successful as the mother in overcoming this . . . ? Actually, I think it's kind of irresponsible." There was the fear of a life not worth living. "I would rather not be alive than have a disease like that," said Claire from Oceanside. "I'm not talking perfection, but this is ridiculous—no hands, no feet." And there was the notion that without cure there was no reason or right to live. "To stop something like that, which is very bad [and] not curable,

you have to start with reproduction," added Kathy from El-
sinore. "And if you know the possibility exists, don't have them
[babies]."

Aaron James Lampley was born healthy. He, too, inherited
ectrodactyly. Walker Lampley brought a complaint—filed by
Paul Steven Miller, the Harvard Law School graduate who had
been refused jobs because of his short stature—against the radio
station with the Federal Communications Commission. The suit
ultimately failed, but Walker Lampley won the war with a
barrage of sympathetic national media coverage. Like most other
disabled people of her generation, "I was raised to just take it,"
she noted. "But I just can't roll over and let this one fall into that
category. This is about my children and all children in the future
born with an unconventional appearance. This station was
spreading hatred. I felt I had to pick up the torch on this one."
As the group identity of a younger generation of disabled people
grows, people like Walker Lampley are increasingly less tolerant
of bigotry. Like her, they are taking a stand for equality, independence, and dignity.

CHAPTER 2

FROM CHARITY TO
INDEPENDENT LIVING

I n the fall of 1962, James Meredith, escorted to class by
U.S. marshals, integrated the University of Mississippi.
That same school season, a postpolio quadriplegic named
Ed Roberts entered the University of California at Berkeley. Just
as surely as Meredith ushered in an era of access to higher
education for blacks and a new chapter in the civil rights movement, Roberts was more quietly opening a civil rights movement that would remake the world for disabled people. The
disability rights movement was born the day Roberts arrived on
the Berkeley campus.

While Roberts's activism would be shaped by Berkeley, it
was first formed in the experiences of being disabled as a teenager—after growing up with all the promises of a full life that
are the birthright of the nondisabled. In 1953, polio swept
through the modest frame home of Verne Roberts, a second-
generation railroad worker, his wife, Zona, and their four sons.

Health authorities quarantined the Robertses' house in Burlington, a working-class town twenty miles south of San Francisco. Everyone would recover from the virus except for fourteen-year-old Ed, the oldest child. He had been a playground rat. He had played quarterback on the football team. He had shagged flies for Billy Martin, the New York Yankees infielder who returned home to northern California in the off-season. Now Roberts, unable to move more than his head or even breathe on his own, hovered near death in a hospital.

Roberts spent the first year of his illness in a dreary county hospital, confined to bed, never allowed to sit up in a wheelchair. Because the muscles that worked his lungs had been paralyzed, he could not breathe for long on his own. He spent eighteen hours a day in an eight-hundred-pound iron lung. It was yellow, alien looking, and as big as a telephone booth. He lay on his back in the tank, which enclosed his entire body except his head. The lung chamber created positive pressure from a bellows powered by a small electric motor. The uniform pressure over his chest, thorax, and abdomen forced Roberts to inhale air through his mouth. The machine became the boundary of his childhood. During the day, he could go up to six hours outside the lung by "frog breathing," swallowing deep gasps of air to fill his lungs.

Roberts saw himself as a "helpless cripple" overwhelmed by depression, powerlessness, and self-hatred. He asked his parents if he would ever go to college, marry, or hold a job. The answer, based on what doctors, nurses, and counselors had said, was always no. It would have been more humane, a doctor had told his mother, if the high fever of the polio had killed him quickly. Instead, the doctor said, Roberts would live as a sickly "vegetable" for the rest of his life. Roberts had no reason to think that the doctors were wrong. His decision was to attempt suicide by refusing food, in defiance of his private-duty nurse. His weight plummeted from 120 pounds to 50 pounds in seven months. The day the nurse left, he started to eat again. It was his first act of self-empowerment, albeit a subconscious one. No one would tell this "helpless cripple" when and what to eat. He would decide for himself.

After twenty months of hospitals, he moved back to his room in the house in Burlington. The iron lung moved with him. Roberts attended school, via telephone. His new classmates (he was now two years behind) sat at attention at their desks at school. Roberts, isolated, listened over the phone, often while lying in the iron lung. When students answered a question, they would pass around the microphone to speak to the classmate they had never seen. Before his illness, Roberts had been, at best, an indifferent student. Homework was boring. He had been slow to learn to read. But from his iron lung, he realized that education would be his power. His mind, he knew, was the one thing that had not been weakened by the illness. As he got healthier, there was no reason—other than his own embarrassment—to keep him from school. He returned, in a wheelchair, for his senior year of high school.

Shy and ashamed of his crippled body, he had rarely ventured outside his home. Over time, he had come to accept his disability, which now was central to his identity. Some regarded him as a freak in a wheelchair, the poor boy in the machine. Yet he had proved wrong all the doomsayers who had thought him better off dead. He had a different life, but it was an okay life. Disproving all those experts had given Roberts a growing sense of his own power. His first day back at school, too, had been a revelation. As he was lifted from the car, he had felt the staring eyes of his schoolmates. Staring was what he had most feared. But the stares that day were not looks of disgust. Those who were discomfited had averted their eyes. Instead, these were stares of fascination and excitement, as if Elvis Presley had suddenly descended upon the school. "It was like being a star," recalls Roberts. "So I decided to be a star, not a helpless cripple."

Despite his good grades, the school principal, a humorless

bureaucrat who did everything by the book, refused to give
Roberts his diploma because he had not completed the driver's
education and gym requirements. The principal got backing
from the assistant superintendent of schools, but Zona Roberts
fought back. A former labor organizer, she raised hell, complaining all the way up the line to the school board. Finally, at her
insistence, Roberts's physical rehabilitation sessions were
counted as physical education, the driver's education requirement was dropped, and Roberts got his diploma. For a disabled
person growing up, says Roberts, to have "parents willing to
fight for you and include you in that fight" is "the most important skill you can learn to be successful." This was an early
example of how only harsh attitudes of others, not his own
physical shortcomings, would threaten to hold him back.

After high school, Roberts spent two happy years at San
Mateo Community College. Thirsting for more education, he
planned on applying to the University of California at Los Angeles, one of four U.S. universities at the time that had special
programs and accessible campuses for students in wheelchairs.
UCLA had set up a disabled students program for disabled
World War II veterans. Roberts, as a disabled man, had been
thinking practically—in terms of wheelchair access and a school
ready to admit him despite his disability. But Jean Wirth, his
academic adviser at San Mateo, insisted that he do what any
other student would do and set his sights on the best, not the
least restrictive, school. She talked him into applying to the
University of California at Berkeley, which had a superior reputation in political science, the area Roberts wanted to study.

But California's Department of Rehabilitation refused to pay
for his four-year college education, as it did for other, less
disabled students. Roberts's counselor, who had a slight limp,
ruled that spending money on Roberts would be wasted since it
was "infeasible" that he could ever work. San Mateo's president,
the dean of students, and Wirth appealed, arguing that Roberts

had excelled at the community college and deserved the chance to go on. When they were rebuffed, the school officials took Roberts's case to the local newspaper, and eventually the state agency was forced to relent in the onslaught of negative publicity. Roberts had learned another valuable lesson: the press was willing to champion the cause—even if overdramatically—of a worthy "cripple."

Even then, Roberts still had to convince officials at Berkeley to admit him. "We've tried cripples before and it didn't work," one Berkeley dean explained matter-of-factly to Roberts. Practically speaking, he was correct. The classrooms were not accessible, and the library and the cafeterias had steps. But Roberts had sidestepped this problem at San Mateo by relying on attendants or friends to lift him out of his wheelchair and carry him into classrooms. The bigger problem at Berkeley was where to live. No dormitory had floors strong enough to take the weight of the eight-hundred-pound iron lung.

But another thing Roberts had learned was not to stop at the first roadblock. He knew he had to keep searching until he found a sympathetic person who was open to bending the rules. Roberts found one in Dr. Henry Bruyn, the director of student health services. Bruyn offered a solution: Roberts, with his iron lung, could move onto the third floor of the university's Cowell Hospital. Living in the student infirmary, making it a one-man dormitory, was not exactly the college experience Roberts had in mind. But it was a way onto what had been a closed campus. As Berkeley tried its experiment, a local newspaper wrote about Roberts in a story with the headline HELPLESS CRIPPLE GOES TO SCHOOL.

At Berkeley, Roberts needed someone to push his wheelchair and help him get dressed and eat. Sometimes a friend helped willingly. But for the most part, it hired attendants, including sometimes his brother Ron, also a student at Berkeley. State funding paid for the attendants. California had the nation's first such program. "It wasn't inexpensive, a couple hundred dollars a month," says Roberts. "But as it turns out, it was a real breakthrough." Money, Roberts suspected, had been the real reason it had been deemed "infeasible" for him to attend Berkeley. Education at San Mateo had been inexpensive: he had lived at home in Burlington and tuition at the junior college was cheap. For a quadriplegic like Roberts, joining the nondisabled world would sometimes require extra spending.

Roberts could stay away from the iron lung for up to several hours at a time. "That was enough time to go to classes and even go out and drink a little," he recalls. Most buildings were accessible, but he had to find back doors and circuitous paths without steps to the elevators. There were innovations to keep up with classwork. He could move the pages of a book, for example, with a stick that he clenched between his teeth. He read while lying on his back in the iron lung. The book slipped into a reading stand on the mirror one foot above his head.

Getting onto a vibrant college campus was a liberation. He had the typical college experiences of the 1960s: he found intellectual discussion exciting, and he experimented with drugs and sex. Each typical college experience pushed him farther. By 1967, Roberts's mother, Zona, had moved to Berkeley to take classes and be near her son. Judy was her neighbor and a student, too. Judy, recently abandoned by the husband she had helped through medical school, and Ed would engage in long discussions of their vulnerability and their feelings of having to fight stereotypes to win opportunities. Soon, their neighborly relationship turned into a romantic one. Roberts was dependent on someone, often his mother or brother, to push him in his wheelchair. A new innovation, a wheelchair powered by a twelve-volt battery, was on the market. But rehabilitation counselors had told Roberts that his weak hands could never manipulate the joystick control. Motivated by love and a need for privacy, however, Roberts learned to navigate one with only an hour and a half of practice. The power wheelchair represented independence. For the first time since the polio, Roberts was free to move when he wished to move, to go where he wished to go, anytime he wanted.

Roberts was alone on the empty wing of Cowell, but word of his experiment traveled quickly. Soon the university began admitting other physically disabled applicants. The first, the following year, was John Hessler, who had heard about Roberts from his physical therapist. A lanky six-foot-seven-inch quadriplegic, Hessler had broken his neck in a diving accident. Roberts, Hessler, and the other disabled students who were soon to join them got caught up in the political upheaval of the times, which burned intensely on the Berkeley campus in the Free Speech Movement, the anti–Vietnam War protests, and other causes. Roberts watched and learned from the civil rights movement and the nascent women's movement. Women rejected that "anatomy was destiny" and were struggling to control their bodies. Disabled people, too, were questioning the medicalization of their lives. Particularly, Roberts noted how feminists used stereotypes about them—as the weaker, milder sex—to their advantage. The women would let their opponents fall into such tired assumptions, then catch them off guard with the force of their anger and the unassailable correctness of their demand for equality. Roberts saw that he, too, could use the charitable and protective instincts of his enemies. When someone saw a severely disabled man and felt compelled to help, Roberts would use that compassion as an opening to blast away at the low expectations, including the assumption that he would never work or could not get around a campus.

Roberts finished his undergraduate degree, got his master's degree in political science, and began work on his doctorate. By 1967 there were twelve severely disabled students living in Cowell. They called themselves the "Rolling Quads." In late-night bull sessions on the hospital floor, Roberts and his friends, in their wheelchairs and iron lungs, would strategize constantly about breaking down the common barriers they faced—from classrooms they could not get into to their lack of transportation around town—and dissect the protests for self-determination of minority students.

In 1968, the dormitory became a formal program run by the state department of rehabilitation. When one counselor tried to evict two men from Cowell, complaining about their low grades, the rest of the Rolling Quads rebelled. "She wanted us all to get A's and to carry a certain number of credits," recalls Roberts. Some of the men were moving through Berkeley slowly, either because their disabilities made it hard to study or because they wanted to delay the inevitable departure from this rarest commune of like-minded brothers. But the counselor was threatening to cut off state funding for those who did not follow her instructions. And to justify the eviction of the two men, she brandished the bureaucratic label of "infeasible" for work. "Nobody was going to threaten our independence, or the program itself," says Roberts. So he led a rebellion, petitioning university administrators and appealing to Berkeley's liberal student body. It was unfair, he argued, for the freewheeling campus to apply stricter rules of behavior to a pocket of disabled students. Thinking back to his own fight to get into Berkeley—and then the protest movements he had seen on campus—Roberts put in telephone calls to the local newspapers, radio, and television stations. "We haven't had a villain like this in a long time," one reporter confided to Roberts. Other students at Berkeley offered words of encouragement on the street. Within a few weeks, the counselor was reassigned.

Back in Cowell, the late-night discussion sessions focused on total self-sufficiency. The Rolling Quads wanted to be their own counselors, or case service managers, so they would never again have to kowtow to a bureaucrat who controlled their funding. They needed to know how to get a job on their own, so they would not become dependent on any state program. They talked about whether the know-it-all assumptions of their rehabilitation counselors were motivated by a need to control their clients if for no other reason than to make sure their own jobs did not become obsolete. The Rolling Quads realized that they would have to think of themselves as consumers of state services, not as clients.

The next battle would come the following year, when the city of Berkeley was renovating the main shopping street south of campus. Curb cuts, at that time, were not a standard part of street design. Because their wheelchairs could not ride over five-inch curbs, Roberts and his friends rarely left campus. But eight members of the Rolling Quads showed up at a city council meeting—eight wheelchairs in one room, Rolling Quad Donald Lorence would explain later, is a dramatic statement in itself— and won a commitment of $50,000 a year to ramp city streets. From these seemingly small victories emerged a sense of political power.

From Campus Life to Independent Living

It was about this time that the idea of living in Cowell began to get stale. Residing in a hospital still stigmatized the Rolling Quads; they were students by day and patients by night. And that was exactly the image they wanted to erase. Despite their polio or spinal cord injuries, they were as healthy as other students on campus. The original idea was to find an expansive communal house off campus, but some members balked. Independence meant having choices about where to live and not needing to live always with other wheelchair users. They could not, after all, spend their entire lives together as part of some sort of disability frat house. Yet, finding apartments that could be made accessible would be a herculean task. Two students had already tried to move out of Cowell, but only one had succeeded in finding a wheelchair-accessible apartment. The other had returned to Cowell, discouraged. Nevertheless, with their new sense of collective power, the Rolling Quads began planning to set up a support group to help each other live independently. An important break would come from an old Roberts connection: Jean Wirth, his counselor at San Mateo. Wirth had started a program there to cut down on the high rate of black and Hispanic dropouts. Traditionally, dropping out was seen as an academic problem. But Wirth understood that often, particularly with her minority students, it was the problems of everyday living that led to school failure. So Wirth asked other students to be peer mentors. If a minority student was about to quit because he or she had no transportation to school, the mentor arranged a carpool. If the student could not afford school, the mentor helped find a job. Wirth's College Readiness Program worked so well that a federal education official asked her to come to Washington to try to replicate the program on a national level. In 1966, at Wirth's request, Roberts flew to Washington to help her write provisions to include disabled students among the listed minorities.

Wirth and Roberts specified that the disabled students' antidropout programs were to be run by disabled people whenever possible. Since this provision was little known and there were only a handful of other schools with special programs for disabled students, the Rolling Quads were virtually assured that their grant proposal to Washington would be received favorably. The Department of Health, Education and Welfare speedily approved $81,000, and the university kicked in $2,000. By the fall of 1970, the Physically Disabled Students' Program, or PDSP, as it was known, was open for business in a newly ramped office on campus.

Roberts and his colleagues drew on their own experiences to figure out what was needed to live independently. In essence, PDSP was Wirth's antidropout program for minorities, but it was applied to disabled students. The PDSP hired disabled counselors who would scope out available and accessible apartments for people in wheelchairs. They put together a pool of potential attendants, who would help prepare meals, push wheelchairs, and do whatever else was needed to help the students. In Berkeley, where people came for the countercultural life-style, it was easy to find attendants who would work odd hours, even if the job was often difficult.

Wheelchairs were a major obstacle to independence. They had been invented for people living at home or in institutions. They had not been constructed sturdily enough for the vanguard of radicals who were redefining what it meant to be paraplegics and quadriplegics by zipping around the spread-out Berkeley campus. Consequently, Roberts and his friends found that their wheelchairs broke down frequently, an event that could keep a student out of classes for weeks. So PDSP set up its own wheelchair workshop, staffed twenty-four hours a day by the self-taught band of wheelchair wizards, who were soon tinkering with their own designs for a better, stronger wheelchair. Others would learn the latest designs to modify cars and vans so that those unable to use their legs could work the brake and gas pedals with their hands. The Rolling Quads also ran PDSP's advocacy department, walking students through the maze of red tape and bureaucracy that accompanied attendant-care funding and other benefits and services.

The student program was radical. The medical model of disability measured independence by how far one could walk after an illness or how far one could bend his legs after an accident. But Roberts redefined independence as the control a disabled person had over his life. Independence was measured not by the tasks one could perform without assistance but by the quality of one's life with help. The health care system offered only custodial help. Roberts rejected this in favor of innovative self-help and group organizing. Disabled people themselves, the newly christened "independent living movement" assumed, knew better than doctors and professionals what they needed for daily living. And what disabled people wanted most of all was to be fully integrated in their communities, from school to work.

Independence. Self-sufficiency. Mainstreaming. Disability as a social problem. These were the principles that guided the PDSP and the disability rights movement of which PDSP was the leading edge. As the program grew, it soon became clear that the fight for rights had to embrace a wide range of disabilities. Traditionally, various disability groups worked separately for their own members, with little sense of common purpose. Even the Berkeley program was for "physically" disabled students and was run by people in wheelchairs. But shortly after it opened, PDSP started getting requests from blind students who saw the similarities in their own struggles for independence. The attendant referral service, for example, was expanded easily to include a pool of readers for the blind. It was not lost on Roberts, who was studying community organizing, that political power expanded with coalition building.

When the PDSP started, John Hessler, Berkeley's second quadriplegic, had gone off to France to study. But Roberts wrote an airmail letter asking him to head the new students' program. Hessler understood that something big was starting and wanted to be part of it. He returned to Berkeley, even buying a modified van. It was common for paraplegics to drive cars and vans with brakes and gearshifts they could move with their hands and arms. But even for a grand thinker like Roberts, the sight of a quadriplegic like Hessler, with his limited arm strength, moving such levers, was mind-boggling. Hessler's driving was so impressive that he would show off his van to new disabled students the program was trying to recruit.

There had been a few other college programs for disabled students. The University of Illinois had been the first, setting up a similar but less ambitious program in 1950 to help disabled veterans returning from World War II. By 1961, there were 163 disabled students, 101 in wheelchairs. Students got the campus ramped, had their own fraternity, and published an annual magazine. A fleet of buses equipped with hydraulic lifts made an hourly route around campus and to shopping spots. There were separate wheelchair sports teams, including softball, as well as a cheerleader squad of women in wheelchairs. There were even wheelchair square dances. Although people disabled by polio would eventually go to school there, most at Illinois were less disabled than those at Berkeley, and few of the Rolling Quads would have qualified for the Illinois program, which required students to be able to fend for themselves, without attendants. Nor did the Illinois program—which was run by university officials—incorporate the self-help approach of the Berkeley students.

The Center for Independent Living

The PDSP in Berkeley was an instant success. A staff of nine full- and part-time workers quickly had a list of one hundred student clients. Disabled students moved out of Cowell quickly and succeeded in school. But from the beginning there was one problem: the nonstop requests for the same help from disabled people who were not students. Staffers at PDSP rarely turned anyone away. But by spring, they found they could not keep up with the needs of the students and others as well. That May, Roberts, Hessler, and the other PDSP leaders got together to discuss how to set up a parallel program for nonstudents. The idea for the Center for Independent Living was born.

Incorporated in the spring of 1972, the Center for Independent Living—or CIL, as it was known—would work on the same principles as the disabled students' program. It would be run by disabled people; approach their problems as social issues; work with a broad range of disabilities; and make integration into the community its chief goal. Independence was measured by an individual's ability to make his own decisions and the availability of the assistance necessary—from attendants to accessible housing—to have such control. Unlike the student program, which had modest resources, CIL operated on a shoestring. The student program donated office space—a large closet—supplies, and some secretarial help. A door balanced on a small table became the center's desk. Roberts, cofounder Phil Draper, and others put aside 10 percent of the pot of their occasional Friday night poker games to keep the center running. A donated Volkswagen van became the center's transportation program. People in wheelchairs could not get onto city buses or into taxis. The van took them to jobs or around town to shop or play. Crucial grants came from Washington and the university. But the money would stop and start the first few years, at times forcing the center to shut down until the next grant came in.

Roberts took over as head of CIL in February 1974, a job he held for eighteen months. He had left Berkeley briefly to teach community organizing to black residents of East Palo Alto. Like Hessler in France, he, too, had felt a gnawing sense of missing something important back on the Berkeley campus. It seemed time to use his expertise as an organizer to help his own people. He started talking more explicitly of disability being a civil rights issue, although there was resistance to drawing such a bold parallel with the problems of black Americans. "We were talking about self-empowerment, self-hatred, and discrimination," Roberts says, "all the same issues." The center's extraordinary new grant writer, Joan Leon, raised a phenomenal $1 million, and the program's financial picture brightened.

Then, in 1975, California's new governor, Jerry Brown—at Roberts's suggestion after he took Brown on a tour of CIL—appointed Roberts the director of the state Department of Rehabilitation. Roberts delighted in the irony of being the chief of the agency that a decade and a half earlier had deemed it "infeasible" that he would ever hold a job. Now he was about to be married to Catherine, who had once been his physical therapist. Starting a family—the couple was soon to have a son, Lee— only underscored for Roberts the silliness of a system that tried to write off people based on the severity of their disability.

Roberts set about altering the California rehabilitation system. Like CIL, the Department of Rehabilitation drew on a variety of services. Funding to these agencies was based on how many people were placed into jobs, something that was easy to measure. This, Roberts complained, forced a practice called "creaming." Rehabilitation counselors tended to help those with the most minor disabilities. Severely disabled people—like Roberts—were written off as too hard to help into jobs. Roberts had responded to this by setting up CIL, which had "independent living," a more vague and hard-to-measure outcome, as its goal. When Roberts assumed his post, he merged the seemingly contradictory principles of independent living and rehabilitation services. He expanded funding for attendants to help disabled people with the things they needed for daily living, from eating to dressing. In California, every disabled person was to be helped, no matter how severe the disability. Although the department under Roberts would reach out to more disabled people, federal funding formulas were still based on the number of people placed in jobs, and the debate over creaming continues to this day. Roberts's reforms turned the department upside down, and many employees quit, bitter about the change. But many, to Roberts's surprise, also realized that deemphasizing numbers and concentrating on quality was the proper direction. Their director's own unexpected success served as testament to the error of lowering expectations for the most severely disabled.

Berkeley was not the only place where the lessons of civil rights and student protest were shaping a new generation of disability activists. In the spring of 1970, one year after she graduated from college, Judy Heumann was denied a license to teach in New York City's public schools. She fought her exclusion and emerged as another powerful disability rights leader. Heumann, like Roberts, was a quadriplegic, the result of polio. Hers had struck when she was eighteen months old, so, unlike Roberts, she never had a sense of self-identity without being disabled. Heumann was the eldest of three children born in Brooklyn to German-Jewish immigrants. A doctor urged Werner Heumann, a butcher, and his wife, Ilsa, to put the child in an institution. Relatives told the couple that their misfortune must have been the result of some horrible sin on their part. Later, the local elementary school principal deemed the young girl in a wheelchair a "fire hazard" and for three years sent a teacher to give her home instruction twice a week for a little over an hour each visit.

But Heumann's mother, with a Jewish immigrant's respect for learning, knew this was not a real education. Besides, her daughter was isolated and not making friends. Ilsa Heumann became a battler, emboldened by small victories, who fought to get Judy into a regular school. At first Judy went to a special elementary school for disabled children—where she realized that the parents of many of her classmates had low expectations for their children and that the teachers, when not prodded by pushy parents, responded accordingly. It was a city policy that when children in wheelchairs reached high school age they would return to their families for home instruction. Ilsa Heumann asked the March of Dimes, where she had done volunteer work for years, to help. But the charity's officials declined, saying they wanted to stay out of politics. Banding together with other parents, Ilsa Heumann brought enough pressure on the school board that it reversed the policy. Judy Heumann entered high school in 1961, a time she remembers for the parallel efforts of black Americans to force their way into closed institutions.

Heumann would pick up her mother's zest for battle. She was accepted at Long Island University, an urban school in the middle of Brooklyn. There she led her own battles, forced to insist on everything from the right to live in a dormitory to getting someone to lift her wheelchair over the steps to the classroom buildings. She organized other disabled students to fight for ramped buildings. She took part in protests against the Vietnam War as well.

Heumann studied speech therapy with the goal of helping elementary school children. But she was denied her teaching certificate, despite passing the oral and written parts of the exam, when she flunked the medical exam. The testing physician questioned whether she could get to the bathroom by herself or help children out of the building in an emergency.

Heumann quickly slapped the Board of Education with a lawsuit, charging discrimination. Then she went to the local newspapers, which were happy to tell the story of a qualified teacher up against a coldhearted bureaucracy. "You Can Be President, Not Teacher, with Polio," said the New York *Daily News* in a headline. "We're not going to let a hypocritical society give us a token education and then bury us," Heumann angrily told the newspaper. When it became clear that the board would likely lose its case, it settled out of court, and Heumann was given her certification. Yet no one would hire her, until the principal of the elementary school she had attended in Brooklyn offered her a job.

The experience taught Heumann that she would always have to fight for her rights. Even then, attitudes would still be barriers. But as a result of the press coverage, Heumann received hundreds of letters, largely from others with disabilities with similar complaints. From the base of those contacts—and ones with disabled friends from special summer camp and from college—Heumann in 1970 started her own disability rights group, Disabled in Action. She was twenty-two.

Unlike Roberts's organizing in California, Heumann's DIA would be explicitly political and it did not provide direct services to help disabled people live independently. Instead, it engaged in political protest. In 1972, DIA traveled to Washington to demonstrate at the Lincoln Memorial after President Richard Nixon vetoed a spending bill to fund disability programs. Then, in the closing days of the presidential election, Heumann joined with a group of disabled Vietnam veterans to take over Nixon's New York reelection headquarters to demand, militantly if unrealistically, an on-camera debate with the president himself.

The following year, summoned by Roberts, Heumann moved to Berkeley to work at CIL. California was a revelation. She was picked up at the airport in a friend's van with a hydraulic lift. She could get the state to pay for her personal attendant. In the growing West, she could find newer buildings that had been made accessible. Most of all, she found disabled people who had come together in a common group identity. From 1975 through 1982, Heumann would serve as the deputy director of CIL, blending her East Coast political activism with the Berkeley disability community's focus on providing independent living services. In California, Heumann, along with Roberts, would continue to rewrite the history of the disabled.

The History of Disabled People in America

Throughout most of its history America has been inhospitable to people with disabilities. In colonial America, the settlement of a vast new rural society meant that early colonists put a premium on physical stamina. The early colonies tried to prevent the immigration of those who could not support themselves and would have to rely on state help. People with physical or mental disabilities who were potentially dependent could be deported, forced to return to England.

The nation's attitude softened somewhat during the Revolutionary War. When the Continental Congress paid for up to 50 percent of the pensions of disabled soldiers, it was the first time the federal government helped the states care for their disabled. A system of marine hospitals was established in 1798 to provide for sick and disabled sailors. The Marine Hospital Service would later evolve into the Public Health Service, and in 1922 some of these hospitals became the first Veterans Administration hospitals. The nation's sense of indebtedness to men who became disabled while fighting its wars was to inspire many major disability programs throughout U.S. history.

There are few historical records of disabled people in the early years of the new nation. What does exist suggests that many disabled people were able to fit easily into society. Gouverneur Morris, who helped draft the Constitution and was later a U.S. senator from New York, wore a "rough stick" to replace the left leg he lost in a 1780 carriage accident. Stephen Hopkins referred to his cerebral palsy when he signed the Declaration of Independence, saying, "My hand trembles but my heart does not."

Larger colonial towns, reflecting Elizabethan poor laws, had built almshouses for the poor and the physically and mentally disabled. These had continued to grow during the first half of the nineteenth century as the nation's population grew and a simple rural society became industrialized and urbanized. Dorothea Dix, a Boston schoolmistress, led reformers in the 1840s who demanded that the states take control of miserable local almshouses, where adults and children, the disabled and nondisabled, criminals, and those with retardation, epilepsy, and mental illness were all thrown together. Dix had found people with mental illness and retardation "in cages, closets, cellars, stalls, pens! Chained, naked, beaten with rods, and lashed into obedience." The result was that states took over such institutions, built more, and set up specialized facilities for the criminals, disabled, and others who had populated the almshouses. In 1854, Congress, at Dix's urging, agreed to break with past practice and to provide federal funding for separate facilities for what were then called the deaf, dumb, and blind and mentally ill. But President Franklin Pierce vetoed the measure, saying that the care of the physically and mentally disabled was not a federal responsibility. Historian John Lenihan noted, "Pierce's veto became a landmark precedent limiting federal intervention in welfare matters for the next half century."

Doctors and educators working with the blind and deaf, following experiments in France, were among the first to understand that disabled people could be integrated into society rather than sent away to institutions. A school for the blind was opened in Baltimore in 1812, and Thomas Hopkins Gallaudet founded his school for the deaf in Hartford in 1817. Samuel Gridley Howe would open the Massachusetts Asylum for the Blind, later the Perkins Institute, in 1832 with a curriculum that paralleled that in other schools. His theory was an early form of "mainstreaming," in which he prepared blind youths to find work and live self-sufficiently in their communities. Howe's success in teaching Laura Bridgman, who had been left blind, deaf, and unable to speak by an attack of scarlet fever when she was two, brought visitors such as Charles Dickens and American educators, and with them a recognition that reformers were right that people who were both blind and deaf could be educated. This success also encouraged Howe to open the first state school to try to train "idiots and feebleminded youth" in 1848. The work of Howe, Dr. Hervey Wilbur, and others showed that mental retardation could not be cured, as they had hoped. Nor could people with retardation be easily educated. As a result, these schools became more custodial in their care than were the schools for the blind and the deaf. As historian Lenihan noted, however, "If the gap with the mainstream of society was not closed, at least retardation was no longer considered an incurable disease tantamount to insanity."

The Civil War forced the nation, for the first time, to deal with large numbers of physically disabled citizens. The South, because of heavy casualties and poor medical care in the Confederate Army, was particularly hard hit. Mississippi, in 1886, spent 20 percent of its state revenue on artificial arms and legs. In the North, a National Home for disabled Union soldiers was established in 1866. The rise of orthopedic medicine began to develop partly in response to the returning Civil War wounded. But, as historian David J. Rothman writes in *The Discovery of the Asylum,* the American reformers' experiments with institutionalization were falling apart by the 1850s, a trend that was exacerbated by the added demands of the Civil War.

These institutions continued to grow, but, losing their grounding in charity, they became places of abuse, isolation, and segregation. The rise of social Darwinism and the eugenics movement at the end of the nineteenth century—two related schools of social thought that challenged whether it was even desirable to have a society with disabled people—brought new hostility.

As the new century opened, Washington, for the first time, was to play an extensive role in welfare. Once again, returning disabled war veterans stirred the nation's sense of obligation. Medical advances, including the development of new medicines, allowed far higher rates of survival for people who became disabled. Nowhere was that more evident than in the returning World War I veterans. So many, who would have died before, returned with disabilities that Washington was forced to establish the Veterans Bureau in 1921 to deal with their needs. Adding to a new national awareness of disability—fed by muckraking journalists and labor unions—was the rise of industrial accidents. Congress passed major rehabilitation programs in 1918 and 1920, guaranteeing federal funds for vocational training and job counseling. Charitable groups also set up employment bureaus for the disabled, including the American Red Cross. A 1921 law established child and maternal health centers to reduce the nation's infant and maternal mortality rate. This would lead to a broader federal role following the Depression. In 1935, Franklin D. Roosevelt signed the Social Security Act, which, for the first time, created a program of permanent assistant to disabled adults.

Roosevelt became the country's most famous disabled person. Americans admired his battle with polio. They sent money to the March of Dimes, which he helped found, and schoolchildren even sent their dimes to build him a White House pool for exercise. Historian Hugh Gregory Gallagher notes, however, in *FDR's Splendid Deception,* that Roosevelt went to great lengths to hide the extent of his handicap. Roosevelt could not walk, although Americans held a contrary impression. "The generally accepted line was that FDR had had polio and was now a bit lame; he had been paralyzed, but now he was recovered. He was a 'cured cripple,' " writes Gallagher. He was never seen in public, nor photographed in private, in his wheelchair. This was still possible in an era before television. He, his son, and Secret Service agents had devised elaborate ways to get him in and out of buildings. If he had to enter in public view, his son and agents would walk closely by his side, and FDR would lift himself on their arms, as if he were a gymnast on parallel bars. He would seem to be walking although he was, in effect, being carried. Washington was a wheelchair-accessible city—or at least the parts frequented by FDR—with ramps at the White House, Capitol, the War, State and Navy Building, and St. John's Church across Lafayette Square. It would be another thirty years before such access was required by law.

Once again, disabled soldiers returning from war, this time World War II, spurred another expansion of federal rehabilitation programs. There was renewed national dedication to helping this most highly visible population of disabled Americans. The Paralyzed Veterans of America formed in 1946 to promote their medical care, and the President's Committee on Employ-

ment of the Handicapped was founded the following year to
convince business of its obligation to hire them once they left
rehabilitation. Most important, however, was the creation of
rehabilitation medicine during World War II by Drs. Howard
Rusk and Henry Kessler. Working independently, these men set
up rehabilitation centers that worked on a revolutionary idea.
They would go well beyond acute care to put together all the
medical services—from physical therapy to occupational therapy—that a newly disabled person required to return to a normal life. The independent living movement that Roberts created
twenty years later was both an improvement on this and a
rebellion from it. The independent living movement endorsed
physiatry's ground-breaking emphasis on looking at the whole
person, but it rejected the medical model that could view that
person only as a patient, in the context of a medical setting.

For the most part, it was government or charitable groups
that helped people with disabilities, but there were a few scattered cases of disabled people rising up on their own. Deaf and
blind people had been the first to set up national advocacy
organizations, beginning in the last two decades of the nineteenth century. Such groups proved effective. Blind relief laws,
providing special financial assistance, were enacted in twenty-
seven states in the 1920s and early 1930s. But when economic
times were good, others argued that to take special assistance
only furthered perceptions that blind and deaf people were incapable of living without charity. Robert Irwin, the blind
Harvard-educated man who led the American Foundation of the
Blind through its early years in the 1920s and 1930s, promoted
self-reliance and opposed automatic pensions or special schools
for the blind.

Disabled people turned to civil disobedience for the first
time during the Depression. Historian Paul Longmore tracked
down the lost story of the short-lived League for the Physically
Handicapped, a group of three hundred disabled New York

pensioners—most with polio and a few with cerebral palsy—
who occupied the Works Progress Administration offices in
Washington to protest that they were being routinely rejected
for WPA jobs. Another important self-help group started in
1958 when Gini Laurie, who volunteered with patients on a
Cleveland polio ward, started the *Toomey j Gazette* as an "alumni"
newsletter for people leaving the hospital. Soon people were
writing in with tips about how they took care of a baby from a
wheelchair, managed on a trip to France, or started their own
mail-order business working at home over the telephone. The
newsletter turned into a journal of self-reliance—today it is the
Rehabilitation Gazette—and soon won a worldwide readership,
including a young Ed Roberts in California.

But it was the rise of a parents' movement that would most
change the course of disability policy in the years following
World War II. A proliferation of new disability groups like the
United Cerebral Palsy Associations, founded in 1948, and the
Muscular Dystrophy Association in 1950 were started by parents. As more children survived disability, more parents sought
to keep them from being institutionalized. They realized they
shared their struggle with other parents who were also frustrated
by the paltry support offered by doctors or social service agencies. Their biggest common concern was to get their children
educated. These new parents' groups took their case to Congress,
which, in 1966, created a federal bureau for the handicapped.
The groups sent permanent lobbyists to Washington, and in
1970 the bureau began providing funds for training special-
education teachers and developing separate materials for teaching the children in these classes.

Section 504

The first civil rights law for disabled people, however, would not
be the end result of a hard-fought battle. Disabled people did

not even ask for it. Nor had they lobbied for it. Section 504 of the Rehabilitation Act of 1973 was no more than a legislative afterthought. The overall act authorized $1.55 billion in federal aid to the disabled to be spent over two years. For President Richard Nixon, as well as for Congress and even disability groups, including Heumann's DIA, this was simply a spending bill. Nixon had vetoed two earlier versions he claimed were too costly. But at the very end of the bill were tacked on four unnoticed provisions—the most important of which was Section 504—that made it illegal for any federal agency, public university, defense or other federal contractor, or any other institution or activity that received federal funding to discriminate against anyone "solely by reason of . . . handicap."

When sociologist Richard Scotch later studied the act's legislative history, he found that congressional aides could not even remember who had suggested adding the civil rights protection. But the wording clearly was copied straight out of the Civil Rights Act of 1964, which ruled out discrimination in federal programs on the basis of race, color, or national origin. There had been no hearings and no debate about Section 504. Members of Congress were either unaware of it or considered it "little more than a platitude" for a sympathetic group, says Scotch. Professional and charitable groups representing disabled people were sophisticated in winning multibillion-dollar federal funding, but had not focused on civil rights legislation.

Roberts and Heumann, however, would soon recognize the significance of what had fallen into their laps, even if the anonymous Capitol Hill staffers who had crafted Section 504 had not. The Ford administration would understand the significance of Section 504, too. The Department of Health, Education and Welfare estimated that compliance would cost billions of dollars and stalled the issuance of the final regulations. When Ford's presidency ended, HEW left behind a 185-page draft of the regulations.

The new president, Jimmy Carter, had made a campaign promise to complete them. But his new HEW Secretary, Joseph Califano, was quickly alarmed by the scope of Section 504, too, and assigned a group of lawyers to write new regulations. Carter and Califano were afraid of the public outcry if alcoholics, drug addicts, and homosexuals were to claim protection under the law, although an HEW team already had concluded they would not be eligible to do so. Califano pleaded for time. Frank Bowe, the head of the American Coalition of Citizens with Disabilities, led a group of demonstrators in wheelchairs, holding candles and praying, to Califano's home shortly before midnight on April 3, 1977, to demand that he sign the regulations immediately and without weakening them. Two days later, activists loosely organized by Bowe's group staged demonstrations in Washington and eight regional offices of HEW. Three hundred people took over Califano's offices, and most remained overnight. The HEW secretary, infuriated, retaliated by refusing to let in food and by cutting off telephone communication. After twenty-eight hours, the demonstrators left.

In San Francisco, however, the sit-in endured and turned into a national attention-grabbing moment of conviction. Led by Heumann, the demonstrators occupied the sixth floor of the regional HEW office in UN Plaza for twenty-five days. When they arrived the first day, recalls protester Mary Jane Owen, they were furious at the condescending treatment they got from HEW officials, who served them cookies and punch, as if they were schoolchildren on a field trip. Heumann was angry about her colleagues in Washington being "starved out" of their occupation. As in Washington, HEW officials in San Francisco, too, tried to shut down the protest at first by refusing to let in food, cutting off telephone lines, and even barring entry to attendants. Some of the most severely disabled protesters were literally putting their lives on the line, since they risked their health to be without catheters, back-up ventilators, and the attendants who would move them every few hours to prevent bedsores, or who, with their hands, would cleanse impacted bowels every few days. None of these deprivations, however, deterred the demonstrators. Instead, they backfired. The protesters' success, in the face of forceful opposition, only bolstered their euphoria and determination.

Particularly helpful was the fact that protest movements held a place of honor in the activist atmosphere of the Bay Area. On the fourth day, Roberts, now the state director of rehabilitation, showed up to give his official blessing to the sit-in, which by then had grown to over 120 demonstrators. "We've got to keep up the pressure," he said from his electric wheelchair on this first of several visits. And then he noted, correctly, that federal officials "have underestimated the commitment of this group." On the sixth day, Representative Phillip Burton, who represented San Francisco, demanded that food get past the guards in the lobby and won the installation of three pay phones. Two other pay phones on a distant floor had quickly broken down, clogged by uncollected coins. Heumann had found other more creative ways to get messages out of the building. The demonstrators unfurled banners with their messages from windows; deaf protesters used sign language to convey information to those watching outside; and at one point members of the Butterfly Brigade, a group of gay men who patrolled city streets on the lookout for antigay violence, smuggled in a set of walkie-talkies. On the thirteenth day, Mayor George Moscone brought in twenty air mattresses and hoses with shower heads, over the objections of HEW regional director Jose Maldonado, who complained, "We're not running a hotel here."

Nevertheless, food donated by a local Safeway store, Goodwill Industries, McDonald's, unions, and civil rights groups was prepared by the Black Panthers, including an Easter dinner of meatloaf, green beans, and mashed potatoes that arrived steaming and covered in tinfoil. Several priests lived with the demonstrators to help out with everything from preparing food to doing pastoral counseling and celebrating Easter Mass. A rabbi came in to lead a Passover seder. There was even clandestine help, including food smuggling, from some of the federal employees who kept working in the building through the twenty-five days of occupation. One HEW deputy wore a ceramic pin with a snake twisting through it and promised that, if his bosses ordered police in to storm the floor and arrest the demonstrators, he would surreptitiously warn them beforehand by turning the pin upside down.

The continued miscalculations of HEW officials were clear again on the twelfth day, when Burton and another Bay Area lawmaker, George Miller, held a congressional hearing in the occupied building. Gene Eiderberg, the low-ranking HEW assistant dispatched to California to testify, disclosed that Califano was considering twenty-two changes in the regulations that would set up what Eiderberg impolitically described as "separate but equal" facilities for the disabled. Among the changes, he said, were exceptions to rules requiring ramps and free access to hospitals and schools and a proposal to have some disabled children educated in special schools rather than at regular schools adapted for them. "We will not accept more segregation," Heumann told Eiderberg heatedly. "When you erect buildings that are not accessible to the handicapped, you enforce segregation. There will be more sit-ins until the government understands this." Roberts, too, blasted Eiderberg's suggestion of a "separate but equal world" for the disabled. "Integration is the key word," said Roberts. "People with disabilities have to come back into our society."

The San Francisco sit-in marked the political coming of age of the disability rights movement. Disabled people had risked arrest and their health by turning to civil disobedience tactics and had surprised a nation—and themselves—with their own power. The protest built on the early efforts at cross-disability activism by the CIL. "People went into that building with some kind of idealism, but they didn't have much knowledge of other disabilities," says Mary Jane Owen, who stayed for the twenty-five days. "Up to that point you had blind organizations, organizations for deaf people, for wheelchair users, for people with spina bifida or people with mental retardation."

Such parochialism changed at San Francisco. On the sixth floor of the federal building, demonstrators created their own disability city, a mini-Woodstock in close quarters where there was no privacy. They not only came together in the joint recognition of their second-class citizenship, but became close friends and administered to each other. One young woman, who walked on crutches, fell in love with the attendant of another demonstrator. One night the young woman and a dozen others sat in a circle during a typical late-night talkfest. They went around the circle, each saying what they would ask for if given one wish. "For Califano to sign the regs," said one. "For a hamburger," said someone else. Then it was the young woman's turn. "I used to know what I would wish for," she said. "I wanted to be beautiful. I wanted to stop being a cripple. But now I know I am beautiful." Says Owen, "We all felt beautiful. We all felt powerful. It didn't matter if you were mentally retarded, blind, or deaf. Everybody who came out felt, We are beautiful, we are powerful, we are strong, we are important."

On April 28, 1977—four years after the law had been passed—Califano caved in to the protest that showed no signs of diminishing and signed the regulations, without changes. And on April 30, the protesters marched out together in victory—thrilled to have won, but bittersweet at seeing their idealized disability city end. They left singing "We Have Overcome."

At the same time, Califano signed the regulation for the Education of All Handicapped Children Act. Congress had passed it in 1975, but Califano had blocked it, too, along with Section 504. When he signed the two together, schools were required to guarantee the best possible public education—instead of the inferior home teaching Roberts and Heumann had been forced to accept—to every disabled child. This gave angry parents a new tool to demand quality schooling, alongside non-disabled children, for their disabled sons and daughters. The new law would give rise to a new generation of well-educated disabled children, who then went on to college in record numbers.

Backlash

Yet the movement that seemed so promising as the demonstrators left would soon falter. What existed in the San Francisco area simply did not exist elsewhere. Although nearby Berkeley had already been labeled a "mecca for the handicapped" by the press, other communities did not have the center of activism that Roberts and Heumann had helped build in California.

Shortly after Califano signed the regulations, costs would come up time and time again as a reason for denying full rights, no matter how hard won, for disabled people. News stories attacked the Section 504 regulations, for example, as an instance of costly and nit-picking federal rule making. Newspapers widely reported the outrage of people in Rudd, Iowa, a farming community of fewer than five hundred people. An HEW regional official had informed the town that its public library had to be made accessible. Town officials said it would cost $6,500 to build a ramp, even though no one in the town used a wheelchair. As historian Edward Berkowitz would later note, there was a sudden realization that antidiscrimination measures for people with disabilities carried a price tag. This was quite different from the black civil rights movement, where the end of separate accommodations had meant financial savings. "Admitting James Meredith to the University of Mississippi cost nothing in an economic sense," Berkowitz wrote. "All of the costs were political. Meredith required courage to attend classes, not ramps and wide toilet stalls with grab bars." But "to admit James Meredith's handicapped counterpart to a university would cost money rather than save it. It would mean that the physical plant would need to be expanded or modified, and it would require the university to pay the administrative cost of complying with the federal regulations."

Architect Ron Mace of Barrier Free Environments says university officials and others wildly overestimated the cost of accommodating disabled people. North Carolina education officials, says Mace, estimated it would cost $15 billion to make state university buildings accessible. In fact, many changes were simple and inexpensive. To accommodate students in wheelchairs, universities moved classes to ground floors rather than install elevators to carry students to higher floors. The total cost to the state, Mace says, turned out to be only $15 million. A 1982 study for the Labor Department, too, found it was "no big deal" to accommodate disabled workers, since 50 percent of changes in the workplace cost little or nothing. A company, for example, could change a wheelchair user's work hours to conform with the schedule of lift-equipped buses. Another 30 percent of the accommodations were achieved for between $100 and $500 per employee—these included such ideas as giving a telephone headset to a quadriplegic telephone operator. At the high end were the 4 percent of changes that exceeded "the low figure of $2,000 [per employee]." These low costs would later win over a generation of businessmen as well as disabled people. But in the years immediately after Califano signed the Section 504 regulations, there were still fear and concerns about limits on federal funding. The courts, so crucial for advances in the black civil rights movement, proved less hospitable to disabled people. The Supreme Court, in *Southeastern Community College* v. *Davis,* ruled that a deaf woman, Frances Davis, could be denied admission to a nurses' training program at a North Carolina community college on the ground simply that her deafness would prevent her from participating in clinical training. Disabled people were not insisting that they be hired for jobs they could not do. Davis argued her deafness did not prevent her from going to school or being a nurse, unless she was refused accommodations along the way.

In 1980, with the election of Ronald Reagan, there was an administration in place that would review the regulations considered ominous to business and government agencies, particularly Section 504 and the Education Act. By 1984, sociologist Scotch would write that "the effectiveness of the disability rights movement appears to have peaked in 1978" and that since Reagan's election "the decline in influence has continued and quickened."

It would be several years after the San Francisco sit-in before the independent living movement, as it started in Berkeley, would grow across the country. But once it began to spread, it spread rapidly. In 1977, according to disability policy expert Margaret Nosek, there were just fifty-two independent living centers in the United States. Within a decade, there would be close to three hundred, all bringing a similar fervor of advocacy and group activism. Most modeled themselves after Berkeley's center, which not only had the distinction of being the first independent living center but was considered to be the most activist and most thriving. By 1976, one reporter noted, the center was already serving "some one thousand disabled persons with a variety of programs, including housing and transportation assistance, crisis counseling, attendant and reader referrals, wheelchair repair, mobility training for the blind, a computer training project, and an education program for rehabilitation professionals." By 1988, the center reported it helped 1,807 clients who received an average of eighty-one hours of assistance throughout the year. Three of every four clients lived in poverty.

A key moment came in 1978 when Congress, listening to testimony from Roberts, gave the federal commissioner of Rehabilitation Services the discretionary power to award money to the states to operate independent living centers. This assured a stream of money so that disabled people would have a significant role in running their own programs. However, because the centers depended on federal dollars, many over time were forced to tone down their overt political activism.

The proliferating independent living centers spread the new philosophy of the disability rights movement to disabled people, their families, and disability professionals in cities, towns, and even isolated rural communities across the country. They proclaimed a new ideal of independence. The centers argued that no one—not even doctors or therapists—knew more about the needs of disabled people than disabled people themselves. Above all, the centers provided a model of disabled people running their own self-help programs, making decisions for themselves.

The post–San Francisco generation of disabled Americans would be the beneficiaries of the Education of All Handicapped Children Act and the new sensibility of the independent living movement. Disabled children who began school in 1977—the first group to be assured rights—would start graduating high school in the late 1980s. It was no accident that the time of their leaving school—for a world where the rights of disabled people were not protected as they had been in school—became a period of new disability activism. As a group, this protected generation was more self-assured about standing up for themselves than had been the more downtrodden generation that preceded them. The Gallaudet student protests and the passage of the Americans with Disabilities Act, an expansion of Section 504, would pick up where the brief flurry of mid-1970s disability rights activism of the San Francisco sit-in generation had left off. These events in the late 1980s and early 1990s would bring about a renewed public sense of the minority identity of disabled people and carry on the self-help and activist vision that had taken root in Berkeley.

CHAPTER 3

THE DEAF CELEBRATION
OF SEPARATE CULTURE

T
he 1988 protest by deaf students at Gallaudet University was a defining moment for the disability rights movement. It was the closest the movement has come to having a touchstone event, a Selma or a Stonewall. True, protesters with a wider array of disabilities had taken over the San Francisco HEW headquarters in 1977. But that was just a blip on the screen of national consciousness. It had come a decade too early for Americans—even for many disabled—to view disability as a civil rights issue. The Gallaudet campus takeover, by contrast, was a made-for-television solidarity phenomenon, thick with drama. Cameras feasted on the sea of hundreds of outstretched arms signing "Deaf President Now," over and over, in a rhythmic choreography. A school that prided itself on preparing deaf students for the hearing world had decreed a deaf person not ready to lead a deaf university.

The uprising that followed resonated for people of all

74

disabilities, who empathized with the students' revolt against the paternalistic care of well-meaning but insensitive people who were not disabled. Gallaudet gave Americans a new rights consciousness about disability. It was reflected in post-Gallaudet journalism, which focused less on "supercrips" and sad cases, according to a study by Beth Haller of Temple University. Newspaper stories began using the words "disability" and "rights" in the same paragraph. Lawmakers, too, made the connection. The Americans with Disabilities Act was introduced two months after the Gallaudet protest and, for a law with such sweep and so many potential enemies, took a rocket course toward passage. Argues Lex Frieden, then of the National Council on the Handicapped, "It would not have happened without Gallaudet raising people's consciousness."

The Revolution of Seen Voices

The Gallaudet *student* protest. That is how the March 1988 Gallaudet revolt is remembered. But the students were the last of the Gallaudet family to get involved. It was the anger of young alumni, battling the sting of prejudice and discrimination in the hearing world, who set it all in motion.

It began in August 1987, when Jerry Lee, the school's hearing president, announced he would leave the university in December. In early February of 1988, six young graduates met, and their discussion turned to the Gallaudet search committee that was winnowing a list of candidates to succeed Lee. To be deaf, the friends agreed, was to struggle constantly against the low expectations of the hearing world. What an insult, then, that the world's premier school for the deaf should buy into this underestimation. There had been brief talk in 1984, when Lee was chosen, of whether the job should have gone to a deaf man. Gallaudet's six presidents over 124 years had served for an average of twenty years, although there had already been three

presidents in the 1980s. This might be the last shot for several
years, the friends realized, at making a stand for a deaf president.
Jeff Rosen, a young Washington attorney at the meeting, says
the group decided to sponsor a campus rally to unite students,
faculty, and alumni into a massive coalition that could not be
ignored.

Support for the rally came from two local alumni entrepre-
neurs, John Yeh and David Birnbaum, who were bitter that the
university had shown little interest in giving contracts to local
deaf businessmen. Once out of the protective cocoon of Gallaudet's Washington campus of Victorian red-brick buildings,
these alumni had confronted the mindless exclusion and condescension of the hearing world. It was an outrage, Yeh and
Birnbaum felt, that their school played into these attitudes by
dismissing deaf businessmen. It gave the lie to the school's
mission of preparing students for the hearing world.

On campus, as Gallaudet alumni director Jack Gannon notes
in his history of the strike week, students paid scant attention
to the discrimination that faced them beyond the school's gates.
Replacing a president seemed little more than a campus administration issue. "Many deaf persons had been conditioned to
accept limits—to believe that hearing is better," explained Ros-
lyn Rosen, dean of Gallaudet's College for Continuing Education. Confusing, too, was that Gallaudet's student body was
made up not just of those with total hearing loss—who make up
10 percent of the 22 million Americans with hearing disabilities—but those with profound and severe hearing loss who could
be helped with a hearing aid. The different groups often formed
cliques, and those who used hearing aids felt more sanguine
about integrating into the hearing world. The task for the rally's
sponsors was to crystallize the presidential selection as a civil
rights battle.

"It's time!," said the fliers Yeh printed up to promote the
rally. "In 1842, a Roman Catholic became president of the

University of Notre Dame. In 1875, a woman became president of Wellesley College. In 1886, a Jew became president of Yeshiva University. In 1926, a Black person became president of Howard University. AND in 1988, the Gallaudet University presidency belongs to a DEAF person." Yeh underwrote most of the costs of the rally, including the printing of thousands of blue-and-yellow buttons that said DEAF PRESIDENT NOW, which became the protest week slogan.

The civil rights theme was hammered home at the rally on March 1, an exuberant revival that moved from point to point on campus, followed by 1,500 excited students, alumni, and faculty, chanting and waving "high fives"—the deaf sign-language applause of hands stretched straight up and fingers fluttering that would soon be familiar on television screens across the country. It was a sunny day with brilliant blue skies, and the sense of deaf pride that coursed through the crowd was electrifying. Jeff Rosen, wearing a red sweatshirt with the words DEAF PREXY NOW, stood on the flatbed of a pickup truck and signed to the crowd, "People have died in the civil rights movement. People were jailed in protesting the Vietnam War. I stand here in 1988 asking, What do you believe in? What is your cause?" Another of the two dozen speakers, Professor Allen Sussman, drove home the point: "This is an historical event. You could call this the first deaf civil rights activity." This was a powerful cry. Even many of the students who listened to him had never thought of the way deaf people were treated as a civil rights issue.

By coincidence, moments before the rally, the names of the three finalists were announced. I. King Jordan, deaf since young adulthood, was Gallaudet's popular dean of the college of arts and sciences. Harvey Corson, deaf since birth, was the president of a Louisiana residential school. Elisabeth Zinser, the one hearing candidate, was an administrator at the University of North Carolina at Greensboro. Also by accident, it was the same day that the new student body president took office. Greg Hlibok would become the national spokesman for the students, a reassuring symbol with his blond and preppy good looks. Tim Rarus, the outgoing student body president, along with Jerry Covell and Bridgetta Bourne, who before the rally had been campaigning for a woman president, would also emerge as leaders of the protest. All four had deaf parents and had grown up with self-confidence, not feeling left out because of their disability.

On Sunday, March 6, some five hundred students and alumni gathered at the main gate to the campus at 8:30 P.M. That was when they had been told to expect an announcement by the board of trustees. But the choice had already been made public, in a press release, two hours earlier. Hearing reporters had been told before the students: Elisabeth Zinser, the lone hearing finalist, was the new president of Gallaudet University. The eruption of anger was immediate. There were speeches, tears, burning of press releases.

Shouting "Deaf President Now," the group spontaneously marched the few miles downtown to the Mayflower Hotel, where the trustees were said to be at a party to celebrate their choice. Policemen lined the hotel entrance as the students shouted and signed speeches. Hlibok, Rarus, and Jeff Rosen were invited upstairs to meet the board. There, they said, Jane Bassett Spilman, chairwoman of Gallaudet's board of trustees, gave her insulting explanation that "Deaf people are not ready to function in a hearing world." Later, Spilman vigorously denied making the remark, saying she had been misquoted by an interpreter. But even this excuse was an example of what the students saw as the school's paternalism. Spilman had served on the board of trustees for seven years and she still couldn't speak to the students in their language. Why hadn't she learned to sign?

The next morning, Monday, students closed down the school. At 5:30 A.M., they began parking university cars and buses, hot-wired by a street-smart student from New York City, in front of all the campus entrances. Gallaudet's provost got past the angry protesters only after security guards cut a hole in a chain-link fence. Classes were canceled, and a hastily assembled group of students, faculty, and staff took a list of demands to Spilman. Rescind the choice of Zinser, they ordered, and appoint a deaf president. Spilman must resign and a majority of deaf members be named to the board of trustees. There could be no retribution against student and faculty demonstrators. Spilman rejected the demands but agreed to address an assembly, confident she could explain the logic behind choosing Zinser.

But the meeting in the field house was a debacle. There were one thousand noisy students. They screamed and rhythmically swayed their arms to sign "Deaf Power," which was formed by holding the left hand over the left ear to signify "Deaf" and raising the other fist in the air for "Power." They signed "Zinser Out," using, as they did all week, the sign for the word "sinner" as a close and mocking approximation of her surname. Spilman and the other trustees waited onstage, protected from shouting students by a line of security police. Before Spilman could speak, mathematics professor Harvey Goodstein, a member of the delegation that had met with her, walked onstage to sign that she had rejected all of their demands. He encouraged the crowd to leave, and most took off, marching again to the Capitol and the White House, snarling rush-hour traffic. A policeman tried to control the crowd by shouting directions through a megaphone. Then, realizing he could not be heard, he disgustedly flung the megaphone into the back of his patrol car and slammed the trunk. Police were reduced to giving the students an escort downtown. A small group of students stayed behind to hear Spilman in what would be an emotionally charged meeting and one more stumble for Spilman.

As the remaining students yelled in protest, some of the departing ones pulled the fire alarm. "We aren't going to hear you if you scream so loudly that we can't have a dialogue. It's very difficult to be heard over the noise of the fire alarm," the hapless Spilman told the students. "What noise?" students shouted or signed back. "If you could sign," one deaf student responded, "we could hear you." Spilman took a hard line, declaring the choice of Zinser was "lawful, proper and final." It was that scolding attitude that led Bridgetta Bourne to tell a newspaper reporter, "We want to be free from hearing oppression. We don't want to live off the hearing world, we want to live as independent people." That day, visiting professor Harlan Lane had scheduled a lecture on paternalism. It was canceled, along with all other classes. "Real life overtook it," he explained.

The students' ardor did not cool. Classes resumed on Tuesday, although all but about 10 percent of students boycotted them. Protesters burned effigies of Zinser and Spilman. Some 1,500 people gathered for another protest rally at the statue of the school's namesake, Thomas Hopkins Gallaudet, teaching the alphabet to a kneeling girl. "We will not give up," Hlibok signed to the crowd to cheers. "Now is the time to . . . show that we can help ourselves and control our own lives and our futures."

Most important, the protest had grabbed national attention. Students at other deaf schools from Georgia to California demonstrated and sent letters of support. Some students and alumni even came from around the country to the Gallaudet campus to help out. Local businesses sent fruit baskets, pizza, soda, and other provisions. A linen company donated forty bedsheets for banners. A local law firm offered pro bono representation. The students, improvising as the protest grew, put together a sophisticated operation. The protest leaders camped out at the alumni house, where, fortunately for them, the school had set up a bank of telephones and TDDs, telecommunications devices for the deaf, for the semiannual Alumni TDDathon. The students used these to make hundreds of calls to reporters and to people around the country to raise funds. Some seventy interpreters arrived on campus to volunteer their services for the students when reporters and others arrived.

Zinser showed up in Washington on Wednesday, declaring, "I am in charge." Full of bravado, and thinking the protest was the work of only a handful of disgruntled students, she believed she could end the unrest. "I like to rise to the occasion of a challenge," she told reporters during a press conference at the National Press Club and hinted that she was ready to get tough with the demonstrators.

But Zinser never set foot on campus. To keep her out, students at the barricades thoroughly searched incoming campus security cars, even checking the trunks. Students even planned to stop Zinser from arriving by helicopter by lying on the ground, if necessary, to prevent it from landing. Zinser summoned a group of student leaders to her hotel but was refused a request to address the entire student body. The students did not recognize her as president, Hlibok explained, and would not give her such legitimacy by letting her address them. There was a setback for the protesters, however, when Zinser got backing from the two deaf candidates she had defeated. Spilman released a supportive letter from Corson. A stricken-looking I. King Jordan showed up at Zinser's side at the press conference. Earlier in the week, he had given a moderate endorsement of the student protest, encouraging students to "continue this in a positive way." Now, he explained, he felt an obligation as a dean to support the school first. Other faculty and staff members, however, voted to support the student demands by near-unanimous margins.

Wisely, the students had focused on taking their cause to Congress. Gallaudet is a federally chartered university, and in 1988 75 percent of the school's budget, some $61 million, came from Congress. Many politicians, who already understood the political power of disabled people, were eager allies. Senator Bob Dole and Vice President George Bush, now locked in battle for

the Republican presidential nomination, had already urged the
school to name a deaf president. So had House Majority Whip
Tony Coehlo. And Michigan Representative David Bonior was
quoted on the front page of Wednesday's *Washington Post* warn-
ing that Zinser's appointment imperiled continued congressional largesse toward the school. On Wednesday morning,
Democrat Bonior and Republican Representative Steve Gunderson of Wisconsin, both on Gallaudet's board, met with Hlibok
and faculty and alumni protesters. Later that day, Zinser and
Spilman called on the lawmakers, too, in an attempt to reassure
members of Congress that they were in control despite the brief
spark of revolt. Instead, Bonior urged Zinser to resign. That
evening, Hlibok and Zinser faced off on the ABC news program
"Nightline," which ran open captions for the first time. Zinser
said that she believed "very strongly" that a deaf person would
one day be the president of Gallaudet. "This statement, 'one day
a deaf president,' is very old rhetoric," Hlibok shot back. "We've
been hearing this for one hundred twenty-four years."

By the following day, it became clear to Zinser that she
could not win. The board had reaffirmed its decision to appoint
her, but the protest showed no signs of dying out as students
pledged to stay on campus the following week, even though it
meant giving up their spring vacation. A symbol of the changing tide had come when Jordan, smiling, showed up at the day's
rally to recant his support of Zinser of the day before and express
his "anger at the continuing lack of confidence that [members
of the board of trustees] have shown in deaf people." It was a
risky move for a university dean. Later Jordan would explain, "I
realized I might just be dean for a week. But I would be a deaf
person for the rest of my life." That evening at about 7:30,
Zinser turned to Spilman and said simply, "I resign." Shortly
before midnight, the university put out a press release to announce Zinser's resignation.

The next morning, Zinser read her resignation statement at

a press conference. She had concluded, she said, "that the best way to restore order and return this university to its business of education" was to resign and allow the appointment of a deaf president. She ended her statement by giving the sign-language hand signal for, "I love you." Even after this victory, the protest was not over. There was still a new president to name, and the students' other demands remained on the table. Shortly after Zinser's press conference, about three thousand cheering students and supporters left campus and marched once more to the U.S. Capitol, signing and chanting "Deaf president now" and "We will not back down."

On Sunday, one week after the protests had begun, seventeen members of Gallaudet's board of trustees met in a downtown hotel to choose a president. In the seven-hour meeting, they decided to give the students everything they were seeking, and more. Jordan, the popular dean, would become the school's first deaf president. The new chairman of the board would be Philip Bravin, an IBM program manager and the deaf head of the presidential search committee who had angered students earlier in the week. Half of the board of trustees would be deaf. There would be no sanctions against the demonstrators.

Outside the hotel, before ecstatic students and in front of television cameras that recorded the moment for the world, an exhilarated Jordan accepted his new appointment. "This is a historic moment for deaf people around the world," he signed, and spoke in his clear voice. "In this week we can truly say that we, together and united, have overcome our own reluctance to stand for our rights and our full representation. The world has watched the deaf community come of age. We can no longer accept limits on what we can achieve."

Spilman announced her own resignation, saying, "In the minds of some, I have become an obstacle to the future of the university. And because I care very, very deeply about Gallaudet's future, I am removing the obstacle." Even to the end, however, she insisted that the "best choice [for president] was a hearing candidate."

A few days later, Hlibok wrote a letter to Zinser, who had returned to her school in North Carolina. "You were, of course, an innocent victim and unfortunate target for our collective anger," he wrote. Zinser would take to wearing a necklace with a silver charm shaped in the hand sign for "I love you."

That it had taken until 1988 for such a stunning expression of deaf pride was no accident. Like other disability group protests, the one by deaf students reflected a growing sense of oppression. It gave voice to anger bottled up over years of being seen as pitiful and sick. Social, demographic, and technological trends, too, had created the sense of an emerging deaf minority group in the 1980s. It was not until 1971 that a television show—an episode of Julia Child's "The French Chef"—was captioned for deaf viewers. Television news first became accessible in 1973 with the titled and rebroadcast ABC's "World News Tonight." By the year of the Gallaudet protest, some 180 hours a week of network, cable, and public television shows were captioned. Deaf people, as a result, were more informed and felt more a part of the world. Even more important, the telephone was becoming accessible. In the 1970s and 1980s came the development of portable, affordable TDDs. Interpreting grew as a profession, as deaf people became more numerous and more independent. Before, interpreting had been left largely to the hearing children of deaf parents.

The disability rights movement, too, had led to new opportunity. More deaf children went to mainstream schools and colleges. Many at Gallaudet would see mainstreaming as a threat to the separate schools that fostered a sense of deaf identity, but by 1985, 44 percent of deaf students were in mainstream public schools and only 29 percent in deaf residential schools. Still, civil rights protections for the disabled often had limited applications for the deaf. Few schools and businesses interpreted these laws to mean they needed to hire costly interpreters for deaf students or employees.

Once again, medicine helped spur a movement by saving people, who then would live with a disability: the number of school-age deaf children doubled as a result of the rubella epidemic of 1964–65. This new generation of deaf, born in the middle of the civil rights and Vietnam eras and molded by the new technology and laws for disabled people, had higher expectations for themselves. They were more militant, too, and talked of their deaf identity and culture. Some were studying at Gallaudet in 1988; others were among the young alumni who had bankrolled the protests.

Yet there was great irony in the fact that it should be Gallaudet students who would succeed in equating disability with civil rights: to them, deafness is not a disability but a culture—like being Jewish, Irish, or Navajo. Some deaf people make this distinction by spelling deaf with a capital *D* when referring to cultural deafness, and with a small *d* when talking about an auditory condition. Deaf people argue that they share their own complex language, American Sign Language, as well as a culture and a group history. Disability is a medical condition, argued the Gallaudet student leaders. Deaf people felt they had long been oppressed by those who saw their hearing loss as a disability or pathology in need of correction. In concert with the broader disability rights thinking, they argued that they had been held back by those who pitied their deafness and felt them, therefore, less capable. As John Limnidis, a hulking Gallaudet football player from Canada who played a small part in the movie *Children of a Lesser God,* would explain: "Deafness is not a handicap. It's a culture, a language, and I'm proud to be deaf. If there was a medication that could be given to deaf people to make them hear, I wouldn't take it. Never. Never till I die!"

Lost Language, Lost Culture

Indeed, there are strong historical arguments for the profound power of a separate deaf culture and for the viability of deafness as a way of life different from, but equal to, traditional hearing culture.

For 250 years, deafness was commonplace on Martha's Vineyard. The first deaf resident, a fisherman named Jonathan Lambert, settled there in 1694. He carried a recessive gene for deafness and, as a result of frequent intermarriage among the isolated islanders, this trait spread through generations of Lambert's descendants. A few villages, like Chilmark and Tisbury, had unusually high numbers of deaf citizens. By the middle of the nineteenth century, one in twenty-five residents of Chilmark was deaf, and in one neighborhood the ratio was one in four. As anthropologist Nora Ellen Groce notes in her book, *Everyone Here Spoke Sign Language,* the result was an easy, almost natural fusion of deaf and hearing cultures.

With such a large population of deaf citizens, the entire community learned to use sign language—even when there was no deaf member of the family—and sign was not for the exclusive use of communicating with deaf residents. Hearing fishermen would use it to communicate from one distant boat to another. People even signed to talk in church. If hearing people were talking among themselves and a deaf person joined them, they would all switch to sign.

The last deaf islander died in 1952, but when neurologist and author Oliver Sacks visited Martha's Vineyard some thirty-five years later, he found that older hearing people still communicated in sign language to tell stories or converse with their neighbors. One of the oldest Sacks met, a woman in her nineties, "would sometimes fall into a peaceful reverie" all the time moving her hands as if she were knitting. "But her daughter, also a signer, told me she was not knitting but thinking to herself, thinking in Sign," Sacks writes. "And even in sleep, I was further informed, the old lady might sketch fragmentary signs on the counterpane—she was dreaming in Sign."

There were no language barriers on Martha's Vineyard and, as a result, no social ones either. Deaf people participated widely in community affairs, from town politics to church events. Deaf and hearing islanders led similar lives. Eighty percent of deaf people on Martha's Vineyard married, about the same rate as that for hearing islanders. In the nineteenth century, only 45 percent of American deaf people married. Both deaf and hearing islanders had an average of six children, while nationally in the 1880s, the average deaf-hearing couple had only 2.6 children. On this island separated by a short span of Atlantic Ocean from the Massachusetts mainland, deaf and hearing islanders held the same jobs and therefore enjoyed similar income levels; they played cards and drank together. Deaf people held town positions from school committee member to highway surveyor and served in the militia.

One difference was that deaf islanders tended to be better educated. The state of Massachusetts paid for ten years of their education, and most went to the American Asylum for the Deaf and Dumb in Hartford while their hearing brothers and sisters who stayed on the island often dropped out of school early to help farm or fish. Some of the "less educated hearing people would occasionally bring a newspaper or legal document to their deaf neighbors to have it explained," writes Groce. By the mid-1800s, greater mobility slowed the pace of intermarriage, and the genetic anomaly that created the deaf community disappeared.

Martha's Vineyard was a nineteenth-century deaf utopia, where deafness was ordinary, not a sickness. Nor was it disabling, largely because the island's hearing residents were bilingual.

The tolerant atmosphere of Martha's Vineyard may not have been universal in America, but for most of the nineteenth century the predilection of the deaf for signed communication was acknowledged and endorsed. The most influential educator of deaf people, and an early advocate of ASL, was Thomas Hopkins Gallaudet. One day in 1813, Gallaudet, a Congregationalist minister, watched a neighbor girl playing with other children in his garden. The child, Alice Cogswell, had become deaf in 1807 when she contracted spotted fever. Unable to communicate with her friends, Alice was aloof and shy. Gallaudet talked to the girl's father, a prominent physician named Mason Cogswell, and found out that no American schools taught deaf children, although a few wealthy families had sent their deaf children to Europe, where exciting new pedagogy had been developed. The next year, Gallaudet, with financial backing from Cogswell and others, set off for Europe to find a deaf teacher to bring to America.

His first stop was England, where he met the Thomas Braid-wood family. They ran several schools of oralism, a method to teach deaf people to speak like hearing people. But after several trying months, Gallaudet's negotiations with the Braidwoods fell through. They insisted on maintaining their profitable franchise over their oralist method for which another Braidwood, John, was already attempting to establish an American school. Frustrated, Gallaudet left for France. In Paris, he went to the Institute of Deaf-Mutes that had been opened in 1755 by the Abbé de l'Epée, a man often wrongly credited with inventing sign language. (Sign language is innate, not invented.) L'Epée had noticed that deaf children had their own communication system, which he combined with French signed grammar in order to teach them. It was at this school that Gallaudet met a young teacher named Laurent Clerc, himself deaf and without speech. Clerc had traveled little beyond the confines of the school, but he accepted Gallaudet's offer of adventure. On the fifty-two-day journey back in 1816, Clerc taught Gallaudet to sign, and Gallaudet taught Clerc to use English.

Together they raised money and in 1817 opened the American Asylum for the Deaf and Dumb in Hartford. Alice Cogswell was the first student. The teachers were fluent signers, and most were deaf themselves. With the advent of ASL instruction, there was an impressive rise of literacy among the deaf, and the school was hailed as a great humanitarian experiment. Other schools, modeled after the one in Hartford, opened around the country. In 1864, Congress created the Columbia Institution for the Deaf and Blind in Washington, the first school of higher learning for the deaf. Edward Miner Gallaudet, the eighth and youngest son of the famous educator, had persuaded Abraham Lincoln to charter it, with the aim of training deaf teachers for the deaf. Edward Gallaudet then became the first principal of the school, which would later be renamed for his father. Originally, sign language was used for all instruction at the Columbia Institution.

It would not be long, however, before the founding of a school opposed to sign-language instruction. In 1867, the Clarke School for the Deaf was established by a millionaire Bostonian named Gardiner Greene Hubbard. His young daughter, Mabel, had become deaf after contracting scarlet fever at the age of five. He had hired tutors to help her keep up her speech, which declined over time. Hubbard's belief in oralism had come from two prominent educators. One was Samuel Gridley Howe, who had established the Perkins Institute, the first school for the blind, where he had won national attention for his success in educating Laura Bridgman, who was blind and deaf. Howe and educator Horace Mann had visited European schools that claimed important success teaching oralism, and the two had returned to America, hoping to replace sign-language instruction with oral methods.

One of the first teachers at the Clarke School was a young inventor and speech expert named Alexander Graham Bell. He was born in Edinburgh and came from a long line of elocutionists and teachers of speech to the deaf. George Bernard Shaw praised his father, Alexander Melville Bell, in the preface to *Pygmalion,* and the father has been credited with being the model for Professor Henry Higgins. In 1873, Alexander Graham Bell, then twenty-six, began tutoring Mabel Hubbard. It was to be a fortuitous union. For one thing, Gardiner Greene Hubbard was a patent attorney, interested in the telegraph and Bell's experiments with the telephone. In 1876, Hubbard helped Bell get the first patent on the telephone, although other inventors were registering similar designs and there would be years of litigation to protect the patent. Bell and Mabel Hubbard married soon thereafter. Some Bell biographies say he invented the telephone in search of a device to help Mabel Hubbard communicate with other people in the same house. Instead, it would only cut deaf people off more from the world, depriving them not only of communication but of jobs and a full place in the hearing community.

Oralism fit well with the conformist spirit of the times. The Victorian era was unsparing toward minority culture. The Welsh language was banned from schools in Wales; English was made the administrative language of the Indian subcontinent. Even the usage of gestures when speaking English was considered improper since, notes Arden Neisser in her history of sign language, "gesturing was something that Italians did, and Jews, and Frenchmen: it reflected the poverty of their cultures and the immaturity of their personalities. Sign language became a code word with strong racial overtones." Speech was God given. It was what separated man from beasts. If one did not have speech, then one did not have language and, went thinking that dated back to Aristotle, was presumably unable to reason. To remain silent, then, was to be prey to the devil.

All this suggested that deafness was a sickness, something that needed to be cured. Oralism held out the hope of correction. It was a laborious method that required intensive one-on-one instruction. By comparison, sign could be taught to many students at once. When someone succeeded in the oral method, however, his ability could be awe-inspiring and his deafness would seem almost irrelevant.

Oralism spread in the nineteenth century, although Bell's own family showed the method's shortcomings. His wife was never considered a good speaker or lip-reader, despite the years of special tutoring from Bell and others. Even Edward Miner Gallaudet, cognizant of the shifting theories of the times, visited oralist schools in this country and abroad and came back advocating that both manual and oral communication be used. After all, it had been accident more than philosophy that resulted in his father's returning from France with Clerc, instead of from England with a Braidwood, in tow.

In 1880, the year of the International Congress of Educators of the Deaf at Milan, oralism was adopted as the universal teaching method. From the end of the nineteenth century through the early 1970s, American educators embraced the method. They taught the deaf to speak and lip-read, and therefore to use the language of the dominant culture. Deaf students were molded in the image of the hearing world, and their inability to speak was seen as a shortcoming in need of correction. ASL was dismissed as a crude slang. Linguists taught it to apes and chimpanzees, but it was considered useless for real thought and communication.

Few deaf people, however, ever mastered oralism. Those who did tended to be people who had lost their hearing after they already had language—the adventitiously or postlingually deaf—or who had significant residual hearing and could use hearing aids. Those who learned oralism could move easily between the hearing and deaf worlds. But lip-reading was a skill of superachievers. "It can be compared with breaking an eighty in golf or painting a masterpiece in oils," writes deaf educator Leo Jacobs. "Speech-reading talent has absolutely no correlation with intelligence." Even in the best circumstances, only 30 percent of speech can be read from lip movements. Oralists can speech-read only those who move their lips distinctly, and even then can only do so in good light or at a near distance. "I can consistently understand somewhat fewer than 50 percent of the people I meet for the first time, but familiarity will raise the level of understanding to 75 to 80 percent," writes Henry Kisor, a talented lip-reader who is book editor of the *Chicago Sun-Times.* "Perhaps 10 percent of the people I come across will always be impossible to lipread." Kisor called his autobiography *What's That Pig Outdoors?,* a reference to his misreading of his son's question, "What's that big loud noise?"

Deaf students in the 1850s who had been taught ASL at the American Asylum for the Deaf in Hartford were equally literate as their hearing peers. As educators insisted on teaching oralism, however, deaf students' academic achievement deteriorated. Many deaf people became functionally illiterate, a trend that continued for the next century. A 1972 study by Gallaudet researchers found that the average eighteen-year-old deaf high school graduate read at only a fourth-grade level. By the 1960s, alarm about this low academic achievement forced educators to find new methods of instruction.

Cued Speech, invented in 1966, used fourteen handshapes formed near the mouth to signal to a speech-reader the sound being made, in order to distinguish similarly formed words such at mitt or bit. But this system was useful only if both people knew it. In the 1970s, most teachers switched to Total Communication, usually a combination of speech and signed English. This was a minor breakthrough since it acknowledged that oralism was not always the best method. There are many different forms of Total Communication, but all, like oralism, depend predominantly on the use of English. One method, called Sim Com, requires teachers to speak and sign simultaneously. Linguistically, this is nearly impossible, since it is the equivalent of speaking in one language and simultaneously writing in another. Speaking tends to slow down, and signing gets sloppy.

ASL is not English. It has its own syntax and grammar. ASL is a separate innate language that belongs to people who become deaf at birth or before they learn to speak. The deaf in every country have their own form of this native language. American Sign Language is different from French Sign Language, even from British Sign Language. In the Southern United States, black deaf people, kept segregated from white ones, developed separate sign dialects. Only in the 1970s would ASL be studied by academic linguists, who then realized it has a highly complex and nuanced structure.

It is only now that researchers are beginning to argue that a deaf child's brain is structured to pick up ASL and that learning ASL first can make it easier to pick up English later. Most proponents of ASL agree that it is important to be bilingual and to learn signed English along with ASL. The deaf children of deaf parents, called "native signers," pick up ASL naturally from seeing their parents use it. Scientists recently discovered that deaf babies of deaf parents use this language, and develop it, first babbling at ten months, at times parallel to the learning of spoken language by hearing babies. Before, linguists had assumed that language was the same as speech and that the maturation of an infant's vocal cords determined language development. Five-year-old native signers possess vocabularies of about five thousand words, the same amount as the average five-year-old hearing child. But deaf children of hearing parents—the case 90 percent of the time—often enter school with a vocabulary of less than fifty words. As a result, some researchers have begun calling for teaching ASL to all school-age children.

Even today, ASL is rarely taught to deaf students. Most teachers use a signed version of English. The argument for this is that deaf students, to get along in the world, need to know the language of the dominant, hearing culture. Another reason is simply practical. Most teachers of the deaf are hearing and English is their native language. It is hard enough to learn to sign in English (and many deaf students complain about the poor signing of their teachers). To learn and use ASL would be like teaching in a foreign language. That would be a considerable burden on teachers. Yet using any other method is an imposition, too, on deaf students, since research is showing that ASL is their natural language.

For ninety years after the 1880 Milan conference the use of sign language would be banned from American schools. Students who disobeyed got their hands slapped or tied down. Deaf teachers—who by 1869 totalled 41 percent of instructors of the deaf—were driven from the classroom. By the turn of the century, that percentage had dropped to 25 percent and to only 12 percent by 1960. Gallaudet became the only institution to use manual instruction, but, more and more in the minority, teachers there quit using ASL and instead signed in a version of English. (In the 1890s, the football huddle was invented at Gallaudet, to keep other teams from reading their signs.) ASL came to be viewed as no more than a slang gesture language.

Alexander Graham Bell's profound influence on educators for the deaf was a major force in the denigration of signing. Bell's motives were mixed. This prominent educator of the deaf also was a proponent of another popular movement of the day— eugenics. To avoid the emergence of a "defective" race, Bell suggested a typically eugenicist solution: Laws to forbid "the intermarriage of deaf-mutes." But there were shortcomings to such an approach, as Bell conceded in a major address on the subject to the National Academy of Science meeting in 1883. Deafness could skip generations. Although Bell's contemporaries were ignorant of Mendelian genetics, Bell realized that congenital deafness ran in families in some way. Many of his students and the deaf residents of Martha's Vineyard whom Bell had visited were not born to deaf parents but had deaf relatives.

For that reason, Bell thought there was genetic logic to drafting marriage banns very broadly to forbid "the intermarriage of persons belonging to families containing more than one deaf-mute." Even such legal proscriptions, the practical Bell knew, would not keep deaf men and women apart. Indeed, it "might only promote immorality," as deaf lovers sought out each other in secret trysts.

Far more effective, then, would be to keep deaf people from associating with one another. Bell looked at the state of deaf education and declared that it was perverse. If keeping deaf people away from one another was a necessary goal, then everything deaf schools did was wrong. "We take deaf children away from their homes and place them in institutions by the hundred, keeping them there from early childhood to the commencement of adult life," he told the scientists at New Haven. And then, when these students became adults ready for marriage, the schools held reunions and published newspapers with "personals" to keep readers informed of deaf social events around the country. The schools created lifelong networks of friends, and in every large city they formed social clubs. "After the business of the day is done, the deaf-mutes of the city meet together for social intercourse and on Sundays for public worship," Bell noted. There were state associations of the deaf, too. "Periodical conventions are held in different parts of the State, attended by deaf-mutes of both sexes. At these meetings they amuse themselves in various ways. Sometimes they hold fairs; have theatrical representations in dumb show, spectacular tableaux, dancing, &c," he said, in words dripping with disdain. More ominous, he added, was that deaf people were beginning to form national associations, and recently the Second National Convention of Deaf-Mutes brought hundreds of deaf people to New York from across the United States.

Bell's address came at the beginning of the international movement to bar sign language from the classroom. The one thing that most united deaf people was their "gesture language." Bell acknowledged that sign was a language that deaf people thought in, a separate language "as different from English as French or German or Russian." But the use of sign, he said, was the biggest deterrent to integrating deaf people with hearing ones. Deaf adults often lacked fluency in English, Bell complained, and communicated with hearing persons by writing "in broken English, as a foreigner would speak." They were unable to appreciate great English literature or comprehend "the political speeches of the day, the leading editorials," Bell told the scientists. Yet there were misguided attempts, he said, to legitimize sign language, including a Canadian school principal's plan to write a dictionary of sign symbols. Bell's remedy was simple: use the oral method of teaching—only 14 percent of deaf students then used speech—and stop letting deaf teachers—who used gesture language in the classroom—instruct deaf students.

To his fellow scientists in New Haven, Bell made an early call for what today we would call mainstreaming. At a time when people with disabilities were being removed to closeted institutions, Bell's "grand central principle" was to educate the deaf and the hearing side by side. Deaf students would be located in the same schools as hearing ones, with limited, separate instruction in some subjects, but in the same classroom as hearing pupils for any subject "in which information is gained through the eye," such as writing, drawing, geography, arithmetic, and sewing. "For other subjects special methods of instruction would be necessary, and these demand the employment of special teachers," Bell said. In another argument that parallels those for integrated education today, Bell called for teaching deaf students in their neighborhood schools. This would save money, he noted, by ending the practice of building costly, distinct facilities.

Most crucial to integration, Bell understood, was to excise irrational "fallacies" and "fear" of the deaf. It was segregation that created unkind myths. Such "incorrect ideas" were created because deaf students were collected "into institutions away from public observation," he noted. Contact between deaf and hearing people would erase these myths. "Whatever the cause, it is certainly the case that adult deaf-mutes are sometimes hampered by the instinctive prejudices of hearing persons with whom they desire to have business or social relations," Bell said. "Many persons have the idea they are dangerous, morose, ill-tempered, etc." A deaf person, he added, "is sometimes looked upon as a sort of monstrosity, to be stared at and *avoided.*" One deaf man in Alabama, he noted, had been shot dead by a man who became alarmed by his unfamiliar hand gestures. Such words won Bell acclaim as a great champion of deaf people. But his progressive-sounding call for full acceptance and integration of deaf people only masked his dark eugenicist vision.

Bell's words carried great weight. Thomas Gallaudet had died twenty-two years before, and the oral method Bell advocated was winning international primacy. By the time of his 1883 speech, Bell was emerging as the nation's foremost authority on educating the deaf. That deaf people needed a hearing savior was dubious, given that they were well-educated, quickly entering professional jobs like teaching, and setting up extensive social networks. Yet Bell's words were considered a compassionate defense of deaf people. Underlying this presumed sympathy, however, was the oppressive belief that deafness was a cause for commiseration. The most merciful thing to do was to end deaf culture and language—even to prevent deaf people from being born. Coming from a renowned expert on the deaf—indeed, from a man hailed as their greatest champion—the oppressiveness of this pity was hard to refute. As disabled people would instinctly understand, prejudice cut deepest when it came from the charitable, not from the most bigoted.

The denunciation of sign language would not change until the 1960s, with the publication of the work of William

Stokoe. The young linguist had come to Gallaudet in the late 1950s to teach Chaucer and English literature. On the Gallaudet campus, Stokoe became fascinated with the graceful sign language students still used outside class. He began to study the signing of students who were the children of deaf parents. Gallaudet administrators frowned on his work. But in 1960, Stokoe, who was hearing, published a seminal paper arguing that ASL was a complex, three-dimensional language, and in 1965 he published *A Dictionary of American Sign Language.* Such manuals of sign language had been out of print since around 1918.

Today, deaf people are beginning to reclaim ASL as their birthright, a natural language that has been denied to them for over one hundred years. The National Association of the Deaf, in a position paper, says that deaf people should have "the right to become fluent" in both ASL and English and the right to choose to use whichever language they prefer in the classroom or elsewhere. Gallaudet and some other schools now teach ASL again. But other classes, according to Gallaudet's official policy, are conducted in signed English. I. King Jordan, who lost his hearing—and almost his life—in a motorcycle accident when he was twenty-one, uses signed English and speaks clearly. On the Gallaudet campus, this is a source of lingering criticism of Jordan, who otherwise has become a folk hero at Gallaudet and among deaf people around the world.

Since the 1988 Gallaudet rebellion, there have been brief flare-ups of student demands to make ASL mandatory for classroom teaching. In 1990, there was tragedy when one of these protesters, a student named Carl Dupree, died of asphyxiation when, following a dispute over a grade with an instructor, he struggled with four campus police officers. Students complained that the security police had only further agitated Dupree by handcuffing the hands he used for speech. Dupree was protesting his grade in a basic English class, required to stay in school, but which proponents of ASL said should be dropped. Controversy over the use of ASL arose again at the 1992 trial of the four security police, who were acquitted of charges of using excessive force: there were several disputes over the exact translation into English of the courtroom testimony given in ASL by deaf witnesses.

The Common and Tribal

The world of deaf people, say deaf authors Carol Padden and Tom Humphries, revolves around a "different center." To be unable to hear is the norm, whereas society sees deafness as a pathology. This is the same complaint of the disability rights movement that rejects the medical definition of disability as an illness. This "different center" is clear in language. In ASL, to say someone is "very hard of hearing" means the opposite of its definition in English. To deaf people, to have no hearing is the standard. To be "very hard of hearing" is to deviate greatly from the standard, or to hear quite well.

The central tenet of the disability rights movement is complete integration into the community. At the end of the rainbow is a day when a person's disability will no longer matter. Integration will come through mainstreamed schools and civil rights laws that guarantee full access to public accommodations and the workplace. Just give us a chance, disability activists say, and we will be like everyone else.

The 1988 Gallaudet uprising was a primal roar of rebellion against decades of an expectation to adopt the dominant hearing culture and its demands for oralism, at the forfeiture of a rich deaf identity. It was a declaration that deaf people should celebrate their differentness. A person's disability will always matter, the students argued, and it will always set disabled people apart. Deaf people, they said, should make their own world. This debate echoes the integrationist argument of the last three decades among black Americans. It was the appealing Gallaudet students, with their clean-cut and All-American good looks, who made the radical argument for disability separatism.

For deaf students, a separate world meant education in their own schools, to be run more and more by deaf presidents. To them, one of the first great victories of the disability rights movement—the mainstream education law—was a threat. It led to cuts in public funding for segregated deaf schools, in part because regular schools began welcoming deaf and other disabled students. Mainstreaming, complained David Wolfe of the National Information Center on Deafness, was "like trying to solve the race problem by making everybody white." Trying to force deaf students to fit into an alien world would only reinforce their sense of inferiority. After the Gallaudet protest, there would be renewed clamor for separate deaf education where students would learn their own language and the values of deaf culture. California's legislature even passed a law to require deaf students to be educated with groups of deaf peers and taught by teachers "proficient" in sign. Governor Pete Wilson vetoed the legislation, which would have largely resegregated deaf students in separate schools or isolated classes.

There are reasons to believe in the idealistic and hopeful integrationist scenario that is most common to the disability rights movement. Disabled people often have more in common with the general population than do members of other minority groups. Disabled people are almost always brought up by nondisabled mothers and fathers, with nondisabled sisters and brothers. They may marry nondisabled spouses and then have children who are not disabled. Most disabilities, however, are not as isolating as deafness, which cuts off communication from others. Many deaf leaders, too, like Frank Bowe, who headed a federal commission on deaf education shortly after the Gallaudet protest, have argued that too much faith in "deaf pride, deaf culture" can cut off deaf people from the benefits of the disability rights movement. "For too long, deaf people have stood by themselves, fought for themselves alone," said Bowe. "But it is time for them to recognize that they share so much with people who are blind, who have cerebral palsy, and we all need to work together." Indeed, many deaf leaders embraced the expansion of rights spelled out in the Americans with Disabilities Act, and Jordan became a visible proponent of it on Capitol Hill.

After Gallaudet, the hearing world became more welcoming. Hlibok, for example, entered law school, saying he no longer questioned his place at a hearing school. Bridgetta Bourne's father, a Department of Defense computer expert, got a promotion. He had been passed over for many years by hearing bosses who, until they watched the daughter's protest, had underestimated his ability.

Separatist deaf pride flourished, too. One writer proposed renaming Gallaudet as Gallaudet and Clerc University, to give proper credit to the deaf member of the founding team. Many objected when the woman chosen Miss Deaf California played a Bach piano concerto for the pageant's talent competition. Should the title have gone to someone with enough hearing to play music, or picked for her ability to do something that other hard-of-hearing people could not appreciate? And deaf people protested more stridently when hearing actors played deaf movie roles—the "moral" equivalent of "putting a white actor in blackface," complained deaf activist Bobbie Beth Scoggins.

Some thoughtful disability rights activists think there is much to learn from the deaf separatist model. Judy Heumann argues that it is important for disabled people, as they overcome segregation, to hold on to their sense of identity and history of struggle. Growing up, she knew she was always "different." Even when she had reached mainstream schools she still never felt "completely accepted by my peers." She yearned for the dignity and opportunities that were second nature to nondisabled people, but she rejoiced in the bonds made with disabled people. Best of all was camp for disabled kids, which she attended every summer from the time she turned nine until she was eighteen. With kids who were blind, deaf, or had physical disabilities and mental retardation, she confessed secrets and found others shared her doubts and worries. "We had the same joy together, the same anger over the way we were treated and the same frustrations at opportunities we didn't have," she says. For the first time, Heumann confided that she suspected people stared at her in her wheelchair and that it made her uncomfortable. To her delight, every other kid with polio had the same feeling. At home she watched "American Bandstand," but disabled kids, she was told, "were not supposed to dance." At camp, "we danced and we danced so well that we felt good about ourselves." A kid in a wheelchair could be just as cool as "American Bandstand" dancers—at camp, anyway—and not be just another sick kid excluded from dances, dates, and even sex. Crippled girls were never expected to get married. Motherhood was thought out of the question. No boy would ever give them a second look, they were told. But at camp, Heumann recalls, they dated and "talked about getting married, where you couldn't talk about it at home." At camp she could feel comfortable and self-confident about being disabled, much as students at Gallaudet could feel secure in their deafness.

There are few places today for this kind of bonding among disabled people. Heumann is heartened by the rise, however slow, of disability culture. There are poets and writers like Vassar Miller and Anne Finger. There are novels like *The Body's Memory*, Jean Stewart's beautiful story of a disabled woman's politicization, to counter literature's more familiar embittered cripples, like Flannery O'Connor's unappealing victim who gets her wooden leg stolen by a traveling Bible salesman. Most common remain the autobiographical memoirs, which are becoming ever more political, like Lorenzo Wilson Milam's *The*

Cripple Liberation Front Marching Band Blues or John Callahan's *Don't Worry, He Won't Get Far on Foot.* Disability studies classes are being taught on college campuses. Lively magazines, including *The Disability Rag, This Mouth Has a Brain,* and *Mainstream* vent the new anger. There are even disability comedians and theater groups. Not surprisingly, the center of disability performance is Berkeley, home of performance artist Cheryl Wade and performance groups like the Wry Crips and remnants of Frank's Church, an avant-garde troupe that used nudity and sexual themes to discuss nondisabled people's fear of disability.

Yet disability expression lags behind the thriving deaf arts. The rediscovery of ASL sparked a deaf cultural renaissance, starting with the decision of the National Theater of the Deaf in 1972 to perform in the expressive native language of deaf people. "Once the resistance had been broken, and the new consciousness established, there was no stopping deaf artists of all sorts," writes Sacks. "There arose Sign poetry, Sign wit, Sign song, Sign dance—unique Sign arts that could not be translated into speech. A bardic tradition arose, or re-arose among the deaf, with Sign bards, Sign orators, Sign storytellers, Sign narrators, who served to transmit and disseminate the history and culture of the deaf, and, in so doing, raise the new cultural consciousness yet higher."

Not all disability activists, however, share Heumann's celebration of a separate disability culture. Robert Funk, one of the founding philosophers of disability integration, argues that deaf culture grew out of the unique experience of having a distinct language. For most disabled people, he argues, "disability will disappear as an issue," once they ease into mainstream society. This is dreaming, says Heumann, noting that the integrationist dream circa 1960s of the black civil rights movement proved unattainable. (Heumann notes that as a wheelchair rider she is more restricted and therefore more pessimistic about full integration than Funk, who uses crutches.) Funk says it will be possible for disabled people, who come from nondisabled families and "all strata of society" to blend into an integrated world. He thinks businesses will come to accommodate disabled workers, and architects will embrace universal design, the idea of making buildings accessible to all, and homes that can be rearranged as owners age.

Today Funk's view is dominant. Civil rights legislation for disabled people was based on making physical and mental limitations irrelevant; but, like all minority groups, disabled people have had to draw on their history of oppression to become politicized and demand those rights. Disability pride is emerging and being embraced just like deaf pride before it. Funk warns that disabled people must not get caught in the trap of identifying themselves as victims, something that he argues has snared blacks and other minorities. Disabled people may succeed in balancing pride and a separatist identity borne of past discrimination, without playing the role of victim. The disability rights movement, after all, is a rebellion against being cast by society as pitiable victims. This is one minority group that understands that claiming the role of victim is self-defeating.

The disability movement would seek civil rights protection in the Americans with Disabilities Act, but the act would not demand affirmative action programs or guaranteed equality of results. Disabled people would optimistically argue that all they needed was integration and an equal opportunity to achieve. Still, there are questions. Will nondisabled Americans understand how disabled ones are reexamining what it means to have a disability? Will disabled people get a true shot at being fully included citizens?

CHAPTER 4

A HIDDEN ARMY FOR CIVIL RIGHTS

L isa Carl just wanted to see a movie. But in 1988 when the nineteen-year-old with cerebral palsy wheeled herself to the ticket booth of her neighborhood theater in Tacoma, Washington, the owner refused to take her dollar bill. "I don't want her in here, and I don't have to let her in," the owner later explained, noting the girl had difficulty speaking and getting around. As Carl told U.S. senators the next year, "I was not crying outside, but I was crying inside. I just wanted to be able to watch the movie like everybody else."

Carl told her story in testimony on behalf of the Americans with Disabilities Act, a bill to extend to people with physical and mental disabilities the same protections against discrimination that had been afforded minorities and women under the 1964 Civil Rights Act. The movie theater owner's rejection had been a case of blatant bigotry. But disabled people knew that, sadly, what happened to Carl was no isolated act of exclusion. In fact, nearly two-thirds of disabled people had not been to a movie theater in the previous year, compared to just 22 percent of the general population. Seventeen percent of disabled people had not eaten a meal in a restaurant, although only 5 percent of nondisabled people had avoided dining out. As compared to only 2 percent of all others, 13 percent of disabled people never shopped in a grocery store. When pollsters from Louis Harris and Associates asked disabled people why they remained so separate, 59 percent explained that they were afraid to go out. They were fearful of being mistreated, as Carl had been at the movies. And 40 percent said their access to public places was restricted by physical barriers, meaning buildings and streets, while 49 percent said transit systems were inaccessible. It was the same poll that found that 66 percent of disabled people were unemployed, although two-thirds of that group said they could work and wanted to work. Either bosses would not hire them, they claimed, or they could not get through the front door of inaccessible workplaces.

No other group of citizens was so insulated or so removed from the American mainstream. Twenty-five years after black Americans had successfully won a legal end to their exclusion from public places and jobs, similar segregation was still a fact of daily life for millions of disabled people. The disability rights victories of the previous decade—a law guaranteeing public education and Section 504—had been not nearly enough to end the isolation. That was why disability activists now turned their attention to winning passage of a broad civil rights bill. For the first time, people with disabilities were asking Americans to recognize that the biggest problem facing them was discrimination. They sought access and opportunity, not charity. Nearly every disabled man and woman has a story like Lisa Carl's, all of which helped fuel the anger and passion that brought about the unexpected and stunning passage of the ADA, the most sweeping civil rights law since 1964. Bob Burgdorf has such a story as well.

Just twenty years old in 1968, Burgdorf was home from college for the summer and about to take part proudly in a new program sponsored by the electricians' union in Evansville, Indiana. The teenage sons of electricians in the Ohio River city would work alongside their fathers and their fathers' friends. When Burgdorf had shown up for his first job, the foreman, noticing how Burgdorf's right shoulder hung lower than the left in his work T-shirt, pulled him aside from the large group of electricians and "summer student assistants" and dismissed him. "We're not hiring any cripples here," he said.

Burgdorf had swelled at the thought of working with his father. His father's oldest son, he had always been proud to be Robert L. Burgdorf, Jr. That morning, he had felt particularly close to his dad as he had tugged on his electrician's belt of tools "slung low over my hip like a holster." The old leather belt filled with pliers, a scratch-awl, and screwdrivers belonged to Burgdorf's father, who had patiently explained how to use each tool.

Even with his paralyzed upper arm, Burgdorf knew he could use any of the tools and do any job. Neither of his parents ever talked about his minor disability. Perhaps it was because his bout with childhood polio, when he was a year old, had been a time washed in fear and ignorance, when the milkman had quit making deliveries rather than come near a "contaminated" house. But Burgdorf's father had taught him not to let his atrophied arm stop him from doing anything any other kid did. He had learned to do everything left-handed, even shoot basketballs.

In his jeans, T-shirt, electrician's belt, and hard hat—his father's uniform—Burgdorf had felt adult and manly. But when the foreman turned him away, Burgdorf would recall later, "My macho bubble was burst." He had wanted to scream, You can't do that. It's against the law. But Burgdorf knew there was no antidiscrimination law to protect a man with a paralyzed upper arm. There would be no chance for Burgdorf to prove himself.

All he could do, then, was retreat to his white 1956 Ford and drive home, where he stripped off the betraying belt and hard hat.

The first version of the Americans with Disabilities Act was proposed by thirteen Reaganites on the little-known National Council on the Handicapped. Seemingly far out of step with the president who had chosen them, these political conservatives had met in a Washington hotel in February 1988 to adopt a sweeping civil rights bill. The legislation had been drafted by the council's thirty-nine-year-old attorney and research specialist, Robert L. Burgdorf, Jr. He was the tall, quiet man sitting at the front of the room, in a suit coat that, unless you knew about it, hid his paralyzed upper right arm.

It had been twenty years since Burgdorf had been refused a job as an electrician's assistant by the small-minded construction manager. In that time, he had gone to law school and become an attorney specializing in disability law. He had plotted the outline of an antidiscrimination law in his head. By the time he arrived at the National Council on the Handicapped in 1984, the bill was virtually in his back pocket. It was Burgdorf's good fortune, therefore, to hook up with Justin Dart, Jr., a member of the council who believed in civil rights for disabled people with a passion that some would say bordered on zealotry. On behalf of the council, Dart, a small, frail-looking man, had embarked on a tour of all fifty states to conduct town meetings with disabled people. He had paid for the trips largely out of his own pocket. At every meeting the consensus was the same: people of various disabilities all said they suffered from discrimination. Sometimes Dart would bring along members of the council, who would be surprised to find people defining protection of rights—not, say, government welfare or health benefits—as their most pressing issue. Shortly after Burgdorf arrived at the council, he and Dart sat in an office and Burgdorf mentioned his dream of a separate civil rights act. Yet Burgdorf doubted, given the political climate and the conservative council, that such a bill would go anywhere. "How are we going to sleep nights," Dart asked, "if we don't try?"

Both Dart and Burgdorf had contracted polio in 1948, shortly before the vaccine invented by Jonas Salk would effectively wipe out polio in the United States. Dart had been eighteen, Burgdorf an infant. It would be many years before Dart came to see the slights, indignities, and lost opportunities of his life as a paraplegic as a form of discrimination. When University of Houston officials in the early 1950s withheld the credits he needed for his teaching certificate, believing a man in a wheelchair could not teach successfully, Dart accepted it as fact that he would have fewer choices. At the university, Dart had organized the first "integration" club. Members advocated that the all-white Texas university start allowing entry to black students. The club was a miserable failure, unable to get university officials even to pretend to listen. Only five students, on a campus of fifteen thousand, joined. Coincidentally, three of the five integration club members were in wheelchairs. If it was their disabilities that allowed them to identify with another oppressed group, they never let on, or even realized it. During all their many hours of discussions on the correctness of civil rights for black Americans, there were "not even five minutes of discussion on disability rights," says Dart. Reflecting on that time, Dart says, "That shows the sort of subhuman perception that existed of people with disabilities, and how it was internalized even by those with disabilities."

It was not until 1967, on a trip to South Vietnam to put together a report for a world conference on rehabilitation, that all the hurts of being a paraplegic would well up into a traumatic understanding of his own "subhuman status." In war-torn Saigon, Vietnamese officials escorted Dart to an "institution" for young children with polio brought in from rural hamlets. In his wheelchair, Dart arrived at a large metal shed with a concrete floor "like the kind you find for a public market in the tropics." Dart was unprepared for the vision of hell inside. One hundred young children had been brought to this flimsy shed, left to die and be buried in an unmarked field outside. Children with his own illness had been treated as bereft of worth, dignity, or future. "It was like a branding iron burning that message into my subconscious or onto my soul, to see how human beings were being treated there." The children had been left on the floor, "with bloated bellies and matchstick arms and legs like you see in pictures from Dachau and Auschwitz, with their eyes bugging out, lying in their own feces and urine and their bodies covered with flies." Once in a while, someone would bring a suffering child a bowl of maggoty rice. One dying boy, with big eyes, had slowly held out his hand to Dart, pleading for help. At that moment, Dart was overwhelmed by a mixture of fury, helplessness, grief, and even guilt. "It was one of those things I didn't believe I would ever see," he says. "I had grown up in Chicago with maids and a chauffeur. I had been privileged. In Japan, I was president of a company [a division of the Rexall drugstore chain run by his father]. I lived in a very comfortable place and had a big staff."

Dart quit his business and dedicated himself to figure a way to help other disabled people. He and his wife, Yoshiko, retreated to a snowy mountaintop in Japan, giving up their comfortable life-style to live in an abandoned farmhouse with no running water, no electricity, and no telephone. The house was at the end of a quarter-mile-long dirt road that turned to mud during the rains, making it impassable for Dart's wheelchair. They had no car. When Dart needed to go into town, several miles away, often he would crawl on his hands, dragging his legs, to the end of the road, and catch a ride on a wagon. The children in Vietnam were not given wheelchairs, so Dart would deny himself use of one, too. Yoshiko describes the period as one where the couple sought to rehabilitate themselves before they could rehabilitate others. Together they read books of philosophy. The Darts, too, started paying closer attention to the accomplishments back home of Martin Luther King, Jr., who soon was to be tragically assassinated by a sniper in Memphis. They began writing to leaders of the student protest movement in Berkeley and elsewhere. Feeling healed, the Darts returned to the United States in 1974, eventually settling in Texas. There, Dart began serving on numerous state disability groups.

Dart's father, Justin Dart, Sr., was a prominent California Republican. The blunt and forceful drugstore magnate was one of Ronald Reagan's few personal friends and the leader of Reagan's "kitchen cabinet," a small circle of California millionaires who had pushed Reagan into gubernatorial politics and, ultimately, toward the presidency. Most people around the younger Dart assumed that his prominence during the Reagan administration had come as a payoff owed his father. This imbued Dart with an aura of power, yet Dart had won the jobs by virtue of his own activism as a Texas Republican. In fact, although he became a prominent spokesman on disability, Dart never talked to Reagan about what he was doing. Nor did father and son, who had a complex and estranged relationship, ever discuss the son's appointment. Only rarely in his life had Dart even told his father—the dashing, athletic industrialist—about his disability advocacy. "As far as I know, my father didn't oppose my being appointed," says Dart. "Otherwise, I assume, I wouldn't have gotten it. But I don't know either that he supported it."

There had been many reminders for Dart and Burgdorf that no matter what they accomplished, in the eyes of many they would always be seen as incapable because of their disability. For Dart it was a severe disability, the loss of his legs. For Burgdorf it was something minor, a withered arm. A parent, too, like Sandra Swift Parrino, the chairperson of the National Council on the Handicapped, could feel the sting of stigma, just by watching how people discounted her severely physically disabled son's attempts to get an education and go to college. It did not matter if disability came at birth or later, whether the person was rich or poor, or even if it did not interfere with one's accomplishments. To be disabled meant to fight someone else's reality. Other people's attitudes, not one's own disability, were the biggest barrier. This frustration gave rise to the ardor behind the disability rights movement.

Patrisha Wright arrived in Washington in 1980 like a spring storm, clearing the air of Washington's clubby disability lobby. Existing lobbyists came from professional and parents' groups. They had succeeded in establishing and then jealously guarding a multimillion-dollar stream of federal funding for nursing homes, sheltered workshops, vocational rehabilitation, and other disability programs in the traditional medical model. These lobbyists had little sense of the emerging movement of disabled people to take control of the programs that affected their lives. Wright understood this new wind. Wright had set up the lobbying office of DREDF, the Berkeley-based Disability Rights Education and Defense Fund. For the first time disabled people would be represented in Washington by a group they ran themselves.

"I do civil rights," Wright explained during a courtesy call to one of the key disability group lobbyists her first week in Washington. "We do budget. We don't do civil rights," he told her icily. "You will," replied Wright, cutting off the meeting as she swept out of the room. The presumptuous newcomer was proved correct. Wright and the lobbyist would become friends and allies in the 1982 battle with the young Reagan-Bush administration to save Section 504 and the education guarantees for disabled children. Other important civil rights victories would follow, like one for a housing discrimination bill. When the disability lobby was faced with its most important challenge—passage of the Americans with Disabilities Act—Wright led the charge.

Growing up in Connecticut, Wright had decided early on that she would one day be an orthopedic surgeon. But a degenerative muscle disease in her eyes left her with double vision. She wandered to California, found work in a nursing home, and then latched on to the deinstitutionalization movement of the early 1970s. Hired to run an experimental program for adults coming out of state hospitals, she would take the principles of the independent living movement, which had begun in nearby Berkeley, and apply them to men and women with retardation and cerebral palsy. Wright had set up a large group home in Martinez, a small town north of San Francisco, and taught the residents to be independent. One morning, six months into the job, Wright was called urgently into the director's office. Two of the residents had been caught in bed together the night before, he informed her sternly. "Far out," replied Wright, figuring that was appropriate behavior for two adults recently freed from lifetimes spent in institutions. Wright was fired. The project fell apart and the thirty-two men and women were scattered to geriatric nursing homes.

For Wright, it was a revelation of the lack of respect given disabled people, all in the name of helping. "I realized that it would not be acceptable to say that because someone was born black or a woman that they should live in an institution," notes Wright. "But it was all right if they were born disabled. We had all these euphemisms. We said we were 'providing,' 'caring for,' or 'protecting' them." In 1977, Wright joined the HEW takeover, volunteering as Judy Heumann's personal attendant. She worked with Heumann for two years, getting schooled in the vision of the nascent disability movement, and then joined the newly formed DREDF, which had evolved as the legal arm of Berkeley's Center for Independent Living.

The first version of the Americans with Disabilities Act had been a bust. Burgdorf's bill was introduced in the closing days of the 100th Congress in 1988 to almost universal disregard. Legislators, on the way home for reelection races, ignored it. Ronald Reagan, in the dwindling days of a presidency thrown into suspended animation by Iran-Contra revelations, apparently did not even know of the bill's existence. The press and the public ignored it.

Now, at the beginning of the Bush administration, the ADA became the property of Wright, of the disability lobby that had been remade in her image, and of Democratic lawmakers. Among Washington officialdom in cookie-cutter dark business suits, Wright stood out in slacks, loose sweaters, and her long, light brown hair flowing straight down her back, as if she had come straight off the 1960s Berkeley campus. Wright was a brilliant tactician, tenacious, detail-oriented, and absolutely driven to win broad civil rights for disabled people. Senators Tom Harkin of Iowa and Edward Kennedy of Massachusetts, working with Wright, rewrote the ADA. This time the liberals were more conservative than the Reaganites on the National Council on the Handicapped. They narrowed the scope of the accommodations to be made, making the bill more palatable to business and therefore more likely to become law.

Burgdorf, Dart, and their conservative colleagues the year before had written a radical "flat earth" bill. Within two years, everything would have to be made accessible—every bus, subway station, restaurant, and theater. A second-floor barbershop would have to install an elevator, unless doing so would likely put it into bankruptcy. The modified bill stipulated that only new buildings, or old ones undergoing major renovation, would have to be made accessible. Such changes could be made for less than 1 percent of a new building's total cost. Also dropped from the original bill was a provision that would have allowed disabled people to sue for punitive damages if they faced discrimination from a business. Beyond Washington's Beltway, activists like *Disability Rag* editor Mary Johnson worried whether Wright was giving up too much.

Even modified from Burgdorf's original bill, the ADA was a striking departure from existing civil rights law. What made disability rights controversial—and trickier than granting rights to blacks, women, and other minorities—was that it could cost businesses money. The 1964 Civil Rights Act had simply required businesses to change their practices. But the ADA would require businesses to spend money, if necessary, to avoid being discriminatory. A restaurant might have to pay several hundred dollars to build a ramp over the steps outside. A developer building an office or a shopping mall more than two stories high would have to include an elevator. A clothing store might have to widen its aisles so someone in a wheelchair could pass through. A company would be expected to make inexpensive modifications to the workplace to accommodate disabled employees. The 1973 Rehabilitation Act amendments had required similar changes of employers, but as a quid pro quo for getting government funding. This time such change was the law without expectation of reimbursement from Washington.

Aware of the potential burden on business, the ADA specified that modifications were to be made only if they were easily achieved and at reasonable expense. A small business might be required to spend a few hundred dollars, a larger one several thousand dollars, depending on the resources of each. The law, however, did not set a dollar figure. It would rely on logic and eventually, if necessary, the courts to determine a company's obligations. To make stores accessible, the rule of thumb was that an owner would usually be able to recoup his investment in new business. And in accommodating workers, companies that had complied with the 1973 Rehabilitation Act had discovered that most changes were simple and cheap. A 1982 study for the Department of Labor found that half the accommodations made in the workplace cost little or nothing. For example, it was easy to put a desk on blocks to raise it for a wheelchair user. Another 30 percent of the accommodations were achieved for between $100 and $500.

Many businesses, particularly small ones, complained that the law was vague and potentially costly. Yet despite these concerns, business groups' opposition to a bill that would open companies up to a potential spate of lawsuits was surprisingly muted, especially when compared to the business community's vociferous fight against the 1964 Civil Rights Act. This time, however, no business lobbyist wanted to look like a bigot fighting a civil rights bill, particularly one that was rushing to passage with strong bipartisan support from lawmakers and the new, sympathetic Bush White House. More important, however, was that businesses had come to see disabled people as a new source of both labor and customers.

There were other costs of the ADA to spread around. New buses and major transfer stations would have to be accessible to wheelchair users. Telephone companies would be required to hire operators who could take a message typed by a deaf person on a telecommunications device for the deaf and then relay it orally to a hearing person on another phone. Government programs could not treat disabled people differently from others.

What the ADA mainly required was common sense and a creative way of thinking about the way disabled people fit into the workplace and society. Burgdorf liked to engage a blind attorney, Chris Bell, in challenging discussions of how guaranteeing rights to disabled people would work. It was Bell who first talked of changing what he called the "social context." He would ask people, "Could a deaf woman be a secretary?" Of course not, they would tell him. How would she answer the office telephones? But why, Bell would counter, should we think that every secretary needs to answer the telephone? In an office with more than one secretary, one secretary could answer the phones and another could do more of the filing and typing.

A Hidden Power

Given the sweep of the ADA, it seemed a formidable task to win passage. For one thing, disability rights constituted a stealth civil rights movement. Although its activists pointed to the black, women's, and gay rights movements as models, unlike those causes, the disability rights movement had never filled the streets with tens of thousands of protesters. It had no Martin Luther King, Jr., to bring it together, no Betty Friedan to write its manifesto. It had no unifying touchstone moment of courage or anger like the Montgomery Bus Boycott, the Freedom Rides, or the Stonewall riots. There was virtually no attention from the public or press. The fight for disability civil rights was a largely invisible, almost underground, movement.

Yet the disability movement had a power unlike any other. Representative Tony Coehlo of California argued that its strength came from a "hidden army" of people who had an instinctive understanding of the stigma of being disabled. Either they had a disability themselves, or someone in their family had one. The ranks of this army were vast, given that more than one in seven Americans had a disability that would be covered under the ADA. It was no surprise to Coehlo, then, that many on Capitol Hill were part of this army. Coehlo was part of it himself. After a truck accident on his family's dairy farm, Coehlo, then sixteen, started having mysterious blackouts and body spasms. When a doctor finally diagnosed the condition as epilepsy, Coehlo was dismissed from a Jesuit seminary where he was preparing for the priesthood. At the time, Catholic canon law barred ordination of those "who are or have been epileptics, insane or possessed by the devil." Coehlo's parents, too, had reacted with terror. In Portugal, where the family was from, epilepsy was a sign of the devil, the cost of some ancestor's past sin. On every job application he was forced to check off epilepsy and then was turned down from one job after another. California made him give up his driver's license. Even when Coehlo was in position to run for Congress in 1978, his opponent meanly called him "a very sick man" and asked voters, "What would you think if Coehlo went to the White House to argue a critical issue for you and had a seizure?" Coehlo won anyway, but he did not forget the rejection he felt because of his disability. He realized, however, that it was the prejudice of others—not the seizures, which were controlled by medicine—that was his biggest barrier.

Coehlo had been the bill's original House sponsor. In the Senate, the first version of the ADA had been championed by Republican Lowell Weicker, the father of a son with Down's syndrome. There had been seemingly momentous setbacks for the ADA when Weicker lost reelection in 1988 and then Coehlo, in 1990, was forced to quit Congress abruptly after acknowledging errors in public disclosure of a controversial junk bond investment. Nevertheless, there were other members of the "hidden army" to step in and capably guide the bill. In the House, Coehlo asked his closest friend, Maryland Representative Steny Hoyer, to take over. What Coehlo and Hoyer knew—but which Hoyer had not discussed even privately with other lawmakers—was that Hoyer's wife, too, has epilepsy. In the Senate, leadership of the bill would fall to Harkin, who would deliver part of his floor speech in sign language so that his deaf brother watching television could understand. Edward Kennedy spoke of his son, Teddy, Jr., who lost a leg to cancer. In addition, the senator's sister is retarded, and the Kennedy family in the 1960s had helped lead the parents' movement that brought retardation out of the family closet. Senate Republican leader Bob Dole had a paralyzed right arm, the result of a World War II injury from enemy gunfire as he tried to rescue one of his men on an Italian battlefield. Senator Orrin Hatch of Utah cried openly on the Senate floor as he talked about his brother-in-law, who had polio and slept in an iron lung at night, and how Hatch had once carried the man up the long steps of a Mormon temple in California.

Crucial help, too, came from Ralph Neas of the Leadership Conference on Civil Rights, who convinced often reluctant civil rights leaders to put disability rights at the top of their agenda. Neas saw that disabled people faced discrimination and realized the benefits, too, of expanding the civil rights coalition. But Neas also understood disability. A 1979 attack of Guillain-Barré syndrome, a paralyzing neurological disorder, left him close to death and unable to speak or breathe without a respirator. After over one hundred days in a hospital intensive care unit, he slowly recovered.

But of all the members of the "hidden army," the most surprising, and perhaps the most important, too, turned out to be President George Bush. He, too, had dealt with the pain of disease and disability in his family. In 1953, the Bush's three-year-old daughter, Robin, was diagnosed with leukemia and died an agonizing death from it. One Bush friend would call the girl's struggle the most searing moment of the future president's life. Bush's son Neil has a severe learning disability, which in part prompted Barbara Bush to make literacy her White House campaign of choice. The youngest Bush son, Marvin, had a section of his colon removed in 1985 and wears a plastic ostomy bag. He became a spokesman for the Crohn's and Colitis Foundation of America, wanting to calm others' fears about the operation and explain that it did not hurt his professional life, his ability to play sports, or his relationship with his wife. Bush talked of the "courage" of his favorite uncle, surgeon John Walker, who was struck by polio at the height of his career and could no longer pick up a scalpel. The polio made Walker, who had been the family's best all-around athlete, a quadriplegic. Bush spoke with admiration of his uncle's total absence of bitterness.

Still, George Bush seemed strangely cast to become the

shining knight for the disability rights movement. Indeed, in 1982, as vice president, he had seemed to be its most formidable enemy. He was poised to wipe out the movement's two biggest accomplishments: the 1975 law that had guaranteed a public school education to all disabled children and the amendments to the 1973 Rehabilitation Act. In 1982, state and local governments were complaining of the expense of educating disabled children. Similarly, businesses and state governments worried about the cost of the largely untested antidiscrimination law. Although the law had passed in 1973, the regulations that put it into place were not promulgated until 1977. The Reagan-Bush administration had been sworn into office in 1981 with a mandate for deregulation. Bush was given his first significant vice presidential chore in being chosen to lead Reagan's Task Force for Regulatory Relief. Its purpose was to pare away at the thicket of government regulations. Among the first regulations under attack was Section 504 and the guarantees of an education for handicapped children.

Disabled people and parents responded quickly and in large numbers. Mail sacks, with some 40,000 cards and letters, were dumped at the White House. Bush understood that he was dealing with a hidden grass roots constituency. "The protest was spontaneous and it was swift," recalls Bush's legal counsel, C. Boyden Gray. "Obviously it was not a cynical, political thing coordinated in a cynical, political way. It was a genuine response. And that demonstrated to me and to [Bush] that this movement had enormous impact." Clearly, disabled people could be mobilized to cause controversy for the new administration. Bush agreed to meet with disability groups to negotiate the administration's plan.

So it was that Vice President Bush found himself face-to-face with disability rights activist Evan Kemp, Jr., across a table in the Old Executive Office Building. Kemp, an attorney who had long identified himself as a Republican, then worked for con-

sumer activist Ralph Nader, as director of the Nader-funded
Disability Rights Center. With his six-foot, three-inch frame
seated in a bulky power wheelchair, Kemp was a commanding
figure. Yet he was a gentle man, given to speaking slowly in a
soft voice.

Trying to convince the new vice president not to heed the
alarmist complaints of business groups hostile to the antidiscrimination law, Kemp used a conservative argument. Disabled
people wanted independence, Kemp told Bush. They wanted to
get out of the welfare system and into jobs. They did not need
a paternalistic government to help them. The "eye-opener" for
Bush, according to Gray, was that disabled people were seeking
self-empowerment rather than looking for "some captured bureaucracy in Washington, D.C., which usually was the thing
that Washington, D.C., interest groups wanted." When the
administration held hearings around the country, disabled people and their parents were visible at every stop to protest any
changes in the disability protections. By March of 1983, Bush
announced that the administration had dropped its objections to
Section 504 and the education rules. Kemp and the disability
groups had prevailed, and the disability movement came away
with a new confidence in its own power as well as with a new
political sophistication.

In 1964, Kemp had graduated near the top of his University
of Virginia law school class. Yet thirty-nine applications to law
firms netted thirty-nine rejections. Some employers told him up
front they doubted a disabled man could handle the demands of
being a young associate, particularly the airplane travel. Luckily,
Kemp had a well-connected uncle, powerful Washington political columnist Drew Pearson, who helped him get hired at the
Internal Revenue Service. Later, Kemp would move to the Secu-
rities and Exchange Commission. Kemp, who had a neuromuscular disease, did not use a wheelchair until he broke his leg in
1971. During his first seven years in government, Kemp had

enjoyed steady raises. Once he began using the wheelchair, he would not get another raise for six years. Finally, he sued the SEC for discrimination and won.

Kemp and Bush came away from the confrontation over rules as mutual admirers. Later, they became potent allies. Bush began paying attention to disability issues. When he spoke to disability groups, the vice president would seek Kemp's touch in drafting a speech. In 1987, Reagan, on Bush's recommendation, named Kemp a commissioner to the Equal Employment Opportunity Commission, the federal agency responsible for fighting employment discrimination. In 1989, Bush, as president, named Kemp the EEOC chairman.

For Kemp and the disability movement, another and perhaps even more significant friendship came out of those 1982 meetings. It was with Gray, Bush's legal counsel. Kemp and his partner in the White House negotiations, Patrisha Wright, the lobbyist for the Disability Rights Education and Defense Fund, spent hundreds of hours with Gray in his office, explaining their vision of disability as a rights issue. Gray, a lanky six-foot, six-inch man whom *The Washington Post* once described as a "stoop-shouldered Ichabod Crane with a somewhat distracted, professorial air," started visiting Kemp's apartment on Q Street in Georgetown for late-night bridge games. Their friendship grew.

Kemp and Gray came from similar, privileged backgrounds. Both saw the law as a means to change society. And, in a city that usually rewarded play-it-safe politics on issues everyone could agree upon, both had taken on what seemed like quixotic or unpopular causes. Around the White House, Gray was sometimes looked at askance for what was considered his eccentric support of alcohol-based fuel for automobiles. He parked his old, battered methanol-powered Chevy in the lot next to the West Wing of the White House. Both Kemp and Gray became vanguard champions of disability rights.

Having lived with a death sentence over his head, Kemp had been imbued with an understated self-confidence. He could rock the boat, even attack a well-loved figure like Jerry Lewis, and know he could handle the fallout. The disability that made him different freed him of any pretense to honor convention.

Gray was not disabled, but he had an instinctive understanding of the fight for self-worth of Kemp and other excluded people. When Gray was ten, his mother died. Gray, an heir to the R. J. Reynolds tobacco fortune, was sent from his North Carolina home to boarding school at St. Mark's in Massachusetts. There in the mid-1950s, and even later at Harvard, he found his Northern classmates automatically assumed he and all Southerners were bigots, rednecks, and stupid. Even the fact that he eventually would graduate second in his class at St. Mark's did not dispel the prejudice. "The stereotype was that you spoke with a Southern accent, so you've got to be dumb," Gray would recall. It was that painful experience of prejudice that allowed Gray to empathize with the desires of disabled people to overcome low expectations and their distaste for being stereotyped.

Gray's growing friendship with Kemp made Kemp's talk of discrimination concrete. For the first time, Gray had a friend whom he could not take to his favorite restaurants, because they had steps that blocked access to a quadriplegic in a heavy electric wheelchair. Even Gray's home was off-limits, made inaccessible by a flight of stairs. During the negotiations over Section 504, David Stockman's Office of Management and Budget drafted a new White House position that applied a cost-benefit analysis to proposed disability benefits. To the bean counters at OMB, it seemed sensible. The less disabled a person—and presumably the more likely that person was to work and live independently—the more help and rights he or she got. The more disabled someone was, the less he or she was guaranteed. When Kemp confronted Gray with a leaked copy of the OMB memo, Gray agonized. Kemp, after all, was severely disabled. And Gray knew he could not justify a position that would put a price tag or a cost-effectiveness formula on his friend's worth. The proposal was killed.

"It was a wonderful period in my life," says Gray of the fight over the regulations. "It was one of the most exciting times." Kemp, says Gray, "was a great teacher, patient beyond belief." He reached out to explain the experience of disability, "not to scream at me," Gray said, or accuse him of being "some Neanderthal reg-basher." Gray, years later from his wood-paneled office atop the West Wing of the White House—at a time when he was being portrayed in the press as the heavy holding up an agreement on a civil rights bill to reinstate employment protections overturned by Supreme Court decisions—spoke nostalgically of the "remarkable collection of individuals" who had come together on the disability rights issue. "Maybe that's what it takes," he said. "Leadership that is not monolithic and closed."

It was such success winning over people in power that gave advocates faith that Washington was ready for a disability rights bill. A key but little-noticed moment came in May of 1988. Kemp and other activists, in town for the annual meeting of the National Council on Independent Living, met in a downtown Washington hotel. Most of the advocates were Democrats, others were Republicans. They divided the campaigns of the 1988 presidential contenders. Each would go to work for one of them. And each, they vowed among themselves, would try to push their candidate toward the same goal: they wanted a statement of rights for disabled people, like the ADA, which had been introduced in Congress that same month.

Kemp took the Bush campaign. Three months later, Bush pledged, "I'm going to do whatever it takes to make sure the disabled are included in the mainstream." Those simple seventeen words, spoken during Bush's image-turning acceptance speech at the Republican National Convention, marked the first time that an American presidential nominee had acknowledged disabled people as a political force. The Republican nominee had scored with his promise of a "kinder and gentler" presidency, and inclusion of disabled people in the mainstream would be a prime example he would mention on several other occasions. For several years Bush pollster Robert Teeter presciently had advised his political clients that disabled people and their families were growing into an untapped constituency.

At the polling firm of Louis Harris and Associates, company vice president Louis Genevie was proving Bush's instinct correct. Genevie was tracking the voting preferences of disabled voters. Immediately following Bush's words at the New Orleans convention and on a few other occasions when he spoke of disability rights, disabled voters in Genevie's survey swung markedly to Bush. After Bush crushed Democrat Michael Dukakis in the November election, Genevie wrote to Bush that disabled voters who had switched to Bush had constituted up to one-half of the four million difference of popular votes between Bush and Dukakis. This made up one to three percentage points of Bush's seven-point margin of victory, Genevie figured. In part, this reflected the tremendous overall shift by all voters to Bush, who started the campaign seventeen percentage points behind, according to one poll. By the time of Genevie's last poll—before Bush's election-eve commercial in which he again embraced disability rights, presumably sending his support up again—the Republican candidate had 44 percent of the disability vote compared to 49 percent for Dukakis. Genevie considered the narrow margin highly significant, given that disabled people, by virtue of their poverty and dependence on government social services and welfare, were considered near monolithic in their support for any Democratic candidate. His polling did not even count family members, who could be equally strong activists. "A candidate ignores the issues of disabled people at his own peril," Genevie would later say.

*   *   *

The disability movement's strength—the ubiquitousness of 35 to 43 million people with disabilities—was also a weakness. The disability rights movement spanned a splintered universe. There are hundreds of different disabilities, and each group tended to see its issues in relation to its specific disability. There were groups for people with head injuries, different groups for blind people, and still others for cancer survivors or those with diabetes, arthritis, learning disabilities, and mental illness, all fighting for specific programs, funding, and laws to address the needs of members of their own group. Sometimes the groups clashed. Wheelchair users fought for curb cuts. In some cities in the 1970s, activists had even secretly taken to destroying curbs with sledgehammers. But blind people with canes, who tapped curbs for a sense of location, often wanted them kept in place. Sometimes there were bitter disagreements among the same class of disabled people. Members of the National Federation of the Blind made a lonesome break with other disability groups and withheld support of the ADA. Federationists reject any special help that might let sighted people conclude that blind people are inferior. They object to crossing beepers at traffic signals or elevators that announce a floor number. They insist on being allowed to sit next to an airplane's emergency exit, and several federationists have let themselves be arrested rather than move. However, other large groups representing blind people, like the American Council of the Blind, dismissed the rival federation's objections to traffic signals and airline seating restrictions— which they lauded as conveniences and understandable rules— and fully supported the ADA.

The ADA brought this fragmented population together in a fight against discrimination. "People with epilepsy now will be advocates for the same piece of legislation as people who are deaf," said ADA lobbyist Liz Savage. "That has never happened before. And that's really historic." There were 180 national organizations that endorsed the bill, from large charities like the National Multiple Sclerosis Society and the American Diabetes Association to smaller ones like the National Ostomy Association, the Association for Persons with Severe Handicaps, and the International Ventilator Users Network. There were groups representing all the major disabilities, including spinal cord injuries, deafness and visual handicaps, mental retardation and mental illness, as well as those for newer or less-well-known conditions, such as AIDS, Tourette's syndrome, and chronic fatigue syndrome. To win passage of the ADA, disabled people had to forge historic alliances not only among different disability groups and politicians but with the professionals who had cared for them for so long. Some disabled people complained that these health-care workers, particularly nondisabled ones, were controlling and paternalistic. Too often, therapists and social workers assumed they knew best instead of trusting the wishes of their clients. Many professionals felt threatened by the new group consciousness of disabled people. They were afraid or reluctant to share decision making or give up power that, in some cases, might even threaten their own jobs. Others embraced the quest for self-control and saw themselves as partners working with, not for, their newly militant clients. More and more of the younger professionals were disabled themselves.

Back home in Austin, Texas, Bob Kafka and Randy Jennings usually fought each other. Yet both came to Washington the same week in 1990 leading delegations of Texans to lobby for passage of the landmark civil rights bill for disabled people. They shared the same goal, although their style and tactics could hardly have been more different.

Kafka, a savvy protest veteran and paraplegic who used a wheelchair, brought thirty militant activists, all disabled and all members of American Disabled for Accessible Public Transit, or ADAPT. They came to disrupt Congress with protests, sit-ins, and other acts of civil disobedience. Jennings and his seventeen colleagues—only one of whom had a disability—were rehabilitation professionals who belonged to the Texas chapter of the National Rehabilitation Association, or NRA. They had come for polite meetings with members of Congress to explain why their clients needed their rights protected. Together these two groups formed a powerful coalition that would successfully raise the consciousness of Congress to the countless acts of discrimination that disabled people faced daily.

ADAPT had been founded in 1983 to empower disabled people to engage in direct action protest. The group made a priority of getting all city buses equipped with lifts. Riding a bus was the most basic symbol of equality, resonant of the black civil rights movement. It meant being able to go to work, to see friends—in short, to be independent. As Atlanta activist Mark Johnson put it, "Black people fought for the right to ride in the front of the bus. We're fighting for the right to get on the bus."

In eight years, there had been several hundred arrests of ADAPT members in civil disobedience protests around the country. The group disrupted every national convention of the American Public Transit Association (APTA), the association of public bus systems. By offering themselves up to mass arrests, they forced each city, from St. Louis to San Antonio, to consider the injustice of excluding disabled people from using buses. But it had been a lonely battle. Even Rosa Parks had shunned them. ADAPT had asked the symbol of the Montgomery Bus Boycott to march with them when they went to Detroit, where Parks lived. She agreed but then, after pressure from Detroit Mayor Coleman Young, who was seeking to please the visiting APTA convention, sent a letter of withdrawal that blasted ADAPT for its civil disobedience tactics, which would "embarrass" the city's "guest."

Despite its outsider image—even most disability groups dismissed it as a marginal maverick—ADAPT's founder, Wade

Blank, had begun to make the organization a player behind the scenes. Once again, the key link was Evan Kemp. The radical and the Republican were diehard fans of the Cleveland Browns. They also had in common their devotion to disability rights and spoke often on the telephone of their latest strategies. The timing of ADAPT's Washington march had been set to Kemp's judgment of when it would be best to pressure Congress and send a message to the White House.

Blank's discreet line to the White House had given ADAPT new power. Several months before the Washington march, ADAPT had taken over the federal building in Atlanta to demand that the Department of Transportation agree not to fund any city purchases of buses unless they had lifts. Some city bus lines were trying to buy the cheaper buses before the ADA went into effect. A curious thing happened in Atlanta: police dragged ADAPT protesters out of the federal building only to be ordered to escort them back in to stay overnight. The police even provided blankets to keep the demonstrators warm as they slept in the lobby and hallways. A call had come from the White House on behalf of the president. Transportation department officials were then flown to Atlanta to negotiate the temporary ban on inaccessible bus buys that ADAPT had sought. In Washington, ADAPT had returned the favor by refusing to chain themselves to the White House gate. Patrisha Wright had urged them to do so, arguing that Bush could do more to pressure House Republicans to support the ADA.

To Bob Kafka, rehabilitation professionals, or "suits," like Randy Jennings, were part of the problem. Rehabilitation services, such as job counseling, training, and placement, were required by an act of the U.S. Congress in 1920. The National Rehabilitation Association formed five years later. Today, rehabilitation is a $2-billion-a-year industry, funded by federal and state governments. One million people were served in 1989, of whom nearly a quarter found jobs. Yet despite those numbers, the system reaches only one of every twenty people who need help, according to NRA officials. Kafka complains that rehabilitation counselors "cream," or take on the easiest clients and do little or nothing for those who need help the most. Few of the thirty protesters Kafka brought to Washington had full-time work. Most were angry over having slipped through the cracks of the rehabilitation and welfare systems.

Jennings, too, wanted to see more of his disabled clients working. Rehabilitation professionals were restricted by funding limits and by the law, which said only someone deemed employable can get help. The ADA bill, he said, would significantly boost the numbers he could serve by, among other things, requiring employers to make inexpensive accommodations in the workplace. The need for a bill like ADA first became apparent to Jennings years before when he found a nineteen-year-old paraplegic a job in a muffler shop but could not get him to work the next day. No city buses had lifts. "This bill is the most significant piece of legislation to come along for disabled people in a long time," said Jennings. "It's civil rights; it's what's needed." Best of all, he said, the ADA would make interaction commonplace. "We'll see people in chairs going to the opera. They'll be sitting with us in the same ballpark," said Jennings. "And for the first time we'll all be able to go together. We won't have to segregate them in a special bus."

Professionals like Jennings, and other disabled people, too, tended to keep their distance from Kafka's ADAPT, which, with its philosophy of civil disobedience and mass arrests, was regarded as a militant fringe group. But ADAPT's Wheels of Justice March was to be a show of grass roots force. An invitation had been extended to all other groups. By coincidence the National Rehabilitation Association's legislative convention was taking place that same week. So the rehabilitation professionals canceled their morning sessions in order to join the protest. That was how members of the two Texas delegations led by Kafka and Jennings came together in front of the White House on a Monday in Washington during an unseasonably warm week in early March 1990.

Some 475 people, many in wheelchairs, spread across the sidewalk in front of the White House for the start of the protest march. Another 250 people joined them at the Capitol. In the scheme of Washington demonstrations—where a march on either side of the abortion issue will turn out up to 250,000 protesters—the ADAPT march had attracted a minuscule number, too puny to rate even a line in the next day's *Washington Post.* Disability marches never attracted large numbers. People who found it physically difficult to get to jobs—and therefore were often poor—or even out to restaurants or movie theaters, found it still harder to get across country to protests. At the hotel where two hundred ADAPT demonstrators were based, only three rooms had bathrooms accessible to wheelchairs. There had been a few demonstrations of similar size on behalf of the Section 504 regulations. But never had so many people, including professionals, representing so many disabilities come together in one protest.

The small numbers belied the protest's power. Boyden Gray appeared at the White House gate to address the crowd briefly. President Bush, he assured the crowd, was committed to signing civil rights legislation for disabled people. "If it seems slow, remember how slow things were twenty years ago," he said, referring to the struggle of the black civil rights movement. The marchers, with Kafka near the front, took off for the Capitol at the other end of Pennsylvania Avenue. At the base of the Capitol, by the elegantly curving marble steps to the West Front, Kafka introduced the speakers. The first was Dart, newly sworn in as the chairman of the President's Committee on Employment of People with Disabilities. One of Dart's first acts, upon getting his new job, had been to change the committee's name from the President's Committee on Employment of the Handicapped, to show the new sensibilities of the emerging civil rights movement. From his wheelchair, Dart lauded the protesters as "the pioneer patriots of the twentieth century." To growing applause, Dart urged, "We are Americans and we will struggle for however long it takes for the same civil rights other Americans have."

Brief remarks followed from a few members of Congress: Kemp, I. King Jordan, the first deaf president of Gallaudet University, and James Brady, the former White House press secretary who had been shot in the head during the 1981 assassination attempt on President Ronald Reagan. But the power of the crowd seemed to surge forth when ADAPT's national leader, Mike Auberger, came to the microphones to tell his story from his motorized wheelchair. He wore jeans and an ADAPT T-shirt. The braids of his long hair came down to his lap, in which he held his speech, written out on a yellow legal pad. In a steady voice, without emotion, Auberger recalled a visit to the Capitol he took as a younger man, a student on a ninth grade class trip to Washington. "Twenty years ago, I walked up these steps a wholly equal American citizen," said Auberger, referring to the steep flights of stairs to the top of the Capitol that loomed above him. Then, with more feeling in his voice, he added, "Today I sit here with you as less than second-class citizens who are still legally discriminated against daily."

As Auberger's voice built with anger describing his devalued citizenship, the crowd responded in shouts and increasing applause. "The steps we sit before represent a long history of discrimination and indignities heaped upon disabled Americans. We have faced what these steps have represented. Among us are those who have been forced to live in institutions against our will. There are those among us who have had our children taken away solely because we are disabled. We have been denied hous-

ing and jobs. These indignities and injustice must not go on."
The crowd rocked with cheers as Auberger concluded, his voice
rising with emotion. "We will not permit these steps to continue to be a barrier to prevent us from the equality that is
rightfully ours. The preamble to the Constitution does not say
'We the able-bodied people.' It says, 'We the People.'"

The cries from the protesters drowned out Auberger's words.
"Access is our civil right," they chanted. At that point about
three dozen ADAPT demonstrators, according to a prearranged
plan, threw themselves out of their wheelchairs. They began a
"crawl-up" of the eighty-three marble steps to the Capitol. Each
struggled up the steps carrying a scrolled paper with the opening words of the Declaration of Independence to present to
lawmakers once they had pulled themselves on their hands and
knees inside the Capitol building.

The sight of paraplegics dragging themselves across each
step was both fascinating and repelling. At the end of the day,
some activists, including editor Mary Johnson, worried that the
grueling "crawl-up" had conveyed precisely the image disabled
people wanted to avoid—of being pitiable, inspirational, and
childlike. Indeed, the cameras had zoomed in on an exhausted
eight-year-old, Jennifer Keelan, struggling forward on her hands
and knees. It would be the one photographic image from the
ADA fight to register in the public memory. Yet the network
news reports that night stressed exactly the message ADAPT
wanted to get across: that disabled people were demanding civil
rights.

For the next day, Tuesday, ADAPT had scheduled its members for a "tour" of the Capitol. It was to begin where tourists
traditionally gathered, in the Capitol rotunda, under the structure's cast-iron dome. But the tour, as ADAPT members knew
and Capitol police suspected, was a sham. The real agenda was
to take over the Capitol rotunda, a place decorated with huge
murals of the signing of the Declaration of Independence and

other key moments in the building of the republic. ADAPT
members would demand that the ADA bill go to the floor of the
House for a vote the very next day.

While the Capitol tour guides, in their red jackets, waited
patiently nearby, 150 ADAPT members gathered in the center
of the rotunda. The takeover began with ADAPT's demand to
speak to leaders in the House of Representatives. Although few
of the shouting ADAPT demonstrators realized it, this, too, was
a carefully staged event. ADAPT leaders planned to take over
the Capitol for several hours and end their protest only when
House leaders were forced to come to see them. That would
demonstrate the group's power. Patrisha Wright, too, wanted
the protest to have impact, so that wavering House members
would feel the impatience of disabled people. But she could not
put House leaders in the awkward position of being seen weakly
caving in to end a protest. Wright called in chits to summon
House Speaker Tom Foley, House Minority Leader Robert
Michel, and Representative Steny Hoyer to hear ADAPT's demands. They would talk to the demonstrators at the beginning
of the protest, not the end.

"I can understand that you're frustrated," said Michel, who
stood in the center of a wide circle of wheelchairs. Activist Mark
Johnson shouted down the Illinois representative: "We're not
'frustrated,' we're pissed off." That set off a chorus of chants,
yells, and horn blasts that reverberated off the rotunda's marble
walls, eventually sending a bemused Michel and a scowling
Foley scurrying from the rotunda. Kafka and other ADAPT
members pulled out chains and bicycle locks to link their wheelchairs together in a phalanx of metal. As Capitol Hill police
moved in to make arrests, one confused tour guide leaned over
the wall of wheelchairs to ask Auberger if this meant the group
did not want to take the scheduled tour.

One Washington disability activist was distressed when
Senator Robert Dole, a stalwart supporter of disability causes,

walked by the rotunda sit-in and said, "This doesn't help us any." Jennings, of the Texas rehab delegation, agreed. Jennings felt Kafka and ADAPT were good at grabbing attention with their shouting but lacked credibility because they then refused to sit down and negotiate. That was not ADAPT's role, countered Kafka. ADAPT demonstrators, he said, knew they were seeking the impossible when they demanded an immediate vote on the ADA bill in the Capitol rotunda. The point was to force a confrontation to show that disabled people—104 of them on this day—cared deeply enough to go to jail for their rights.

As Kafka sees it, forcing confrontation and getting arrested gave disabled people a sense of empowerment after lives of dependency. "Most people see disabled people as childlike and helpless," said Kafka. "We're not Jerry's Kids. We're not going to be passive recipients of charity anymore. We're changing our image. We're demanding our rights." These rude protests grab attention because they challenge widely held expectations of disabled people to be unfailingly polite, explained activist Eleanor Smith. Exhausted after driving over twelve hours to Washington from Atlanta, she had moved her wheelchair into the elevator at her hotel on arrival in Washington. "What floor would you like?" asked a woman in her early thirties who was standing near the control panel. "Three," said Smith, who is forty-seven. "Aren't you forgetting your manners?" asked the woman's husband, who added in a treacly tone, "It's 'Three, *please.*' "

While U.S. Capitol police carried the ADAPT protesters down an elevator only big enough for one wheelchair at a time, members of Jennings's Texas NRA delegation were making the rounds of congressional offices. Seven of the women met with Representative Pete Geren, who had been in Washington only six months, after winning a special election. He had been lobbied on the ADA within twenty-four hours of his arrival in the capital but said he was listening seriously to complaints from small business about the cost of compliance. The women got straight to the point. Rehabilitation professionals, they explained, could show business how to use the bill to their advantage, to get good employees.

Accommodations did not have to be expensive, noted Elizabeth Gaspard, who used a silver lightweight wheelchair. The chronic pain in her feet, she said, made it hard to walk long distances or to stand. For her, accommodation meant simply that her employer left a chair in the photocopying room so she could rest on it when she did her copying. As a high school student, when the pains began, she feared an end to her future dreams of career and family. Fortunately, rehabilitation and vocational counselors were around to tell her how to get along at school. Now she was proud that she had graduated from college and become "a taxpayer, not a tax user." ADA, she explained, would protect her. "Equal employment won't do a thing for me if transit passes me by on the street or I can't get in the front door. How could I be a competitive employee?"

Meanwhile, across the street from the Capitol in the Rayburn House Office Building, the Energy and Commerce Committee was marking up the ADA bill. Tom Sheridan, a lobbyist for the AIDS Action Council, stood outside the committee room, urging lawmakers to vote against several amendments that would exclude people with AIDS from the protection offered by the disabilities act. Many disability activists were envious of the public fascination with the gay rights movement. The week before ADAPT arrived, a national newsweekly devoted a cover story to ACT-UP, the AIDS activist group that takes angry, confrontational politics beyond ADAPT's version. But Sheridan watched in awe the score of disability lobbyists, representing hundreds of disabilities from epilepsy to mental illness, working outside the committee room. Because of the influence of these established groups, including the National Rehabilitation Association, federal and state governments would spend

$60 billion on disabled people in 1990. People with AIDS do not have the same network of federal programs to give them such clout on Capitol Hill, Sheridan noted. Although the gay rights movement was far more visible, more cohesive, and much more in the public's consciousness, gays and lesbians in 1990 could only dream of the type of national antidiscrimination legislation that was moving quickly through Congress for disabled people.

Because AIDS is a chronic disease, people with AIDS or who are HIV-positive were protected from discrimination under the ADA bill. The alliance between the disability and gay communities helped spur the bill. But that alliance worried some lawmakers. "I don't want to hand out anything more to those damn homosexuals," Ralph Hall, a Texas Democrat from the rural district descended from former House Speaker Sam Rayburn, told the NRA women at their next visit. Hall, like all other members of the Texas congressional delegation, was getting stacks of letters from fundamentalist churches urging him to oppose the ADA because it included rights protections for people with AIDS. Gay people, Hall argued, get AIDS because, by their own choice, they engage in risky sexual behavior. "We don't make judgments when we help people with head injuries," shot back Valerie Jean Schwille, who had followed in her father's footsteps to become a rehabilitation counselor. "We don't ask first, 'Were you speeding in that car crash?' Or, 'Did you have too much to drink?' We still help them." Hall conceded, "You've got a point there."

On Wednesday, the ADAPT demonstrators, off the high of their sit-in the day before, planned an even bolder action: to close down the subway system that links the Capitol to the House office buildings. The plan went awry when four groups of demonstrators got lost in the subterranean maze of walkways under the Capitol. As he flew out on to Independence Avenue in his motorized wheelchair, Mike Auberger cursed himself for his botched strategy and made a mental note "never again" to diminish the group's power by dividing into small units. The demonstrators regrouped to take over the office of Representative Bud Shuster (R-Pa.), author of an amendment to exclude sparsely populated areas from making new buses accessible. There were fifty-nine more arrests.

After two days of steady arrests, Thursday was spent in courtrooms. "When I was born, I had a problem with my left arm, which was paralyzed. There were a lot of things I couldn't do. But I didn't break the law," explained D.C. Superior Court Judge Robert Scott. He told the ADAPT demonstrators how, despite his disability, he went on to law school and was eventually appointed to the bench. Then the sixty-eight-year-old judge meted out punishment, some of the toughest, ADAPT leaders said, they had ever received. Auberger was fined $500 and put on supervised probation for one year—in essence, putting ADAPT's captain out of action by forcing him to avoid arrest or else be brought back to Washington to serve jail time.

Scott's tough sentencing infuriated the ADAPT activists. Even worse, they felt Scott had slighted those who had trouble speaking by addressing questions to people next to them instead of letting them struggle with their words. Another ADAPT leader who got a heavy fine, Stephanie Thomas, who is married to Bob Kafka, said Scott is a familiar disabled type—one who hides his disability to "pass" in the nondisabled world. Scott, in an interview later, noted his long-standing reputation for being a no-nonsense judge and said he treated the protesters the same as he would anyone else. "If they expect because they are in wheelchairs to flaunt what is clearly the law and not expect anything to happen," he said, "they're crazy."

Tied up in court all day, the ADAPT activists reluctantly ruled out taking further action. They returned to their hotel dispirited, unsure what Friday and another day of courtroom appearances would bring.

Friday started with one more reminder of exclusion. Auberger, Thomas, and the three others sentenced by Scott showed up, as ordered, at the parole office—only to find that there was no wheelchair ramp to the building. A court officer eventually met them outside, but Timothy Cook, the group's attorney, quickly filed a half-million-dollar lawsuit against the court. The 1973 amendments to the Rehabilitation Act, the prototype for the ADA, required that any federal building be accessible. One of the strongest selling points for the ADA was that this 1973 law, which had been pushed by rehabilitation professionals, proved such antidiscrimination measures could be effective without being burdensomely expensive.

If the day before the court proceedings had gone poorly, the remaining ADAPT members to be sentenced could hardly have been more surprised by the reception they got from Judge Bruce Beaudin. It started when Arthur Campbell, whose severe cerebral palsy makes speaking difficult, asked if someone could read remarks he had written out. The judge agreed. "Take this courtroom," Campbell wrote. "We cannot use the jury box. . . . We cannot get on the witness stand. . . . And we cannot get on to the judge's bench."

Beaudin was moved by Campbell's words, and soon everyone in the courtroom was speaking, telling their most personal stories of discrimination and struggle. For many it was the first time anyone in authority had listened to their tales of pain. People who could not speak, like Claude Holcomb of Connecticut, slowly spelled out their statements, letter by letter, on boards they carried marked with the alphabet. People who rarely talked at all, out of shyness and fear, spoke with eloquence. The courtroom took on the air of a revival meeting and a political rally. People clapped, shouted, and cried.

George Roberts of Denver asked that ADAPT founder Wade Blank be allowed to tell his story of being abandoned by his parents "on the doorstep of an orphanage" to spend twenty-five lonely years in institutions and nursing homes until he got help to sue to get out.

Even Judge Beaudin was choking back tears by the time the

last speaker, Wayne Spahn of Austin, told his story. "When I was a baby, they wanted to put me away. But my mother and father fought and I stayed home with them," he said. "All we want is education and jobs, good jobs, to try to get out in the community and be like everybody else."

It ended with Beaudin praising the demonstrators. "The rightness of your cause is a big one," he said. He imposed minimal $10 fines. "I'm going to take a break, I can tell you that," Beaudin said, teary now himself. And with that, the judge stepped down from the bench and went around the courtroom, shaking the hand of each of the activists.

With the support of a powerful coalition of disabled people and their families, politicians, and disability professionals, the ADA moved swiftly through Congress. On July 26, 1991, Bush signed the ADA into law with three thousand joyous members of the "hidden army" on the South Lawn of the White House. The President greeted one of the guests, Lisa Carl of Tacoma, Washington, who "now will always be admitted to her hometown theater," the president noted. To applause, Bush declared, "Let the shameful wall of exclusion finally come tumbling down." He put his pen to the bill. Then Bush turned to Evan Kemp, who was sitting next to him on the podium overlooking the Washington Monument, and gave him an affectionate kiss on the head.

Bush's administration would promptly issue regulations for the ADA. There would be no four-year fight like that over Section 504. The law took effect in 1992. Many companies, particularly large ones, complied eagerly and reaped the rewards—new customers, new workers, and good publicity. Passage of the ADA was an earthshaking event for disabled people. It signaled a radical transformation in the way they saw themselves—as a minority that now had rights to challenge its exclusion. But it was an odd victory; as radical as the ADA's passage would be for disabled people, nondisabled Americans still had little understanding that this group now demanded rights, not pity.

CHAPTER 5

INTEGRATION: OUT OF SHADOWLAND

The postmaster in a small town was told that he would have to make his post office building accessible to people in wheelchairs. There were twenty formidable steps leading to the only public entrance, and the revolving door there was too narrow for even the smallest wheelchair. The postmaster objected to any renovation for disabled patrons. He sputtered in protest, "I've been here for thirty-five years and in all that time I've yet to see a single customer come in here in a wheelchair."

For disabled people, there is more at stake in such exclusion than just the right to buy postage stamps. Segregation—whether the result of stairs or attitudes—creates harmful myths and stereotypes. Worse, it sets up a self-fulfilling prophecy for failure. That disabled people are invisible or separated, Americans like the postmaster have long assumed, is proof that they do not need inclusion or are not even capable or worthy of it.

"Most people assume that disabled children are excluded from school or segregated from nondisabled peers because they cannot learn or because they need special protection. So, too, the absence of the disabled coworkers is considered confirmation of the obvious fact that disabled people can't work," writes disability rights attorney and theorist Robert Funk. "These assumptions are deeply rooted in history. Historically, the inferior economic and social status of disabled people has been viewed as the inevitable consequence of the physical and mental differences imposed by disability."

The result of this history, argues Funk, has been treatment of disabled people as a "dependent caste." An American apartheid has existed for them. School districts fund separate schools of special education in which the instruction is often inferior to what is offered to nondisabled students. Cities, rather than put wheelchair lifts on all buses, establish parallel "paratransit" systems of vans: separate and unequal transportation, since these first-come, first-serve systems usually require passengers to reserve a ride at least twenty-four hours in advance. In most cases, a nondisabled person is not allowed to ride the van with a disabled friend. Charities set up "sheltered workshops" for people who because of their blindness, cerebral palsy, or other disability—people who may be exceptionally intelligent—are paid at a piece rate, often for pennies a day, toiling at some dull task like sorting nuts and bolts. Although some sheltered workshops have begun teaching real work skills in hopes of graduating their employees to regular jobs, most workshops remain little more than segregated adult day-care centers. States still run separate and isolated institutions and state hospitals—often resembling prisons more than homes—to house people with retardation and other disabilities.

The story of the small-town post office is a favorite of Harold Russell, who ran the President's Committee on Employment of the Handicapped in the 1980s. But he is best known as the star of

the 1946 movie *The Best Years of Our Lives* about a World War II
veteran who returns home paralyzed. Russell himself had come
back from war without use of his arms.

As more and more disabled people like Russell survived after
a trauma, they and their families began insisting on having the
same opportunities to live and work as anyone else, rather than
be forced into an institution or remain behind closed doors in a
family's home. This was particularly true of people who became
disabled after birth. They saw no reason suddenly to forfeit the
first-class citizenship they had grown up to expect as a birthright. Yet the postmaster's reaction was the norm; in a society
where disabled people are remote, we have not understood the
need to adjust attitudes, programs, and laws to fit the changing
reality of disabled people who now seek independence.

As a result, integration—into the work force, the classroom,
the community—has become a primary goal of today's disability
movement. It was first demanded by parents, beginning in the
1950s and 1960s, and now it is disabled people themselves who
are most forcefully demanding to come out from the shadows.

For me, it was a group of autistic adults who made it clear
that integration is not just a goal for a few with the mildest
disabilities but a feasible and common good and a right for all.
These were the autistic men and women clients of Community
Services for Autistic Adults and Children. CSAAC (pronounced
SEE-sack) helped them find work and live in their own homes
in Montgomery County, Maryland, a suburb of Washington,
D.C. I visited Susan Goodman, then CSAAC's director, in her
spartan office of dully colored linoleum and cinderblock in a
converted Rockville, Maryland, schoolroom.

Of the universe of people with disabilities, Goodman explained, those with autism are usually the most segregated of all.
"Because people with autism are the most difficult to serve, they
are the first to be written off," she said. For decades, she added,
people with autism were society's disposables, "relegated to the

back wards of institutions and for the most part termed hopeless."

They were discarded because autism is a rare and lifelong brain disorder with no known cure. They were ignored because some can barely speak and are seemingly unable to communicate with others. Many seem trapped in their own world of fears and visions. Some scream, yell, bang their heads, or engage in other self-injurious behavior when they are frustrated. Autism affects approximately 200,000 Americans, and symptoms usually appear in the first three years of life. Little is understood about what causes it, nor is it known why four out of five people with the condition are male. In addition, at least 70 percent of people with autism are considered to have some degree of mental retardation. Another 10 percent are savants, clinically retarded but spectacularly gifted in some areas such as music, numbers, art, or memory. One CSAAC client, Richard Montgomery, has calendar memory. Ask him any date and with invariable accuracy he instantly tells the day of the week it falls on. But despite this extraordinary talent, Montgomery could not do the basic mathematics that would help in his job of affixing price tags to merchandise in the back of a Kmart department store.

The CSAAC program, Goodman explained, aimed at no less than turning upside down the perceptions that autistic people make up a "hopeless" population. Its purpose, she said, was to show that "with the proper support these people can live and work in the community." CSAAC was started in 1979 by several parents of autistic children, who were distressed at the lack of programs to help their adult sons and daughters live at home or on their own, instead of going into institutions. It grew to sponsor fifty-two autistic teenagers (including Goodman's son) and adults working in twenty-eight businesses and to gain national recognition for pioneering work in taking autistic adults out of institutions and placing them in what is called community-supported employment and living. CSAAC even made a point of finding its clients jobs outside the traditional ones usually offered people with developmental disabilities like autism and mental retardation, the so-called "food, filth, and flower" positions as pot scrubbers, janitors, and lawn crew workers.

I visited Goodman in 1989, the year *Rain Man* won an Academy Award as the year's best movie. *Rain Man* is the fictional story of Charlie Babbitt's discovery that he has an older brother who is autistic. The family had hidden Raymond in a private, tree-lined mental institution. But Charlie, a young hustler, learns of his lost brother's existence when he questions the mysterious distribution of his late father's three-million-dollar estate. The self-centered Charlie (Tom Cruise) discovers and then kidnaps Raymond (Dustin Hoffman) in a vengeful plot to gain what he believes is his rightful share of the inheritance, taking his brother on a colorful road trip across America. It is Raymond's liberation, but even more important, it brings Charlie's revelation that this brother is not the simple disabled man he had first seen. Rather, Raymond is a complex, fascinating, and endearing man. He is an autistic savant who memorizes the phone book and can count 246 falling toothpicks as they hit the ground. During a stop in Las Vegas, Raymond's memorization skills help Charlie win nearly $90,000 at the blackjack table. (Kim, the retarded savant who was the model for *Rain Man* story writer Barry Morrow, works as a payroll clerk and keeps the salary, hours, taxes, and deductions of eighty-four employees in his head.) Naturally, the bonds of brotherhood blossom by the time Charlie and Raymond reach Los Angeles.

The film fades with Raymond on an Amtrak train, escorted by his doctor back to his private institution in Ohio. Charlie has lost his plea to keep Raymond with him. An autistic man like Raymond, argues the doctor, cannot cope outside the institution. The evidence comes in a climactic scene where Raymond panics in screaming, head-bashing terror at the incessant whine of a smoke detector he has triggered in his brother's apartment.

But this is one movie where a typical Hollywood, happily-ever-after ending would have been more appropriate than the sad departure scene of *Rain Man.* Tom Cruise was right. The Rain Man didn't have to go back to the institution. Raymond could have coped quite well on his own. He could have gotten a job. He could even have lived in his own apartment. Approximately 300,000 similarly disabled adults, some with far fewer skills than Raymond, have done so. The autistic men and women I met in Maryland proved it.

Among those was Mary Sauerbier, who, like Raymond Babbitt, is autistic. But Sauerbier takes two buses by herself to work Monday through Friday at FIC Corporation, where she dependably assembles fuses for nuclear submarines and military aircraft. Before getting the job, she had lived over twenty years as a castaway in a locked unit at a regimented institution, doing nothing all day. Now the quiet woman shares a house with three other autistic women and two counselors. Instead of eating bland institutional food, she enjoys cooking steak dinners. Instead of wearing communal clothes, she shops at Bloomingdale's. Sauerbier had traveled to Disney World in Florida and was saving up for a boat cruise to the Caribbean. I met, too, her work partner, Bill Novotny, also autistic, who, like Raymond Babbitt, could precisely rattle off baseball batting averages and, after seeing *Rain Man,* had memorized lists of previous Academy Award winners.

It was not out of do-gooder, hire-the-handicapped instincts that businesses employed the autistic workers. The reason was more selfish: they got dependable workers. Some traits of autistic people, particularly their frequent need for ritual and an ability to do repetitive tasks, made them especially prized workers. At FIC, Sauerbier wraps fuse lamps, a tedious, exacting job that requires twisting slender metal threads around a small resistor. Floor supervisor Nancy Mitchell admitted she was "skeptical" when Sauerbier first came to work. What she said she found, however, was that "Mary is quite meticulous. She's a perfectionist. If she wrapped five thousand lamps, they would all be wrapped exactly the same way." In some tasks, particularly ones that were repetitive and dull, Sauerbier and Novotny could perform at a level up to 200 percent higher than their coworkers, according to their job coach, Carla Lubore. Sauerbier has taken a sick day only twice in eight years at FIC. "We have breaks," said Mitchell. "Fifteen minutes in the morning and fifteen minutes in the afternoon. They'll go back quicker than we do." Indeed, Sauerbier broke off an interview with me at precisely 10:15 to pick up a small knife and get back to scraping excess plastic and metal from fuse screws. At the other end of the work floor, her colleagues continued to chat over coffee for several more minutes.

In addition to two good workers, the bosses at FIC got an extra supervisor in Lubore, the job coach, whose salary was paid by CSAAC. Whatever Sauerbier and Novotny were expected to do, Lubore learned it first. She broke down any new job task step by step and then taught it to Sauerbier and Novotny. A few CSAAC workers get to the point that they no longer need the help, but in most cases a job coach works beside an autistic employee every minute of the workday.

Novotny and Sauerbier are success stories, but they were relatively easy cases for CSAAC. Both, after all, have rather mild autism, are good workers, and display none of the behavior problems such as head banging and screaming that make many people with autism troublesome clients. But CSAAC does not shy away from getting jobs for even the hardest cases, people with minimal skills and the worst behavioral problems. With the right support from CSAAC's staff of job coaches and a psychologist, argued Goodman, any autistic individual could become a successful worker. Sam Dashner was one such case.

When I approached Dashner at the back of the hardware store where he works, he ran up, arms flailing, and put his face right in front of mine. He started rattling questions nonstop. "What's your name? Where do you live? How did you get here? What kind of car do you have? What's your name?" Before I could answer, he was repeating the same rapid-fire litany of questions. There is an engaging friendliness in Dashner—but he is hyperactive and easily distracted. A job coach had to be assigned to work with Dashner at all times. Dashner tags prices—all of which he has memorized—on store merchandise.

One problem that makes this Rain Man a most unlikely candidate for a job is his fear of rain, but CSAAC psychologist Marcia Smith taught Dashner to control his anxiety, which before had often erupted in outbursts of anger. Smith showed Dashner how to check the weather report each morning before leaving home. At the slightest chance of precipitation, he learned to carry a raincoat and umbrella. When it does rain, Smith has instructed him to repeat over and over again, "That's too bad, it's raining." These devices make Dashner feel more in control and remind him that there are simply some things that no one could change. After learning these tricks, said Smith, Dashner's outbursts became rare. A man who before coming to CSAAC had been ruled unable to work by other programs was now employed part-time, making more than minimum wage. Dashner enjoys working, lives in a group home, and supports himself with the money he earns.

Smith's job is half Sigmund Freud, half Sherlock Holmes. She has to figure out the unarticulated cause of a client's frustration—which may be something as seemingly irrational as a springtime drizzle—and then devise a strategy to help the autistic adult cope. "We all have incentives to make us work," she explained. "For most of us, our incentive is our salary. For some of our clients, you may have to pay them every fifteen minutes with a smile or a pat on the back, instead of with a paycheck every week." For a worker whose outbursts came when he was hungry, Smith found a simple solution: making sure the job coach kept plenty of snacks nearby at all times.

Roger Beach, who employs two autistic men at his printing company, found this system worked well. "Any person who works for a company has their quirks. In a program like this, not only are the quirks identified, but the job coach is there, trained to handle them," Beach notes. "A pressman may have a bad day and starts being rude to people around him. That happens every day in business and you just try to live with it."

Even in the worst-case scenario, when one of the autistic workers does act out, the job coach is trained to defuse any problem quickly. When a worker in the back of one store, frustrated for reasons he could not express, sat down on the floor and had an eruption, the job coach pulled the man out of sight. Then he hit his beeper to signal a "Triple Zero," an emergency call that brought another CSAAC staffer within ten minutes to help out. During the brief commotion, three women coworkers nearby ignored the problem and kept on working.

Such tolerance by coworkers is the rule rather than the exception, said Pat Juhrs, a CSAAC founder. When nondisabled people work next to disabled people, they begin to understand disabled people more, she explained. "Coworkers begin to see them as employees, instead of as handicapped," according to Juhrs. "They look to them as an asset to their company and as taxpayers, rather than as a burden to society." Occasionally there is prejudice. At Beach Brothers, a printing company, one worker threatened to quit if she had to keep working alongside autistic employees. Roger Beach told her she could leave. The woman stayed and eventually, said Beach, began treating the autistic employees the way she did any other fellow worker.

Even more noticeable than the growth in workers' perceptions of disabled people, adds Beach, is the social growth of his autistic employees. Frank Morgan, loquacious and lively, would tell other employees at the printing plant about the *Sound of*

Music sound track his father played for him, or what he bought on his last grocery shopping trip. But when Morgan first came to the printing company ten years earlier, from an institution where he had lived for twenty-three years, he used only two words, "hi" and "fine."

CSAAC succeeded because it made a simple, humane assumption: that people with autism deserve a place in the community like anyone else. Yes, autism is a perplexing and difficult disability. But people with autism are not, as tradition has it, to be regarded as sick. Nor is it realistic to insist that they have to be cured of "bad" or different behaviors as a prerequisite to living among others. Agitated behaviors are not regarded as pathological, but rather a frustrated effort to communicate. CSAAC insists that it is the responsibility of society to make a place for the person with autism. People with autism should be placed in real jobs and taught meaningful work skills. It is up to coworkers and neighbors to accept them, or at least tolerate them.

Although community-supported work programs like CSAAC save money by employing people with severe disabilities, instead of simply institutionalizing them in expensive facilities, such operations are still hard to find. Only 74,657 people were enrolled in such programs in 1990. Still, that was up sharply from the fewer than 10,000 served as recently as 1986. By 1990, workers in supported employment earned a mean hourly wage of $3.87 and 81 percent worked at least 20 hours per week. Sixty-five percent of them had mild to moderate mental retardation and another 24 percent had long-term mental illness. The rest included people with autism, cerebral palsy, sensory disabilities, and traumatic brain injury. These workers decreased their dependence on entitlements like Supplemental Security Income the longer they worked. Despite these savings, of the $11.7 billion dollars states and the federal government spent on programs for people with developmental disabilities in

1988, only $62.5 million was spent on community-supported employment.

Despite the success of programs such as CSAAC, the assumption too often still prevails that it is impossible to integrate people with autism into society. At the Behavior Research Institute in Providence, Rhode Island, for example, the priority is the management of autistic behaviors. BRI uses controversial "aversive therapy" to treat teenagers and young adults with autism. BRI seeks to alter the most troubling behaviors of clients with an escalating series of punishments that include pinching, slapping, being sprayed with water vapor or a vapor mixed with ammonia, cold showers, or being strapped into a sensory deprivation helmet that plunges the offender into blackness and the constant sound of radio static. Students are also rewarded for "proper" behavior or for successful completion of tasks and exercises. Rewards included hugs or the piling up of privileges to spend time in a playroom, an in-house midway of games, toys, and even a small merry-go-round.

Dr. Matthew Israel, BRI's founder and director, maintains that his system of rewards and punishments is a caring therapy that allows him to help clients who have been failed by other programs. He was supported in his use of aversives by the American Psychological Association and other professional groups, which argue that a therapist needs the freedom to draw on a variety of treatments in order to correct a person's aggression or self-injurious actions. Critics of aversives, however, charge that Israel uses scientific jargon to legitimize a treatment so harsh that it would not be allowed for any other population, including prison inmates. "You can't say a little bit of cruelty is all right," said Gunnar Dybwad, a Brandeis University professor emeritus of sociology who was an early advocate for the rights of people with developmental disabilities. At best, aversive therapy is ineffective and only further agitates the autistic students, Dybwad argues, escalating the hair pulling and other self-injurious behavior that the program seeks to eradicate. At worst, he says, such treatment of young students is inhumane.

In 1985, twenty-two-year-old Vincent Milletich died after BRI workers "pushed his head between his legs, cuffed his hands behind his back, put a helmet on his head with radio static hissing into his ears and masked his face. He went limp and was declared dead on arrival minutes later at Rhode Island Hospital in Providence." A court later found no evidence of a link between the school's treatment and Milletich's death. But the Massachusetts Office for Children quickly moved to suspend the licenses of seven BRI group homes, located just over the Massachusetts–Rhode Island state boundary. Mary Kay Leonard, director of the Office for Children, called BRI's punishments "excessive," and state inspectors later testified how BRI records noted that one female student had received more than one thousand physical punishments—including finger pinches, muscle squeezes, vapor sprays, and spankings—in a three-day period to correct aggression such as banging her head. Some parents withdrew their children from the school, complaining that their children had been injured by the aggressive punishments.

But other parents of BRI students came to the school's defense most fervently. They argued for their right to have this school of "last resort" as an option, claiming that BRI often took students rejected by other schools. A group of parents sued the Massachusetts office for $15.4 million in damages when Leonard's attempt to bar the use of aversives threatened to close down BRI. The right of parents to choose won out. In a settlement, Leonard sent a letter of apology to the parents, and her office paid $580,000 to the school and parents in attorneys' fees.

Israel studied psychology under behaviorist B. F. Skinner at Harvard, where he received a doctorate in psychology in 1960. Fascinated by Skinner's 1948 novel, *Walden Two,* Israel had set up two Boston communes in an attempt to create the utopian community based on behaviorist principles. Later, suspecting that the communal houses failed because they were self-centered and provided no service, he applied behavior modification techniques to treating autistic children. Skinner himself gave contradictory statements about the use of aversives. At times he denied that punishment could effectively change human behavior, but at the time of Israel's legal problems he said that some people might be "out of reach" of positive reinforcement. When Israel showed his former professor film of his work, Skinner, according to Israel, expressed shock at the level of disturbance of BRI clients. "I didn't know," Skinner was quoted by Israel as saying. "These aren't people; they are animals."

On my visit to Providence, BRI struck me as a human-sized Skinner box or a scene from some fictionalized Orwellian future. In the basement of BRI's nondescript building, "students" were lined up at workbenches, doing mundane tasks in several classrooms, as young, fresh-faced staffers, many newly armed with college psychology degrees, carefully patrolled the rooms and watched over shoulders. Upstairs, in a locked room with banks of television screens, staff monitors watched each classroom through closed-circuit hookups. Not only were the clients constantly watched and graded but the classroom workers were, too, who could also win rewards such as extra pay or vacation based on their performance. In the first classroom I visited, one young man tired of his exercise of picking out matching shapes on a computer screen. He indicated he wanted to stop by removing his hands from the computer screen. But his teacher demanded that he continue and pinched him on the palm for disobeying. The young man, wearing a protective white helmet, made a guttural noise of protest and tried to get up. In a second, two staffers had thrown him facedown on the floor. This only made him more agitated. Then came a squirt in the face with the ammonia water. The man spent a minute on the floor, trying to move and protest, but was restrained by one staffer's knee in his back and another's grip on his arms. When he gave up his struggle, the man was returned to his workbench.

I met one mother, her face wan and lined by years of stress, who had moved her family to New England so that Israel could work with her son. He had been rejected or expelled from numerous other schools for his violent behavior. Within weeks at BRI, she had seen tremendous improvement and was grateful for the simple progress of being able to take her son out to lunch at a restaurant and have him sit through the meal.

Later, over tea in Dybwad's office at Brandeis, I asked him how he would respond to the strong argument of such a desperate parent, who had devoted her life to finding an effective program that would help her son. "I defend parents very strongly," he said. "If I tell a parent to cease and desist, they have a right to say, 'Tell me what else to do.' " Dybwad saves his strongest blame for public school officials, who leave such parents with few options. Research has shown that the most effective treatment of autism—and other developmental disabilities—is to stimulate the child with an intensive program of learning and playing, starting by the time the child is three. Dybwad is not alone in this belief. Perhaps the most compelling support comes from Temple Grandin, a lecturer on autism who calls herself a "recovered autistic." Today she can describe how the constant attention of a nanny and her mother helped pull her out of her childhood autism. "I argue with our school system, which has failed to deal with these children and deal with them early," states Dybwad. "Because obviously a child doesn't start early gouging its eyes out." As with most disabilities, claims Dybwad, this country has proven programs to help people with autism. But they are not in place because of a lack of will and a continuing prejudice that the lives of disabled children are of less worth than those of nondisabled ones.

Critics like Dybwad claim that Israel's aversive therapy at best has only short-lived results. At BRI I also met Janine, a young girl who had been one of Israel's star pupils. Visitors to BRI first see a tape of the institute's work. One of the most disturbing images is of Janine on the day in 1981 when she was admitted to BRI. She jumps up and down, slapping her face with both palms. She cries. Her teeth chatter. She bashes her head on the floor, hits her head with her hands to the point that blood trickles from her mouth. When her helmet comes off, her scalp is marked by scabs and blood where the young girl has yanked out divots of her own hair. The next image of Janine, shot eight and a half months later, shows her playing happily on a swing. Her parents became leaders of the group that sought to keep BRI open. When a reporting crew from the ABC television newsmagazine "20/20" came to BRI in 1985, it filmed Janine, by then a teenager, sitting on a couch with her parents, calmly and happily singing the theme from "Sesame Street." Her helmet was off, her hair had grown back in, and she had even started wearing makeup, a sign of new self-esteem.

Four years later, on my tour of BRI, staffers took me to every classroom but one. When I asked to go back to see what was behind the locked door of that classroom, I met Janine. She had regressed. The helmet was strapped on again. There were fresh, oozing scabs on her scalp. Flanked by two staffers, she sat at her bench sorting colored rings. One staffer gave Janine frequent pinches on the palm—each one counted out and recorded—to try to correct her nearly constant moaning. A second staffer sat by in case Janine acted out. A small television camera, only a few feet away, broadcast Janine's behavior to the monitor in the locked video room upstairs. During fifteen-minute breaks between tasks, Janine would dive into a beanbag chair in the middle of the classroom, wrap herself tightly in a blanket, curl up into a fetal position, and moan softly to herself. She seemed to have become inured to the frequent hand pinches and other punishments. Israel said he was considering employing his harshest punishment, an electrical shock device known as the Self-Injurious Behavior Inhibiting System, or SIBIS, that would require a court's permission to use.

SIBIS was invented to stop such behavior as hair pulling and head banging exhibited by an estimated 160,000 people with retardation or autism. A band of electronic sensors is wrapped around a user's head. When the device detects sudden motion, like that of the head being hit, it sends a mild electric shock through the wearer's body. The sensation is described as feeling like a hard snap of a rubber band. This negative reinforcement is supposed to teach people not to hit themselves.

Some professionals, like Israel, argue that SIBIS is a useful and humane tool of last resort to stop people like Janine from hurting themselves. Others, like Tom Nerney, the former director of the American Autism Society, have fought for state bans on SIBIS, which he calls a crude and ineffective "torture." Instead, he points to nonaversive programs such as CSAAC to prove that there are humane, effective options.

A scientific panel brought together by the National Institutes of Health backed the use of such aversive devices in 1989. Nerney called the NIH process flawed, noting that some conference members were scientists who had helped develop SIBIS or whose universities had a financial interest in it. Dr. Duane Alexander of NIH, for example, was an unpaid member of the scientific advisory board to the American Foundation for Autistic Children, whose founders, Leslie and Mooza Grant, invented SIBIS. Despite the objections of Nerney and others, SIBIS has been slowly winning acceptance by psychologists and educators around the country, even being sold directly to school districts to use on children with autism or retardation.

BRI would come to rely heavily on SIBIS. Only a few students were considered candidates for being shocked when I met Janine. Three years later, in the summer of 1992, SIBIS was used on at least forty-two of BRI's approximately sixty-three students. Dependence on the shock device drew the institution into a soaring spiral of punishments. The initial benefits soon faded as students adapted to the shocks and Israel debated how to make the punishment effective again. He considered a new generation of the shock device that delivered three times the electrical jolt. But Dr. Ogden Lindsley, the chairman of BRI's senior peer review board, scoffed at that as too soft and "a blueprint for adaption" once again by the students. Lindsley's advice to Israel was to up the pain threshold so dramatically that once shocked the student would truly be deterred from acting out again. "You should punish maximumly to get rid of the ongoing behavior," Lindsley explained. "These kids are case-hardened. We need something different."

The Rise of Institutionalization

For the first half of the century, Americans with mental retardation (called "idiots" or "feebleminded"), mental illness, cerebral palsy, and, until as late as the 1940s, those with epilepsy, were viewed as a menace that threatened to lower the health and intelligence of future generations. As a result, these people—with disabilities that were not fatal—were segregated in isolated institutions. There they lost control of their lives and their liberties, solely by virtue of their disability. Often they faced involuntary sterilization. Oliver Wendell Holmes may have been one of America's most distinguished jurists, but even he voiced the standard prejudices of the day. "It is better for all the world, if instead of waiting to execute degenerative offspring for crime, or to let them starve for their imbecility, society can prevent those who are manifestly unfit from continuing their kind," Holmes wrote in the 1927 Supreme Court majority ruling in the case of Carrie Buck. Doctors at the State Colony for Epileptics and Feebleminded of Virginia, where the eighteen-year-old woman was a resident, had sought to sterilize her after she had given birth to a child. Buck's own mother lived in the same institution. (Both Buck and her daughter, and probably her mother as well, were of normal intelligence. But poor women thought to be incorrigible—like Buck and her mother, who both gave birth to illegitimate children—were often institutionalized and written off as "feebleminded.") Wrote Holmes: "Three generations of imbeciles are enough!"

The Nazi eugenics experiments, however, largely discredited such thinking, and following World War II a new approach, thought to be more humane, emerged. Such disabled people were no longer treated as threats but as patients. They were considered sick people in need of help, education, and correction, not elimination.

For those so sick they could not be cured, institutions were considered compassionate places that provided food and shelter. Neither treatment nor activity was prescribed since it was assumed that no benefit would come of it. People with mental retardation were mixed indiscriminately with those who had serious problems of mental illness. The most difficult patients were segregated among other troublesome ones, where they copied the screaming, moaning, head banging, and other behaviors they saw every day. This modeling, rather than being viewed as the understandable outcome of mistreatment and neglect, was blamed on the person's disability, not the environment in which the person lived. People with severe retardation did such things, it was assumed, and could not be made to stop.

It would be misguided to equate slavery and institutionalization on a scale of moral horrors, but it is instructional to note the parallels. Slavery was a malignant system that treated human beings as property, while institutionalization arose out of a reformist impulse to protect and help people believed unable to care for themselves. Yet, as with slaves, people in institutions were regarded as "inferior." They, too, were cut off from their families, and their own possibilities for marriage—a right now common for people with mild retardation—were ended. Slavery existed, above all, because economically it was a profitable labor system for the South. Disabled people were never sent to institutions for economic reasons. But at institutions they were put to work, often backbreaking work, for long hours and without pay. Many state facilities had their own farms, where inmates grew crops and raised animals to feed the institution. Others worked as maids, janitors, and cooks or made blankets and other items for sale to raise money for the running of the facility. As with slavery, institutional life exposed people to deficient diets; cheap, often ill-fitting, and inadequate clothing; and cramped, lightly furnished barracks where they slept with large groups of people. As late as the 1960s, it remained common for inmates at state hospitals to be bathed by stripping off their clothes, forming them into a line, and spraying them with water from a garden hose.

There was inordinate cruelty, too, from "masters." Just as enslaved women were routinely considered the sexual property of their white owners and foremen, people in institutions have also often been subjected to sexual assault. Slavery, notes one history textbook, "robbed the Negro of his manhood, encouraged infantile and irresponsible behavior, and put a premium on docility. In short, slavery deprived a whole race of the opportunity to develop its potentialities and of the freedom that white men treasured so highly." So, too, has institutionalization regarded adults with disabilities as children, placing them in wards where they model the screaming, rocking, and worst behaviors of their peers, expecting them to be docile patients, and removing their basic rights to choice, opportunity, and claim to community.

Such institutions became places of shame and scandal. State hospitals became prisons of bedlam. In the late 1960s and 1970s, parents, professionals, journalists, and even some residents, like Bernard Carabello at Willowbrook in New York, would expose the horrid conditions of these institutions. In 1965, Robert Kennedy, then a U.S. Senator from New York, visited two state institutions where he revealed overcrowded wards of patients, many naked and wandering about aimlessly or lying in their own feces and urine, and what he described as "young children slipping into blankness and lifelong dependence." In December of that year, inspired by Kennedy, Burton Blatt of Boston University, along with photographer Fred Kaplan, who toted a hidden camera attached to his belt, made a similar tour to record the "depths of despair" in the locked back wards of five state institutions. Their shocking photographs and text of Dark Ages conditions were published in an inflammatory book, *Christmas in Purgatory.* Kaplan's grainy photographs taken secretly of residents, many naked and sitting on bare floors, eerily echoed the disturbing photos of emaciated and benumbed survivors of Nazi concentration camps. They recorded children with legs and hands bound and, at one institution, one thousand crying babies abandoned and lined up in separate cribs without interaction with any adult. The stench of feces was so strong that Blatt and Kaplan had to send their clothes to be dry-cleaned after each visit.

This sort of exposé created policies to transfer some of the 195,000 residents of state institutions to community group homes and foster families in the 1970s and 1980s. Federal court judges took an interest, declaring that states like Alabama had violated the rights of residents with retardation by letting them live under such conditions. Advocates of institutional reform won help in 1971 by getting such institutions regulated and funded under the joint state and federal Medicaid program. As a result, existing institutions are now structured to somewhat resemble homes. There are dayrooms with televisions and only small groups share bedrooms. There are limits, too, on how many live in a unit and requirements to design some sort of work or activity program for each resident. It is a sizable improvement although, as Dybwad notes, "It's not hard to predict that when bureaucrats are building a house, it is not a home."

The closing of institutions was spurred by the rise of the concept of "normalization." This represented a sociological approach, rather than a medical one, to disability. People with disabilities thrive, the theory argues, when they leave institutions and are placed in "normal" settings—in homes, schools, and jobs alongside other, nondisabled people. An import from Scandinavia, normalization was spread in this country in the 1970s by Dybwad and his wife, Rosemary, and Wolf Wolfensberger of Syracuse University. Labeling people creates a cycle of failure, they argue. When doctors label someone as mentally retarded or mentally ill, that label is a direction to the public to consider that person a deviant who, according to societal norms, should be segregated. Nondisabled people have been conditioned to consider labeled people as hopelessly ill and of no potential. A child placed in an institution, the Dybwads and Wolfensberger argue, would make little progress because instructors would expect little of him and he in turn would expect little of himself.

It is better, they say, to see the person as "normal," deserving, like everyone else, of the same right to full participation in society. That means an opportunity for the same education, work, and even for love, sex, and possibly marriage. Normalization means the right to have choices and to claim the "dignity of risk."

Yet today deinstitutionalization has stalled. Some 100,000 people remain in state hospitals. It was not until 1991 that the first state, New Hampshire, would close the doors to its last institution, Lincona. "It's a classic chicken and egg problem," says Paul Wehman, a professor at the Medical College of Virginia at Virginia Commonwealth University. "If you shut down all the institutions, you don't have all the community programs in place yet. But if you don't put a ceiling on institutions, there are no incentives for community programs." Most federal money continues to be directed to large state institutions, although group homes and community programs are less expensive in the long run. State institutions are more costly because of their extensive size and staffs. States spend, on average, $56,000 yearly for each person in a state institution, according to a 1988 study by David Braddock of the University of Illinois at Chicago. Community programs like CSAAC cost slightly more than half that amount, according to Goodman.

Neighborhood resistance has remained strong to group homes, despite numerous studies disproving myths that such facilities mean high crime rates and lowered property values. There has been opposition to closing institutions from unions that stand to lose some ninety thousand jobs nationwide. Particularly influential has been a small but vocal group of parents. All mothers and fathers worry about who will look after their disabled children after they die. Those who put their trust in large institutions tend to be older parents, in most cases the ones who on the advice of doctors decades ago made the difficult decision to put a child in an institution.

Dr. Bernard Rimland is a hero to parents of autistic children for his research that discredited once-dominant psychological theories that branded the mothers and fathers of autistic children as "refrigerator parents." His studies in the 1960s shattered Dr. Bruno Bettelheim's emotional causation theories that autism was triggered by the parent's lack of love for their infant and firmly established the biological origin of autism. Rimland is also the father of an adult son with autism. He praises community-supported programs like CSAAC but says they should be just one more choice for parents, along with state and private institutions. "What will guarantee thirty years down the road that CSAAC will not fall on hard times?" he asks.

Only in the rarest cases do young children go to institutions anymore. Today families get support like respite care and other social services, as well as the right to put their children in public schools, so that disabled children can grow up at home. Younger parents, like Goodman, have come to see their disabled child's protection in his or her ability to become self-reliant. It is an independence, they see, that comes only when their sons and daughters are fully included in their communities. And if all severely disabled people had such opportunities, none would need to live in institutions, argues Goodman. These parents have little patience for gradual integration. Backed by law, they sue school districts to give their children a chance to go to integrated, neighborhood schools. By the time the children get out of high school, they have inherited the same assumptions that they have a right to integration and opportunity.

Proponents of institutions use as their most powerful arguments the disastrous deinstitutionalization of another population—people with mental illness. After World War II, mental health reformers had argued for closing state mental hospitals and caring for people with mental illness in the community. State hospitals provided no effective therapy. Drugs were used almost indiscriminately. State legislatures rewrote laws to make it difficult to commit people to such hospitals against their will. In the 1960s, Congress began funding community mental health centers, which, along with halfway houses, were supposed to provide outpatient care for people with chronic mental illness. That care, it was argued, could be provided at less expense than at large institutions.

But that vision was never realized. The doors of hospitals swung open, but people with mental illness had nowhere to go. Governments never provided the money for community programs. Some hospitals simply took construction grants and built nonrelated facilities—in some cases, swimming pools and tennis courts for other patients. Few halfway houses were ever built. Community mental health centers eschewed treating people with difficult chronic illnesses and instead turned to easier and more profitable patients. The result was a tragedy that can be seen in the large numbers of homeless people—some 30 percent—with serious mental illness, mostly schizophrenia and manic depression.

Advocates for those with mental retardation have learned from the grim mishandling of those with mental illness. By law, no one with a developmental disability is allowed to move into the community unless the move is carefully planned. Those leaving institutions go to a group home or apartment, where they are supervised. Usually a staffer lives or stays at the house. Those with mild retardation who can live on their own—some are even buying their own homes—still have someone come by periodically and check on them. Every year, case workers evaluate their progress. A work program during the day is mandatory. Only on the rarest of occasions does someone with mental retardation leave an institution and wind up homeless, but these tend to be people with mental illness as well as retardation. Little by little, the dream of integration is being fulfilled.

Knocking on the Classroom Door

In 1973, children's advocate Marian Wright Edelman launched the Children's Defense Fund with a survey. One U.S. Census figure haunted her. Some 750,000 American children between the ages of seven and thirteen did not attend school. Who were they and why were they being denied an education? Edelman, whose civil rights advocacy had been born in forcing Mississippi to fund Head Start programs of early childhood development for poor black children, felt certain that she knew the answer. They were black children, she assumed, shut out of segregated school districts. But the survey returns showed the highest number of nonenrolled children lived in predominantly white areas, such as Portland, Maine, Appalachian Kentucky, and western Massachusetts.

"Handicapped kids were those seven hundred fifty thousand kids," Edelman recalls finding to her surprise. "We'd never thought of handicapped kids. But they're out there everywhere." Schools had simply turned them away, saying they were unable to educate them. Children were rejected if they had developmental disabilities like mental retardation or autism, which raised doubts about whether they could learn. But even intellectually superior students were left uneducated, because conditions like cerebral palsy made it difficult for them to speak or because muscular dystrophy, spina bifida, polio, or paralysis forced them to use wheelchairs and the school building was filled with stairs.

Edelman's detective work helped lead to a parents' campaign to pass a 1975 federal law, the Education for All Handicapped Children Act, which guaranteed an education for the nation's 8 million children with disabilities. Public Law 94-142 was the disability movement's equivalent of *Brown* v. *Board of Education.* Like black Americans, disabled ones were looking to the schools for equity and social justice. Millions of disabled children have since gone through school under the act (now renamed the Individuals with Disabilities Education Act, although still best known by the old title), often in "mainstreamed" schools with children not disabled. The law requires teaching disabled students in the "least restrictive environment," that is, with non-disabled children whenever possible. The law covers children with disabilities such as mental retardation, who traditionally were segregated in their own schools, and those with chronic illnesses like AIDS, who often find themselves turned away at the schoolhouse door.

The U.S. Supreme Court has acknowledged the right of all children to an education—no matter how severe their disability or how much the cost. Timothy W. is about as severely disabled as a child can be. He has profound mental retardation as well as cerebral palsy and a seizure disorder. In addition, he is blind and a quadriplegic. His New Hampshire school district argued that he could not learn "even the most rudimentary skill" and that it made no sense to spend the estimated $15,000 a year required to keep him in school. But Timothy, according to his mother and child-care workers, "responds to talking, touching, motion, familiar voices, taste, smell, pain, temperature, bright lights and music." Although he does not talk, he smiles when he is happy and cries when he is sad. But the 1975 law, a federal court noted, is clear that *"all* handicapped children between the ages of three and twenty-one have the right to a free appropriate education." The Supreme Court let this lower court's ruling stand. The law, much like the CSAAC program for autistic adults, works from the assumption that we cannot presuppose that a person with disabilities is limited. (Indeed, the popular Head Start preschool program to raise the school performance of poor children came out of Sargent Shriver's knowledge of early intervention programs that had raised the IQ levels of children with retardation.) Timothy may have seemed unlikely to be educated, but he could learn something. And both he and his peers would learn about interacting with a diversity of people just by virtue of his being in the classroom.

Parents of disabled students speak the language of a civil rights movement. They demand an end to "segregated" schools filled only with disabled students. Instead, they want their children—from those with almost imperceptible learning disabilities to those with severe disabilities such as children who now live long enough to leave hospitals and come to class on respirators—to attend neighborhood schools with nondisabled children. "Mainstreaming" is the practice of putting disabled students in the same school *building* as nondisabled students but generally separating them into smaller, special education classrooms. Sometimes a child takes a few classes—music, art, shop, or academic ones depending on the student's skill level—with nondisabled schoolmates. Often, however, "mainstreaming" has been no more than an empty promise of equality, as disabled kids are kept isolated in their own classrooms. Sometimes they even have separate lunch hours. As a result, parents today have begun insisting on an "integrated" education, which means that the disabled student sits in the same *classroom* with nondisabled peers.

In September 1990, Sacramento school officials said Rachel

Holland's moderate retardation and short attention span meant that she could not keep up with nondisabled students in her kindergarten class. The girl's parents sued, making a cutting-edge argument before state courts to expand the interpretation of the 1975 act to guarantee their daughter's right to a totally integrated education. Special education, the girl's parents argued, set her up for failure—because less was expected of students segregated in separate classes. It was another case, they claimed, of separate but unequal programs justified on the basis of a person's disability. "When Rachel is placed with retarded children she tends to act retarded," said her father, Robert Holland. But she learned more when a private school placed her "with her regular friends and in a creative environment," in which a teacher modified assignments for her and other students helped her learn. A special hearing officer agreed with the family, forcing the school district to include the girl in a regular first-grade class.

Parents such as Rachel Holland's cite studies showing that even children with the most severe disabilities learn better in integrated settings. Disabled students set higher goals for themselves when they have nondisabled peers to model. And the teachers in integrated classrooms are more likely to push them as well.

Getting into mainstreamed schools and even integrated classes, however, is no guarantee of acceptance. Former Representative Steve Bartlett tells the story of a girl with Down syndrome from Harlingen, Texas, whose parents fought to get her into a regular school, only to find that insensitive school officials excluded her from pep rallies and refused to let her pose with her schoolmates for her class picture. The principal at one Chicago high school barred Jim Stan, an eighteen-year-old with cancer, from graduation ceremonies on the ground that his presence would be disruptive, since he could not walk. Bad publicity forced the coldhearted principal to relent. Sascha Bittner, a seventeen-year-old with cerebral palsy, had to bring a lawsuit to force her San Francisco high school to reverse a decision to prevent her from attending a class picnic because her motorized wheelchair was too heavy to transport. Similarly, another California high school allowed Christine Sullivan, who has cerebral palsy and uses a wheelchair, to attend regular classes but refused to let her bring her service dog, Ford. A judge ruled that the school had denied the girl her "choice" of ways to "overcome the limitation created by her physical disability," in effect dooming her to fail.

Particularly important for parents is that their sons and daughters get a chance to make friends and not feel like outsiders. Studies of disabled children show that they master social skills far more easily when they go to school with nondisabled children. In addition, the other classmates learn empathy and many take on a sense of responsibility for helping a disabled classmate.

That was clear when I visited a noisy homeroom at the Levy Middle School in Syracuse, New York. There was rap music flying off the walls of this homeroom of five students with autism and eleven other "typical" students. Eddie, one of the autistic kids, made himself a cup of calming herbal tea on the stove in the adjoining kitchen. Michael, another autistic student, and his friend Dante had pushed the desks aside in one corner of the room to play a game of Nerf basketball. Tasha, an autistic girl, leafed through copies of *Glamour* and *Mademoiselle* with Maria and Rachel. Jamal, also autistic, rode one of the two exercise bicycles. Two other boys read the newspaper sports page, and another played a game on the computer. The homeroom was rowdy by design, with plenty of things that stimulated the autistic kids but also attracted "typical" kids from throughout the school to want to voluntarily interact with these different students.

The tactic payed off. When Ben, a six-foot-tall boy with

autism, started slapping himself, another student took his hands reassuringly, then put them in his lap. Jamal, modeling the behavior of these other students, also learned to help Ben, telling him soothingly, "Don't cry." Ben and Dante became good friends, with Ben taking Dante, who lives in the city, to his home in the country. "These [autistic] kids are ready for the world with all its complexities and the community is learning how to deal with them," explained Luanna Meyer of Syracuse University, who helped design the program. "We're not postponing this inevitable need to prepare these two groups of people for how to deal with each other."

Most of the autistic students take gym, music, art, and shop classes with their nondisabled classmates. Some, accompanied by a teacher's aide, take regular classes, like reading, and two of them are in the top ten of their science class. All of them work two days a week in the community, at sites including a hardware store and a library. Pattie Johnson, the special education teacher who runs the homeroom, was initially skeptical of the fully integrated approach. "I've worked with kids who have been segregated and there's a big difference with these kids," she remarked. "Their behavior is so much better and their intellectual level is much higher, too. People who are segregated before high school are still working on separating nuts and bolts." Three of the students at the Syracuse school had been at BRI in Rhode Island. There would be even bigger surprises to come. Three years after I met Ben, he had become a columnist for his high school newspaper. He was taking academic classes and was proud of the B he earned in biology class. He even passed the mathematics section of New York's statewide Regents' examination. Not bad for the autistic kid whose teachers believed he could not even spell.

Ben, the adopted son of Sue and Bob Lehr, is the prototype of the student written off as incapable of learning because of his disabilities but who, in reality, is held back largely because of others' low expectations. In Ben's case, the key to letting others see his potential came with a new and controversial teaching technique called facilitated communication. It required little more than a keyboard and human touch. A "facilitator"—usually someone with a day or two of simple training—holds the person's hand lightly and follows it over the keyboard. Often, over time, a facilitator can reduce the support, moving the touch to the arm, shoulder, or back. Although the power of touch is not fully understood, this gentle assistance seems to allow people like Ben to type out thoughts and feelings that they otherwise could not articulate. However, critics, including many researchers in autism, say it works on the same principle as a Ouija board: the facilitator, consciously or even subconsciously, moves the person's fingers to the correct letters.

Douglas Biklen, a Syracuse University special-education professor, first saw facilitated communication in action in 1989 in Australia, where teacher Rosemary Crossley used it with students with cerebral palsy. That made sense, since cerebral palsy does not affect intelligence, although people with it often have difficulty speaking and moving their hands. So Biklen was skeptical when Crossley started using the method with an autistic student. But the extraordinary results he witnessed made him a convert. He returned to the United States to teach the method, attracting parents, teachers, and speech pathologists to his training sessions. He began using it not just with students with autism but with those labeled retarded as well.

While autism researchers criticized Biklen for failing to do the testing that would provide qualitative scientific proof, parents eagerly embraced the method based on observation of their own children. In South Dakota, Marilyn and Steven Schiller were convinced when their eight-year-old son, Kurtis, began rattling off the surface temperature of Venus and other arcana about the planets. At school he was being taught his colors, but it turned out he had been reading his father's astrophysics books, not just staring at the pretty pictures. In Syracuse, Richard Meives told his father "I love you," a first for the twelve-year-old with Down syndrome and autistic-like behaviors who was thought incapable of expressing spontaneous emotion.

Yet some autism researchers, like Eric Schopler of the University of North Carolina, call facilitated communication a cruel hoax being "recklessly" promoted to play on parents' unfounded dreams for their children. After all, he asks, what parents wouldn't prefer to believe their child really has a 130 IQ and can say "I love you"? Biklen counters that skeptics cannot deal with facilitation because it shatters their own theories. Biklen's surprising conclusion is that autism is not a thinking deficit as much as a physical one, with uncontrollable and sometimes violent body gestures, odd words, and grunts blocking real speech. Ben Lehr has said as much. "Listen to what I type, not what I say," he has typed.

Many parents side with Biklen. If the facilitator is doing the cueing, they ask, then how could Schiller pass his father's quiz on the planets when his mother—who did not know the answers—was holding his hand? If someone was making up his words, why were tears streaming down Mieves's face when he typed, "I want a real friend"? And how could it have been that a Chicago boy, thought at first to be typing gibberish, was really spelling all his words backward? Parents often find themselves fighting for the use of facilitation in schools, where officials are often skeptical about buying the computers in the absence of scientific proof. Schopler thinks facilitation may help 2 percent of people with autism; Biklen, who was once quoted at putting the figure at 90 percent, now says simply that the number is high.

It is not that facilitation is pure joy for families. Even for the most devoted parent advocate, there is sheer terror and profound guilt for having underestimated their children. "It's wonderful, but it's not fun," said Rebecca Susag of Minnesota. She regretted not pushing her autistic daughter, Marta, further in school. Suddenly, she faced protecting a ten-year-old who, after all, still had a severe disability but was harder to protect now that she could express her own wants and choices. Susag's friend Jennifer Otto felt guilt over having never told her multiply disabled twenty-eight-year-old son about God. And Ben Lehr began talking about going to college, although success at that level certainly would not come easily for the young man who still sometimes throws tantrums at school.

School districts have balked not only at facilitated communication but at the costs of integrating disabled students. Schools spend an estimated $6,335 per year on each student receiving special education services, compared with $2,686 per year for students in regular classes. "It's not just a matter of having ramps and special rest-room facilities," explained Carol Arnesen, special education director for Orange County, California, schools. "Sometimes, it's special medical equipment, changing tables for older children who are incontinent, specialized cafeteria services because many are tube fed. . . . It's like running a mini-hospital."

Temple University Professor Margaret Wang figures that the cost gap could be closed. Schools spend at least $1,000 per child with a disability on useless testing, she claims, and existing segregated special-education schools add cost for separate transportation and buildings. Meyer argues that integrated programs can save school districts money. Most, rather than set up programs like the one at Levy Middle School, will pay the tuition at private schools, even residential schools, which can cost $50,000 to $100,000 a year, says Meyer. But the Syracuse program spends about $10,000 per autistic student, which includes the cost of extra aides who sometimes accompany the autistic students to regular classes.

Yet long after the 1975 law that opened schools to disabled students, they continue to get a second-class education. Some 67 percent are still taught in separate schools, classes, and resource rooms, while only 31 percent spend most of their day in a regular classroom, according to the U.S. Department of Education. Forty percent of students with disabilities drop out of school, compared to only 15 percent of their nondisabled peers. The problem is not a lack of know-how. Successful models, like the Syracuse program, provide a quality education for even severely disabled students. The problem is largely one of a lack of will on the part of school districts, which continue to see disabled students as a burden, to be separated and given low priority, and teachers who often expect too little, coddling disabled kids and teaching them less. The state-funded Massachusetts Developmental Disabilities Council concluded that segregation in that state had *increased* in the 1970s and 1980s, contrary to the intent of the 1975 schooling law. The council blamed schools for failing to set up integrated programs, as well as disincentives in federal and state school funding regulations, which reimburse towns at a higher rate if they send disabled students to private residential schools like BRI.

Particularly worrisome is that special education often becomes a catchall category for any student having trouble in class. A child may be there because of a disability, because a teacher cannot motivate him, or because his grades are falling due to some problem at home. Getting into these classes often stigmatizes children and relegates them to an inferior status. Nearly 10 percent of all students are enrolled in special education, according to a 1991 report to Congress. Fifty percent of these are categorized as having learning disabilities; 24 percent with speech or language impairments; 11 percent with mental retardation; 9 percent with serious emotional disturbance; and 6 percent have hearing, visual, orthopedic, or other health impairments. Yet state-by-state fluctuations show that determining who goes into special education is an inexact science. In Massachusetts, 17 percent of students take special education classes; in Hawaii, less than 7 percent. In Connecticut, nearly 19 percent of students in these classes are labeled seriously emotionally disturbed, yet in Idaho less than 3 percent are classified that way. Minority students are especially likely to be placed in special classes, further raising suspicions that these classes are simply dumping grounds for unwanted students. In Massachusetts, 27 percent of minority students are labeled as special-education students, compared to only 16 percent of white students.

The number of students requiring special education will continue to grow, warns Wang. She cites the rising number of teen pregnancies. "Teenage mothers tend to have premature or low-birthweight babies, and these children often develop health and learning problems," she writes. "Many of them become permanently disabled, needing a lifetime of medical care and supportive services." In addition, a new generation of "crack babies" are entering school, challenging teachers with their short attention spans. A 1991 report by the Department of Education notes that the number of students identified with disabilities has increased every year since 1976 and is expected to continue that trend through at least the end of the century.

Despite the often begrudging commitment by schools, a better-educated class of young disabled people is providing the shock troops for the disability rights movement. The first generation of disabled students fully protected by the Education for All Handicapped Children Act began graduating from colleges in the early 1990s, the first disabled Americans to grow up assuming that they have safeguarded rights to equal opportunity. Their success under this law has encouraged parents of younger disabled children to settle for no less than full inclusion.

Integration on the Playing Fields

These new militants consistently demand full integration. This creates some often surprising controversies, like the one over the Special Olympics.

By drawing six thousand athletes from ninety-four countries, the International Special Olympics Games in Minneapolis became the biggest sporting event in the world in 1991. Forty-five thousand spectators at the gala opening ceremonies took in the pageantry of athletes in brightly colored warm-up suits basking in the thrill and glory of competition; seventy-five corporate sponsors poured millions of dollars into the event.

It was a far grander event than the first Special Olympics in 1968. Then, doctors had warned the event's creator, Eunice Kennedy Shriver, that the participants' fragile hearts could not withstand a run of more than 400 yards. But in Minneapolis, Savvas Vikelis ran a victory lap with the white-and-blue flag of his native Greece wrapped around his sweat-soaked body after he won a gold medal in the 13.1-mile half-marathon. In 1968, the experts had warned, too, that people with retardation could not swim. "One old shibboleth was that they had misshapen bodies and would sink to the bottom of the pool," recalled Sargent Shriver. "There must have been a dozen lifeguards around the pool at those first games. We didn't want a child to sink." He pronounced the last word in a voice dripping with sarcasm. The lifeguards, he explained, were deployed to assuage the lawyers worrying about liability. His wife knew otherwise. An accomplished athlete herself, she taught children and adults with retardation to swim in the pool behind the Shriver house at the summer day camp she had started in 1963.

The disability movement is filled with disabled people and their family members who have devoted themselves to disproving the accepted wisdom of various experts. Eunice Shriver, the younger sister of John F. Kennedy, was one of those debunkers. It started with a promise to her father to take up the issue and to look after her older, retarded sister, Rosemary, who lived at a Wisconsin institution run by a Catholic order of nuns. The Joseph P. Kennedy, Jr., Foundation, which she had helped set up in the 1950s, would research new ways to educate and serve people with retardation. But it was the Special Olympics for which she would be best known. The games presented people who until then remained a closeted and dreaded population in a positive way to the world. For dispelling fears and myths about retardation, Shriver rightly became a hero, and the Special Olympics gained status as a revered American institution.

Yet in Minneapolis there were signs that the Special Olympics was having trouble keeping up with the new militancy of younger parents demanding full integration. There, many parents, like Barbara Gill and her son Amar, boycotted the event. Barbara Gill objects to Special Olympics because it is a segregated and special recreation that would place her son in a program with only other similarly disabled children. "We have separated people with disabilities into a shadow world," complained Barbara Gill. "It's an imitation world and it can never be as rich or meaningful as the real world." The Special Olympics, she argued, was just one more separate but unequal place in the shadows.

The week before Vikelis won his gold medal, Amar Gill, who is retarded, and five other twelve-year-olds won medals in the Milk Carton Boat Race at the Minneapolis Aquatennial Festival, a yearly celebration of the city's lakes. Amar helped his friends, none of whom were disabled, build the fifteen-foot long boat of plastic milk cartons and wood, painted green and shaped like a dragon. He paddled, too, along with the others. To Barbara Gill it was an important moment because "he felt accepted. He felt he was part of a team."

When the Shrivers started the Special Olympics, recreational activity for disabled people was a rarity. Then, 75 percent of children with retardation got less than an hour a week of physical education, says University of Minnesota professor and recreational therapist Stuart Schleien. Today, however, parents like Gill complain that the existence of segregated events like the Special Olympics only removes the pressure for creating truly integrated programs. When Gill's friend Sue Swenson asked her playground to help her multiply disabled eight-year-old son, Charlie, play with his friends, she was told to send him instead to a segregated program like the Special Olympics. "It just furthers the pity impulse and the impulse to separate because it's special," complained Swenson.

Schleien argues that separation in recreation is especially illogical, since physical ability is the one place where people with retardation often match up best against all others. Schleien, for example, has successfully integrated adults with retardation into a long-standing Minneapolis bocce league. Although for most people the Special Olympics evokes images of cute children with Down syndrome struggling to cross a finish line, the competitors also include adults, the clumsy, and the athletically gifted. Mental retardation does not necessarily affect physical development, particularly among those with mild retardation.

Indeed, Special Olympians have gone on to fame by setting international track records, winning boxing titles, and playing in the National Basketball Association and National Football League. One former Special Olympian is one of the most widely recognized names in sports today. He declines, through a spokesman, to talk about his participation. Past and present Special Olympics officials will confirm the accomplishments of this athlete and others, but they refuse to make the names public, citing reasons of privacy. That there is such a stigma to going public, argued Gill, is just one more reason not to have separate games.

Jack Hourcade of Boise State University complains that the Special Olympics only masks the wide-ranging abilities of people with retardation because it is a segregated event, with a "childlike atmosphere" that includes "huggers" at the finish line, an appeal to charity, the use of yellow school buses to transport athletes, and the presence of clowns at events.

At the Minneapolis games in 1991, Special Olympics organizers worked hard to dispel stereotypes. Press officers pushed the stories of accomplished adult athletes, like twenty-three-year-old Andrew Leonard, a five-foot-tall power lifter who could dead lift four times his weight; and Loretta Claiborne, a thirty-six-year-old who had run twenty marathons, including the Boston Marathon. Special Olympics officials even handed reporters a guide to proper usage of disability language. Despite their efforts, the media tend to cover the games as a feature story, not a sporting event. So it was not the accomplished athletes who drew the cameras but the cute kids, like the irresistible Chinese girl who thought the race was over halfway through and then, waving her little American flag, joyfully jumped into the arms of a hugger.

The future of the Special Olympics may lie in its tentative acceptance of integration. In Minneapolis, a concept called "unified sports" was on display internationally for the first time. About 4 percent of members of bowling, volleyball, basketball, and other teams were not retarded. Unified sports matches up teammates of roughly equal athletic ability. The idea first emerged in the early 1980s when a Massachusetts softball team decided to integrate itself. Gus Piazza of the Massachusetts softball team that pioneered the concept says the unified teams meet the ideals of integration: disabled athletes get opportunities, and friendships develop. The result was a fairly skilled level of play, as high or higher as on any coed softball league anywhere in America. Piazza says he has watched his teammates with retardation "lose their shyness" and blossom both socially and athletically. Before that year, the Soviet Union, denying even the existence of retardation in that country, declined to participate in the Special Olympics. But in Minneapolis, the first Soviet team to compete was particularly curious about the unified events and announced it would try this American innovation of mainstreaming back home.

Some Special Olympics critics, like Schleien, think unified sports is a step in the right direction. Others, like Barbara Gill, remain skeptical. She argues it would be better to guarantee her son "space in the real world" and the chance to join any league along with his friends who are not disabled. It is not enough, she says, for Amar to grow up having to rely on the willingness of "some good people to be in the shadow world for a while."

Not by Law Alone

Laws alone cannot guarantee integration. Even after *Brown* v. *Board of Education,* blacks faced George Wallace blocking the schoolhouse door. Even after the 1964 Civil Rights Act, there would be decades of racism, hostility, and neglect. Compared to black Americans, disabled ones have found an advantage in the fact that public reaction to them is often motivated by compassion and charity, even if it is mixed with fear and revulsion. And because at least one in seven people have some disability or chronic illness, many Americans are likely to have someone in their own family who is disabled, giving them some understanding of what it means to live with a disability. Yet integration for blacks, compared with integration of disabled people, has been a more consciously adopted societal goal. There are affirmative action programs, minority set-asides, college scholarships, and other efforts to open up opportunities.

Integration has been more quirky and halting for disabled Americans. Even after passage of the 1975 Education for All Handicapped Children Act, school systems continue to run separate schools. Often they respond only when sued by parents, even though the courts, almost routinely, have ruled in favor of the children, even for ones as severely disabled as Timothy W. The history of segregation has been every bit as devastating for disabled Americans as it has been for black ones. Today, the unemployment rate among disabled people is 66 percent. Only 15 percent take part in postsecondary programs. Many depend on some form of welfare. For those with developmental disabilities, for example, 65 percent of their total income comes from public sources, compared to 17 percent for all Americans. Twenty-five percent of people with developmental disabilities live in families with incomes below the poverty line.

In the long run, integration will cost society less. A good education allows a disabled student one day to become a worker and a taxpayer rather than a costly tax burden. But school districts, hard-pressed for resources, tend to resist steps that will ease the drain on someone else's budget in the future. They avoid training a regular classroom teacher to include a child with severe dyslexia or ramping the schoolhouse door.

Recognizing the political reality of fiscal limits, the disability rights movement has been forced to accept a long, slow road to achieving full integration. Even the Americans with Disabilities Act, for political expediency, rejected an instant "flat earth" philosophy in order to phase in integration over time. Cities, for example, are required to equip buses with lifts, but only the newly purchased buses. It will be decades before the older buses—in essence, segregated facilities for wheelchair users—go out of use. Laws that guarantee nondiscrimination in employment and public accommodation mean little for a young disabled person who, due to antiquated Medicaid and Medicare laws, has no option but to live in a nursing home. And laws that govern construction of new homes require only a small percentage to be wheelchair accessible, ensuring that people who use wheelchairs almost always will be unable to visit friends and even family in their own homes for years to come.

The result is that disabled people and their families often have legal protection but few true options. As the ex-chair of the education committee of the Association for Retarded Citizens of Maryland, Nancy Rhead is a fervent advocate for integrated schooling. She understands that schools are the first public institution to shape people's attitudes and are therefore crucial to moving people into the mainstream. All this became painfully clear for Rhead one day when she walked through a store several paces behind her son. David has mild retardation and mild cerebral palsy that gives him an odd gait. "It was chilling," Rhead recalls of seeing the cruel stares directed toward her son. But she knew that people who got to know her son at school found him gentle and friendly. "If you grow up with these kids in your gym class and cafeteria, you get used to people being different. You get comfortable with it." That was Rhead's ideal world, but in Rhead's real world, she did not always have the choice of sending David to integrated schools. He went to a regular public high school when he was eighteen. But because he could not pass the state's newly instituted basic-skills test in math, reading, and language, he was moved to a segregated special-education school. He mourned the lost familiarity of his old school and friends, and his performance slipped. Ideally, there would have been space in a community-supported work program—similar to CSAAC—in his community. But instead, David became one of four thousand adults with retardation on a waiting list for the few such publicly funded positions that do exist in Maryland. So Rhead had to send David to a private residential school—the very sort of option she opposed as an advocate.

David attended the Benedictine School for Exceptional Children on the Eastern Shore of Maryland, run by Sister Jeanette Murray, a dynamic administrator who had adopted community work and living programs in her separate school. Students went through high school in segregated classes, but then were moved into community-supported work programs and group homes every bit as state-of-the-art as those funded by CSAAC, upon which they were modeled. David's three years at the Benedictine school gave him the good job habits and social skills that later allowed him to live in his own apartment several miles from his mother and to work with a lawn maintenance service. He became active in his community, doing volunteer work at the local library and even testifying, with other neighbors, at a county hearing in opposition of a plan to end a bus line that served his area and which he depended upon to get around.

Today, blacks and women often choose to go to separate colleges for the comfort and experience of being with peers of a like identity. But disabled people have few of the options offered other minorities. Nancy Rhead chose a segregated school because it was the only real possibility open to her. "Families ought to have the opportunity to make a choice," says Rhead. "But that's not true right now."

Go-slow integration only creates a cycle of failure and frustration. When a family chooses a segregated school, there is less pressure to integrate other school programs. When a parent enrolls a child in a private residential school that uses aversive therapy, it becomes harder to argue that such punishment is outmoded and should be abandoned. When disabled people are herded into sheltered workshops to earn below-minimum-wage salaries for piecework, employers lose the impetus to hire good workers, and taxpayers foot the bill. When separate recreation programs like Special Olympics exist, parents get turned away when they seek inclusion for their sons and daughters at neighborhood playgrounds. Disabled people remain segregated, and nondisabled people do not get to know them. The only force for overturning the status quo is a growingly militant generation of disabled people and their parents, whose anger and targets will surprise those who remain unaware of the growing frustration.

CHAPTER 6

PEOPLE FIRST

" **O**ne thing we're going to vote on is a revolution!" Deepfelt cheers erupt from the crowd at the first-ever convention of People First of Connecticut. "Resolution" is the word that T. J. Monroe wanted, but revolution, really, is more like it. Monroe and the three hundred people in the hotel ballroom are trailblazers of the self-advocacy movement, a new and spreading crusade of people with mental retardation to make their own decisions about everything, from where they live to what they are called.

"You have to do two things today," Monroe exhorts his rapt followers. "You have to make thunder. You have to speak for your rights." For his listeners, just gathering at this meeting in 1990 is a daring and heady act of subversion. Others have always laid out their lives for them, telling them what to do and what to think. "You're not gonna get in no trouble speaking for yourself, because there aren't going to be laws in this room," Monroe reassures the audience. "I want to hear thunder!"

By the end of the day, a revolutionary declaration of independence will be passed with raucous joy, unanimity, and plenty of thunder. The resolutions concern issues of the greatest importance to people with retardation. Close down all state institutions for people with retardation. Give us paid sick leave, vacation time, and holidays at our job sites and at sheltered workshops. Recognize our right to have relationships, even to have sex with those we choose in our institutions and group homes. And, because "retarded" is an ugly word that makes us seem childlike and dependent, change the name of the state Department of Mental Retardation, and avoid the word whenever you can. Refer to us as people with retardation, if you must. See us as people first.

Self-advocacy is the new rights movement of people with retardation. It is the parallel cry of self-determination by another group of disabled people rebelling against being long underestimated, deprived of choices, treated as eternal children, and thought to lead lesser lives. Self-advocacy is both part of the overall disability rights movement and a separate version that focuses on issues affecting people with mental retardation. (Many self-advocacy chapters include members with other developmental disabilities, including cerebral palsy and sometimes autism and head injuries. Often these other self-advocates have been institutionalized in facilities primarily for those with retardation.) In California, self-advocates picketed the state capitol to protest cuts in social service programs; others in Denver went on strike at a sheltered workshop, where they were paid at piece rates, to demand the same pay as nondisabled employees there; self-advocates affiliated with the Kennedy Institute in Washington, D.C., started a voter registration and education project; and in Connecticut Monroe helped self-advocates still living at a state institution call a well-attended press conference to demand their release from the institution into group homes.

There are 10,000 self-advocates at 374 chapters of People First and similar groups, according to an informal nationwide survey in 1990 by Rick Berkobien of The ARC. That compared to 200 known chapters in 1987 and just 55 in 1985.

The movement's impact belies its numbers or newness. Most significantly, professionals and parents' groups have begun to include people with retardation in decision making about the programs that affect them. Often this is just tokenism, not real power sharing. But in 1991 the Association of Retarded Citizens voted to change its name to The ARC, to reflect the demands of self-advocates to stop using the word "retarded." It was not an easy name change for the nation's largest group of parents and professionals advocating for people with retardation. It became difficult, for example, when fund-raising, to explain what The ARC was all about once it no longer had a defining word in its title. But the name switch was the first demand of the self-advocacy movement, and The ARC's action showed the new regard for joint decision making.

Self-advocacy is a second wave of revolt against the professionals who have run programs for people with retardation. The first came in the parents' movement starting in the years following World War II. Parents' groups formed mainly to obtain more social services for their retarded children, but also to protest the condescension of doctors and professionals who assumed these mothers and fathers were too guilt-ridden or inadequate to make proper decisions for their children. Those groups, including The ARC, which began in 1950 as the National Association of Parents and Friends of Mentally Retarded Children, changed the way professionals regarded parents, eventually leading parents and professionals to team up in their advocacy. Now self-advocacy is enlarging that circle. The parents' movement, says Gunnar Dybwad, one of its founders, is "getting tired," and the freshest thinking about improving the lives of people with retardation is coming from those with the disability. Jean Bowen, an adviser to Connecticut People First, believes self-advocates will be more forceful fighters for their rights than their parents ever were. "Parents have been told to have such little expectations for their sons and daughters to contribute anything that they have been willing to settle for less," she says. Underpinning the self-advocacy movement is a faith that people with retardation—even the most severely retarded person—can be taught to make good choices. "This is a free country. You can talk for yourself" is the way T. J. Monroe explained it at the convention. "You might need some help, but you can talk for yourself."

As Monroe points out, however, if self-advocacy is a revolt against professionals and the nonretarded world, it also, paradoxically, remains dependent on people who are not retarded. Retardation means that a person has much greater difficulty learning than others. So people with retardation often need help in making the choices and judgments that constitute their own acts of self-assertion. Almost always, a self-advocacy chapter relies on a facilitator, a nonretarded adviser who helps break down complicated information but who, ideally, leaves decision making to the advocates. The facilitator treads a fine line. Usually a chapter's character is determined by the adviser. Some chapters are primarily places to socialize. Others press an agenda dominated by political activism. That is the case with Connecticut People First, whose chief adviser, Bowen, as director of the Western Connecticut Association for the Handicapped and Retarded, is active nationally on issues of the rights of people with mental retardation.

And if in Connecticut self-advocacy is a revolution, it is one that is encouraged, at least at arm's length, by the very regime that is being challenged. Speaking at the Connecticut People First convention, following a warm introduction by Monroe, is Toni Richardson, the state commissioner of the Department of Mental Retardation. "You are going to create a new world where everyone is included," she says, comparing the self-advocates to

Martin Luther King, Jr. "All of you are responsible for a new era and I take my hat off to you."

In the end, Richardson knows that self-advocacy will create more headaches for her. The people her department serves are being encouraged to complain about the way they are treated. But there are potential advantages, too. Richardson's department faces budget cuts in fiscally troubled Connecticut. The self-advocates could become effective political allies to help push for more money for, among other things, the new group homes she would like to open. But the biggest selling point for self-advocacy, says Richardson, is that it is the right thing to do.

Richardson has known Monroe since 1969, when, fresh out of college, she took a job at Southbury Training School, where he was then living. Working in one of Southbury's cottages as a residential aide, what she calls a "bottom of the heap" job, Richardson helped people eat, get to the bathroom, or get ready for bed. Later she became a teacher and then director of educational services at the institution. "A lot of the people who are part of self-advocacy now, I knew personally at Southbury twenty years ago. I remember what they were like, and what we, the staff, thought about their abilities. Now I see them in a whole different way, as colleagues and friends," says Richardson. "I'm not sure if they grew, or if we just grew in the way we looked at them."

Richardson was careful to stay at the edge of the conference, lest she seem to be co-opting or constraining the self-advocates. Her department, however, encouraged state-run group homes and institutions to let residents attend the conference, even making state buses available to transport anyone who needed a ride. This was crucial aid, since many of the self-advocates, particularly those in wheelchairs, would have had no way to get to the convention hotel in Middlebury, a small town in southwestern Connecticut. In addition, Richardson's department provided a $5,000 state grant to finance the meeting, the biggest single contribution. Another $10,000 was raised with the $20 convention registration fee and in candy sales by People First members.

People with retardation span a wide range of capabilities and experiences. This is reflected among the Connecticut self-advocates. Most live in group homes or with their parents, although a few live by themselves. Some, however, will return after the conference to a cottage at an institution that has been home for most of their lives. Most have mild retardation, which is not surprising given that 89 percent of the up to 7.5 million Americans with mental retardation are classified this way, according to The ARC. (Other experts, like Marty Wyngaarden Krauss of Brandeis University, say it is more helpful to consider a smaller population, the 1.7 million whose retardation limits their ability to live without help each day.) Some of the Connecticut self-advocates can read and write, while others have trouble making themselves understood. Most have jobs, although many are segregated in enclaves with only other disabled people.

The self-advocates run a model convention, starting with registration and coffee in the morning and concluding with a dinner-dance that ends at midnight. There is a seriousness to their work. The men come in coats and ties, the women in neat skirts and dresses. Monroe has worked for several months planning the conference, along with several self-advocates and advisers. He has carefully decided every detail, from not having a head table—to avoid putting "all the big people up front"—to the issues for the resolutions.

There are powerful moments when Monroe opens the floor to anyone who wants to speak. For two hours, two roving microphones are passed from one self-advocate to another. Most have never spoken before a crowd before. To do so is both nerve-racking and empowering. One man is so anxious that, speaking at hurtling speed, he lapses into the Sicilian dialect of his birthplace. The crowd applauds him wildly anyway, even though no one has understood a word that he said. The self-advocates speak of their friends, their lovers, their families, about being married or wanting to be married. They talk about their jobs, about not making enough money, or about the pride they take in their work. Many share their pain of being considered abnormal and inferior. "We are human beings, not animals," proclaims forty-five-year-old Harriet Snurkowski, who recently moved into her own apartment after living in her mother's home.

Ultimately, self-advocacy comes down to the issue that has always been at the heart of how we deal with people with retardation: how much protection do they need? Is protection necessarily good, compassionate, and progressive? Institutions for people with retardation were first built in the nineteenth century by reformers seeking to help a vulnerable population. But today, these institutions are being depopulated and even shut down as professionals have come to agree that it is wrong to isolate people from the community around them. Today, such protection is seen as a paternalistic response that mires people in dependency, prevents them from learning how to take care of themselves, and, in the long run, costs society more than independence would by forcing government to continually look after a group made dependent.

At the same time, people with mental retardation, by definition, function at a significantly lower intellectual level than others, and that affects how they learn and how they make decisions. The Connecticut self-advocates are adults, but by virtue of their retardation they are sometimes vulnerable adults. This distinction is clear during two afternoon workshops at the convention.

A standing-room-only crowd of seventy attends a workshop titled "Doing the Right Thing: How to Flirt." A woman adviser to the People First chapter in New Haven shows videos of a party and then leads the group in some spirited role playing. You like someone you meet at a party, but how do you let the person know you are interested? Among the tips are to compliment the person on the clothes he or she is wearing and learn his or her name and use it frequently in conversation.

Ten steps directly across the carpeted hallway is "Saying No: We Don't Want to Be Touched," a solemn session run by the director of a local rape crisis center. Again, there is role playing. Participants get on an imaginary bus and are approached by a molester who sits next to them. Among the tips for spotting a molester are that he compliments you on the clothes you wear, asks your name, and uses it repeatedly to win your trust.

Of the two seminars, the one on flirting succeeds precisely because it starts from an assumption that the people in the room are adults and, like others their age, are interested in flirting, dating, and sex. The antirape session misfires because the moderator assumes, correctly, that the participants are vulnerable but incorrectly that their vulnerability and retardation make them children.

People with retardation are thought to be more likely the victims of rape, because some people will try to take advantage of them. That is clear when the woman from the rape crisis center begins the workshop by asking for a definition of physical assault. Hands shoot up. One woman tells of being raped at an institution, but when she reported it no staffer would believe her. Another woman tells of being raped by a neighbor who, just a few weeks before, had knocked on the door of her group home when she was alone.

Thirty adults have come to the antirape seminar because they desperately want to exorcise their own bad experiences and to learn how to protect themselves. But the moderator does not address the personal tragedies of real-life adults who have had horrible experiences; instead, she keeps everything safely in the third person of role playing. She shows a video of elementary school children being approached by caricature-evil child abusers with arched eyebrows and smarmy smiles. She leads the group in unison in shouting out how to spot danger ("You get that uh-oh feeling in your stomach") and then repeating what to do ("Say no! get away! tell a responsible adult!").

Ultimately, self-advocates are saying they are willing to take risks—like anyone else—to live like other adults around them. They want places to turn to for support, but they also want the feeling of respect and self-confidence that comes from taking chances.

Hard Choices

There is a delicate blend of success and failure in any person's life, but people with retardation are rarely trusted to handle either, complains Monroe. Self-advocacy is about taking risks. It is like, he says, "when a child gets on a bicycle for the first time and falls off and gets a little bruise. Are you going to keep that child off the bicycle? No, you let him get right back on. That's how people learn." His own life is full of success and learning from failure. Political leadership fits him neatly, as if it were his birthright. Wherever he moved at the convention, crowds of self-advocates seemed to form automatically around him. Physically, Monroe resembles Polish Solidarity leader Lech Walesa. He has the same bearish good looks, the familiar broad mustache—not to mention the charisma. He speaks emphatically, punctuating his remarks with sweeping hand gestures. Nattily dressed in a dark gray pinstripe suit, white button-down shirt, and a red tie, Monroe is expansive and open. He is a populist hero and role model to the self-advocates, who know the outlines of his story. From the age of eight, he spent eleven years at the Southbury Training School, a state institution where he says he was raped and abused, and then another dozen years living in a large group home.

Now, at thirty-eight, Monroe has acquired the symbols of success: his own apartment in Hartford, a Japanese-model compact car with a sunroof, and a full-time job as a veterinarian's assistant, cleaning cat cages and giving flea baths to dogs. Monroe is a familiar figure, too, around the marble halls of the state capitol building, where he buttonholes legislators to urge them to spend more money on community group homes or to change guardianship laws. Several weeks before the convention, Monroe had been one of three thousand activists invited to the White House to witness the signing of the ADA.

But Monroe's own transition from institutional to community life has often been a rocky one, sending him from heights of self-confidence to suicidal feelings of failure. Reporter Kathleen Megan revealingly described Monroe's split public and private lives in a profile for *The Hartford Courant.* The public Monroe is the confident and effective activist who gets invited to the White House and is a commanding presence running the People First convention.

Monroe's private life is more troubled. There are bills past due, an unkempt apartment, a gnawing loneliness over scarce friends and lost family. Megan wrote of social workers from Connecticut's Department of Mental Retardation visiting Monroe's Hartford home to "dig him out" of trash and piles of mail scattered around his three-room apartment. "They scrubbed and scraped his kitchen counter and teased him gently about the 'science experiments' in his refrigerator. They helped him sort through the mountain of clothes—many of them too small or twenty years old—that covered his bed." Monroe sleeps, instead, on a "dusty, olive-beige bedspread that lies wrinkled on the living room floor." Sleeping in a bed brings back bad memories of life at Southbury—of being doused with cold water to wake up or of a teenage friend who died in a dormitory bed next to him. "When the social workers left, the apartment was serene, the rugs smooth, the bed clear, the kitchen tidy. T. J. should have been relieved, but he was not. 'I feel that I can't do it. They come in and they do it and then I feel like I'm supposed to do it, but I can't. . . . No one really teach me how to do it." In the end, Monroe blames his poor housekeeping on his loneliness. "Why should I clean if no one comes?" he asks.

Loneliness throbs as a persistent unhappiness in Monroe's life. He does not curse the retardation that has made him an outcast, shunted off to an institution, and shunned by others. He is angry, however, about being given up by his mother and father. Monroe talks readily, and with deep sadness, of never having a family. It is a sense of loss, Monroe knows, that he shares with other people, not just ones with retardation who have lived in institutions.

When he was only sixteen months old, Monroe and his four-year-old brother, Raymond, were sent to live with foster parents. His foster father, however, did not welcome him, calling him "freak" and "moron." When he was six, Monroe was separated from his brother and foster family and sent to Southbury Training School.

Shortly after he arrived at Southbury, a social worker introduced him to an eleven-year-old sister he never knew he had. Peggy also lived at Southbury, then an institution of 1,700 children and adults, segregated for boys and girls. He would see her at movies on campus, and sometimes staffers would allow them to talk for a few moments or let him give Peggy a kiss and a hug. Six years later, Monroe learned about the existence of another sister, Mary Anne, after a social worker helped this oldest sibling track down her brothers and sister. (A third sister, whom none of the siblings remembered, called Monroe after reading about him in Megan's article.) Records from Southbury say that Monroe was "obsessed" with finding out anything he could about his lost family.

He had little success learning about his parents until one night in 1988 as he played video games at his favorite Hartford bar. The bar owner introduced him to a lost aunt. That night she took Monroe to another bar in Waterbury and led him to his mother. She was distant and unexcited about this renewed contact with her son. Monroe felt let down. "I didn't kiss my mother, I didn't hug my mother. I shook hands with her," says Monroe.

A couple of weeks later, Monroe drove his sister Mary Anne back to Waterbury to meet their mother. She did not want to be seen with them and wanted them to leave quickly. She sat in the backseat of the car and told them about their father, who had abused her and had died drunk in a Waterbury alley. Now she had a new life: two children by a common-law husband. She had never told her new family about her other children. She wanted Monroe and Mary Anne to go away. "Didn't you ever wonder what happened to us?" Mary Anne asked. "No," said her mother. Confusion, hurt, and anger all bubbled up inside Monroe: "I wanted to say, 'Why not? We were your kids.' "

Self-advocacy was an import from Sweden. There the start of the movement can be precisely traced to a day in 1968 that Bengt Nirje, director of the Swedish Parents Association for Mentally Retarded Children had a routine conversation with a group of retarded young adults. Nirje was trying to develop programs to make sure that people with retardation experienced the same daily routine—working, relaxing—as anyone else. This was a simple, but then radical, concept known as normalization. Asking questions of a group of young retarded men and women, he realized they knew what they liked and disliked better than he or any of the social workers and other professionals did. From that meeting came an epiphany: that retarded people could and should have a role in their own choices.

That may seem obvious now, but at the time, psychologists argued that people with retardation could have no sense of self and therefore were incapable of making decisions. They were automatically placed in institutions, which were set up so that doctors or other staffers could make all decisions. Those that lived at home with family relied on their mothers and fathers to make most decisions for them. Nirje realized that with support and teaching people with mental retardation could make decisions on their own. Nirje then led the creation of groups of disabled men and women, the first self-advocates, who met to discuss their choices in treatment and training. Says Dybwad, who was a key proponent of these ideas in the United States, "It was one of those occasions in history when the right man listened at the right time."

Normalization, promoted in the United States at an influential 1969 White House conference, would eventually lead to a revolution in the treatment of people with developmental disabilities. It was the philosophy behind the closing of institutions and mainstreaming people with retardation into regular schools, homes, and jobs in the community.

But it was parents and professionals who promoted normalization. It would be several more years before people with retardation began to advocate for themselves. The change dates back to November 1973, when a Canadian advocacy group for people with retardation, inspired by the first self-advocacy efforts in Sweden, held that country's first conference on how to set up such groups. The meeting took place on Vancouver Island in British Columbia.

Not too far away, in Oregon, a brochure about the conference landed on the desk of the administrator of the state's largest institution. Larry Talkington, director of Fairview Hospital and Training Center, was part of a new breed of institution directors who were carrying out state mandates to "downsize" their facilities. Talkington showed the brochure to Dennis Heath, one of his young social workers. Heath and three retarded men drove to British Columbia to check out what the Canadians were up to. Heath remembers the meeting as a flop. The social workers, teachers, and parents "stood up front and talked about how to let people with retardation advocate" but did not let the one hundred people with retardation in the audience speak. Nevertheless, they returned to Oregon convinced that self-advocacy could be made to work. The following fall, the first state People First convention met in Oregon. Two hundred self-advocates had been expected. Some 560 showed up. There were workshops on how to get placed in the community and what to say when someone called them retarded. Most powerful was the chance to walk up to an open microphone and talk at the plenary session. "They were superstars and they were leaders," says Heath. "There's power in the microphone. Once they get the microphone, they have the power of being able to illuminate their voice to where everybody, for once, hears them. But now they had to share too, and they learned a whole new dynamic." They learned, he said, to listen, to share, to negotiate, to "disagree without getting angry."

It was during the planning of the 1974 conference, Heath recalled, that one of the pioneer self-advocates—who it was is forgotten—objected to the constant use of the words "retarded" and "handicapped." "I want to be treated like a person first," he said. From that came the group's name, People First of Oregon.

Spreading the gospel of self-advocacy was harder than those early advocates expected. It was the very beginning of deinstitutionalization efforts, and people in large facilities were not being given choices, much less the opportunity to protest and advocate. The idea of self-advocacy was still too new for people with retardation and too scary for their parents. Laws continued to restrict the right to basic choices. As late as 1980, thirty-three states still had laws prohibiting marriage by people with retardation, and not until 1974 did a U.S. District Court enjoin the federal government from providing funding for the then still-common practice of sterilization of women with retardation. Self-advocacy did not catch on in the mid-1970s.

Over the next fifteen years, however, the larger disability

rights movement began to grow. But because the increasing
number of centers for independent living offered little to people
with mental retardation, people with retardation were not immediately included in the larger movement. Self-advocacy, then,
became an attempt to join as well as copy the growing disability
rights movement.

Trends in the treatment of people with mental retardation
also fueled the rise of self-advocacy. People who had grown up
in institutions began moving to group homes or apartments.
Children were staying at home with their families and going to
mainstreamed schools. In the community, people with retardation became practiced at making their own choices. It was only
a small step from learning to make their own decisions to
political advocacy. There are signs of the growing influence of
self-advocates. In 1992, the federal government began training
the first two People First members to join teams of doctors and
university researchers who do on-site review visits of programs
that receive federal grants to provide services to people with
mental retardation. The self-advocates, Nancy Ward of Lincoln,
Nebraska, and Tia Nellis of Chicago, will not be expected to
understand complicated scientific and medical work of these
programs. That will be left to the academics and doctors. But the
team members with retardation will judge whether the services
provided are the type of thing that would help them and their
friends, says Deborah McFadden of the U.S. Department of
Health and Human Services, who is the woman who decided to
include self-advocates. In addition, McFadden's department will
provide $1.8 million dollars between 1993 and 1996 to state
advocacy programs that train either self-advocates or their parents in how to fight for services.

Still, some observers of self-advocacy, like journalist Victoria
Medgyesi, are coming to believe the movement will succeed only
when people with retardation join up with other disability
groups and leave behind the nonretarded professionals who now

serve as their advisers. These professionals, argues Medgyesi, who wrote a handbook for self-advocates, will "never share real money, power and control." There have been a few tentative matchups between People First and ADAPT, the Denver-based disability rights group that uses civil disobedience tactics and mass arrests to fight for accessible transit and getting disabled people out of nursing homes. "I didn't know much about people with mental retardation," said ADAPT activist Stephanie Thomas after attending the second national convention of People First in 1991. "What I learned is that having mental retardation certainly doesn't mean that you're dumb." For their part, says Medgyesi, self-advocates have come away from ADAPT protests impressed to see other disabled people make their own decisions without relying on an adviser. In Tennessee, People First members, with guidance from ADAPT activists, took another step toward full independence when they sued the state to improve conditions at a state hospital. The Tennessee advocates were suing the same department of mental retardation that provided the bulk of their own monies. But after a lengthy and emotional debate about the risk to their own funding, Beth Sievers and the other self-advocates decided on their own that they had a moral responsibility to speak out.

Self-advocacy in Action

Self-advocacy has brought out wisdom and qualities of leadership from some unexpected sources. Nancy Cleaveland, the president of the People First chapter at the Southbury Training School, is such an unlikely civil rights leader. She has lived at the institution since she was nine. There, other people have always made basic decisions for her: what to eat, when to eat it, when to get up, where to live, where to work, when to watch TV, when to sleep. Even simple things that most people take for granted, like taking a shower, are regulated. Now, at fifty-two, Cleaveland is demanding the right to make important decisions in her life. Most of all, she wants an apartment on "the outside" with her longtime boyfriend, Richard Carlson, another resident of the institution.

But the decision to leave is not Cleaveland's. It belongs to a beloved eighty-two-year-old aunt, Marion Mattoon, her only family, who is her legal conservator. Cleaveland, with Jean Bowen's help, has asked a legal service attorney to sue Mattoon for control over such decision making. To Cleaveland, it is an issue of her "right" to live with Carlson. "Nancy is being incarcerated," argues Bowen. "She is being held against her will, kept from her preferred place to live." Mattoon calls it foolishness to think that Cleaveland and Carlson can make it on their own. Her niece, she says, has been "brainwashed" by advocates and lawyers. "Everybody wants to paint the picture so rosy. But it's not rosy," says Mattoon, a retired special education teacher who taught people with retardation. She knows that a few previous attempts to move Cleaveland into a group home ended disastrously.

I returned to Connecticut two months after the People First convention to attend one of the probate court hearings that would determine Cleaveland's future. I wanted to understand the two seemingly irreconcilable images that had been painted of Cleaveland. There was the Cleaveland who was said to be easily led by others, and who, after a lifetime of retardation and institutionalization, had few of the skills needed to live successfully outside the protective confines of her cottage at Southbury. Then there was the Cleaveland who had become a stalwart self-advocate, a leader among her peers who had developed very strong ideas of what she wanted in her life. I also wanted to see Cleaveland in action, leading one of the weekly sessions of the People First chapter at Southbury Training School.

The Wednesday meeting of the People First chapter took place in the dining room of Cottage 15. A dozen advocates sat

around three dining tables as Cleaveland opened the meeting by
holding up the front page of the local newspaper. It was the week
after Election Day. At the previous meeting, Bowen had brought
in pictures of all of the major candidates and talked a little about
each one. "I did it as straightforward as I could," she said. But
at the end, all of the advocates decided they would support
Lowell Weicker, the independent candidate for governor. The
advocates liked the fact that Weicker, as a U.S. senator, had been
the first sponsor of the Americans with Disabilities Act and,
partly because he has a son with Downs syndrome, had been a
leading supporter of disability legislation. A half-dozen of the
advocates had gone into town to vote. Most, since they had
limited reading skills at best, had asked for someone to help
them mark their ballots. Now, ten days later, Cleaveland was
holding the newspaper front page with a banner headline pro-
claiming, NOW IT'S GOVERNOR WEICKER.

"This is our new president," Cleaveland told the advocates,
before Bowen, who sat next to her at the end of a table, corrected
her. "I mean governor," Cleaveland said. Bowen then explained
that there was a new state senator for Southbury and suggested
that the advocates invite him to one of their meetings so they
could voice their concerns, much as they had to his predecessor.

From there, Cleaveland took the meeting off on a rambling
course. There was no set agenda, but those sitting around the
table got the chance to speak up. The minutes of past meetings
show that the group discussions often turn to familiar topics:
moving out of Southbury, jobs, improving lighting and safety at
the institution, ending the use of punishment by Southbury
staff, reestablishing ties with lost family, relationships and sex.
On this day, the talk turned to work and getting out of the
institution. Mark, a handsome man in his thirties who had come
to Southbury only a few years earlier, after sustaining a head
injury, complains that his job in a sheltered workshop is boring
and that he makes too little money. "I think you should speak

up for your rights," Cleaveland tells him, advising him to tell
the Southbury work coordinator that he wants a different job, or
to ask his parents to step in. "I don't want to ask for help. I want
to take care of myself," says Mark. Carlson then explains how he
"stood up for my own rights" to get his guardianship changed.
Bowen notes that she helped Carlson get a lawyer and asks Mark
if he, too, would like to talk to a lawyer. He agrees.

Cleaveland reported on her latest court appearance. "I came
here when I was nine years old," she tells the other advocates. "I
feel I need to get out with Richard in an apartment. I don't know
how an apartment is gonna look. I feel Richard and I should look
at it first." Then she asks Carlson to talk about what kind of
apartment he wants. Carlson buries his face in his hands. "Don't
be shy, honey, nobody's going to bite ya," Cleaveland coaxes.

Cleaveland is both loving and motherly toward Carlson. The
two are "a very traditional couple," Bowen says. "Richard is very
romantic, thoughtful and very gracious to Nancy," she adds.
"Nancy's very jealous. She's protective of Richard and doesn't
like other women around." She is also sentimental. Cleaveland
keeps a stack of dog-eared photos of Carlson in her purse. Every
night, she picks one of them to take to bed with her. Once, she
saw the bedroom Richard shares with several other men at
Southbury and was pleased to see that he has several pictures of
her tacked to his wall by his bed.

But would the relationship between Cleaveland and Carlson
flourish outside of Southbury? Cleaveland understands that living with Carlson, who is less capable than she, is fraught with
risk. She has been hurt before when Carlson, who has a five-year-
old child by another woman who once lived at the institution,
flirted with other women. Mattoon doubts that her niece can
count on Carlson.

A few of the students with mental retardation that Mattoon
taught in her special education classes have married over the
years. Some have even reared children. Mattoon runs into these

former students in the small town where she lives. Some have even dropped by with their spouses to visit Mattoon, in her large white wooden house on the town green. But Mattoon doubts that her niece can attain such a level of independence. Cleaveland has mild retardation. She can read simple sentences and writes letters to state representatives and social service officials in a girlish hand printing. Carlson also has mild retardation, but is less verbal than Cleaveland.

Ultimately, Mattoon worries that if living with Carlson does not work out, Cleaveland will have nowhere to go. She worries that, if Cleaveland cannot take care of herself, there will be no one to care about her after Mattoon dies. With her limited reading skills, Cleaveland, says Mattoon, goes to a restaurant and has trouble reading the menu. "She knows there's going to be a hamburger there nine times out of ten, so she orders a hamburger. Or she finds a picture on the menu and says, 'This looks good, I'll have this.' " Cleaveland copes creatively. But Mattoon sees her niece's serious limits.

Mattoon has been Cleaveland's conservator for twenty-five years. Cleaveland was sent to Southbury after her parents divorced. Her mother, Mattoon's sister, needed to work and could no longer care for her retarded daughter as well. When the mother died, Cleaveland was in her late thirties. Mattoon agreed to be Cleaveland's conservator. No other family member wanted the responsibility. It was not an easy job. Cleaveland would telephone her aunt often when she needed help with a problem at the institution—from dealing with noisy roommates to getting a job. On the decision that was most important to Cleaveland—whether she could live with Carlson—she and her aunt clashed. Cleaveland tried to explain why she thought she deserved a chance to live with Carlson, but Mattoon would not budge.

The case landed in the courtroom of Southbury Probate Court Judge Mary Kay Flaherty. From the beginning, Flaherty was clear that Cleaveland did not need a conservator. That was an antiquated designation, once common for people with retardation but now used almost solely in cases where a person is in a coma. Cleaveland's status had never been changed, largely because the case had remained in the probate court in Mattoon's small hometown, where the judge knew Mattoon and saw no reason to challenge her control over her niece's life. Under current standards, Cleaveland should have a limited guardian, someone who would make choices only on important issues. Flaherty also had to rule on which decisions would be left to the limited guardian and which would be left to Cleaveland. Legally, the issues to be decided were: who would make her personal finance decisions? Who would decide if Cleaveland needed elective or emergency surgery? But choices such as who to live with would fall to Cleaveland.

An informal hearing took place around a conference table in the conference room next to Flaherty's office. Sitting next to Katherine Williams, her legal services lawyer, Cleaveland listened intently to the debate over her future. She leaned her elbows on the wood-and-chrome conference table, sitting forward on her chair with the tips of her toes pressing the floor. She looked younger than her age, betrayed only by a strand of gray in her short black hair. Despite the November cold, she wore a stark white cotton knit dress with a small flower print. She wore a string of costume jewelry pearls and matching earrings. Flaherty sat at the other end of the table. To her left was Diane Roy, Cleaveland's caseworker from Southbury, who, at Flaherty's request, had put together a report from a team at the institution that found Cleaveland "is functioning at the upper level of mild retardation." Williams argued that Cleaveland should be her own guardian and that she needed no limited guardian. "Part of being an adult," Williams said, "part of having control of one's life, part of having control, is being able to make your own mistakes and decisions."

Making Cleaveland's reach for independence more complicated was Mattoon's distrust of professionals who, to her, seem
to jump from one fad to another. When Cleaveland was born, her
mother was told it was best to put her daughter in the institution. Then there were attempts to get her into the community.
The first, in the early 1960s, was a gloomy Dickensian horror.
She was sent to work as a housegirl for a family in a small
Connecticut city. But the family, which had promised her freedom, treated her like their indentured servant. She lived in a
dank corner of the family basement, marked off by a sheet
hanging on a curtain rod. Cleaveland remembers it as a painful,
lonely period.

There had been a couple more recent attempts to put Cleaveland in a group home. The first was a large home, with some
twenty people, where she slept in a room with several women.
Rather than being comfortable like a home, it felt like just
another institution to Cleaveland. The last attempt to move
Cleaveland had come several years before. But there Cleaveland
had a personality clash with a vindictive staffer.

These decades of stops and starts had left Cleaveland and her
aunt skeptical of whatever was being hailed at the moment as the
latest innovation. To Cleaveland, however, the bottom line was
that she wanted out of the institution. But to her aunt, the
institution had been the one constant. Although Mattoon
thought it was silliness to talk about Cleaveland and Carlson
living together like man and wife, she was willing to let her
niece try living in a group home again. But she wanted assur-
ances that Cleaveland would be allowed back to Southbury if the
arrangement went awry.

Thomas Howley, Southbury's director, was not prepared to
give Mattoon that guarantee. For one thing, the current policy
of the state Department of Mental Retardation was to move as
many people as possible into the community, and Southbury was
slowly but steadily decreasing its numbers. A long-term state

plan called for reducing Southbury's population from 968 residents to 320 within twenty years. If Cleaveland left and her placement did not work, Southbury would take her back within "a reasonable length of time," a few months, for example, but not after, say, two years. Said Howley, "Once you've been out awhile, to come back is just as traumatic as it was at first to leave." This was not good enough for Mattoon, who wanted Southbury to be a guaranteed safety net. "Southbury has been good to her," she said. "Where else would she be? There's no other place for her to go."

By law, Cleaveland could not be moved into the community unless her move was carefully planned, with her input. She would go to a supervised group home or apartment. There would always be someone, a social worker and service providers, monitoring her. Almost certainly, someone would be living with Cleaveland, possibly on a twenty-four-hour basis, and at least several hours a day. She would be provided with work.

In the end, it was Cleaveland who steered a commonsense middle ground. She understood that there was risk if she and Carlson left Southbury together. It was Cleaveland who ultimately decided that she wanted to start out by living in a group home with Carlson and other men and women, or to have Carlson in a separate residence nearby. That way they could have their "privacy" but also time to work out being together. Finally Flaherty agreed, making Cleaveland her own limited guardian. Cleaveland turned down her first chance to live with Carlson in an apartment in Danbury, because it was far away from her aunt and Carlson's mother. It would take nearly a year to find a place that fit what Cleaveland and Carlson wanted. First Carlson moved out to live with a family near Danbury. Then Cleaveland moved to a similar house nearby. The move gave her new self-confidence. She loved her new job in a cafeteria. She called

Richard on the phone every day and was pleased when tensions eased with her aunt, whom she would once again call for advice. Eventually, Cleaveland and Carlson ended their relationship, which was doomed by distance. Cleaveland, however, thrived on her own.

Speaking for Yourself

Television has trained a generation of self-advocates. Walk into any group home or institution and a television screen is almost certain to be flickering. "These people now listen and see television. And there they get an introduction to civil and governmental affairs that you never had when you were a boy," says Dybwad. "They have time to listen. They know a lot about local politics. They hear the local political dialogue. They know how to express themselves because they learn it on television. You have to put this in consideration to understand why this movement is so effective today." David Beem, who ran for city council in Salem, Oregon, in 1988—collecting only a few hundred votes but getting national attention and an endorsement from civil rights leader Jesse Jackson—got little education during the ten years he lived in a state institution. "I didn't know that much about reading and writing so I watched TV and watched politics," he explained.

Television changed T. J. Monroe's life. It was from the tube that Monroe first made the connection between disability and rights. His inspiration: Raymond Burr from reruns of the old "Ironsides" series. "He got shot and was in a wheelchair and everybody wanted to feel sorry for him," Monroe explains. "But Ironsides did not want to be pitied. He wanted to do everything for his own. That popped something in my head." The Burr character, Monroe says, "would fight for a lot of people's rights. I decided to open up my eyes."

Another insightful self-advocate, Tom Hopkins, devotedly

watches the current affairs and cultural offerings of the Public Broadcasting System. Hopkins, a leader of Capitol People First of Sacramento, told me about watching a PBS show a few nights before. The documentary had tried to answer why the high school dropout rate was so high among Hispanics and blacks. "One expert who was interviewed said that teachers had low expectations of Hispanic and black students," Hopkins explained. "They didn't think they would learn. So they didn't teach them much. As a result, they failed and dropped out. And I was thinking, that's the way it was with me as a retarded person. People didn't think I could learn, so nobody taught me anything useful."

Hopkins graduated from high school with minimal skills in writing and reading. He went to a sheltered workshop run by some local charities, where he hoped he would learn carpentry skills. Instead, he was paid a piece rate for occasional tasks. (He has no concept of how much he was paid. "I think it was forty dollars an hour," he says. It was forty cents an hour.) He counted screws into small plastic envelopes. Other times he folded fiberglass insulation and would go home "itching like crazy." But most of the time there would be no work at all and Hopkins would sit around with the other men and play cards. "I became the greatest solitaire player the world's ever seen. I didn't learn diddly," says Hopkins. "It was day care for grown-ups. That's all it was."

After four and a half years and never being taught carpentry skills as he had been promised, Hopkins quit. "I got involved in People First and found out I wasn't the only one getting shafted. The system was set up to demean us, to exploit us and to treat us like slaves," he explained. "The workshop was segregated from society. Why were we separated? How come we were in the boonies? Other people worked downtown. How come we can't fraternize with other [nondisabled] people?" Hopkins talks about the social service system as a "retarding environment" that does more to hold him back than his own mental limitations.

In 1985, Hopkins and one of his fellow advocates, Sandra Jensen, met then Vice President George Bush. What was supposed to be a two-minute picture-taking session in the vice president's office turned into a thirty-minute discussion of their self-advocacy activities. Hopkins talked thoughtfully about his disappointment in the sheltered workshop. Jensen, a woman with Down syndrome, spoke emotionally of how her parents had been told that, with an IQ of 30, she would never be able to live anywhere but in an institution, but now she lived on her own. Says disability rights activist Evan Kemp, who was present at the meeting, of Bush: "He never had his preconceptions about any group turned upside down so quickly."

A few years later, Bush got another explanation of self-advocacy, during the signing ceremony for the ADA bill, when T. J. Monroe self-assuredly walked up and presented him with a carefully printed letter. The president thanked Monroe, put the letter in his inside jacket pocket, and promised to read it later.

"Dear Mr. President," Monroe's letter began. "I am writing to you about self-advocacy. My name is T. J. Monroe. I am president of People First in Connecticut. What is a self-advocate? Self-advocate means knowing your rights and responsibilities. Self-advocate means standing up for your own rights. Self-advocate means speak for yourself and make your own decisions, being more independent, standing on your own two feet and sticking up for your rights as a self-advocate.

"We have to be happy. We are as good as any other person. Speak up and let other disabilities know we can help other people to grow and stand together on our big issues. People with disability can work hard for things they know are good for them."

"Sincerely,

"T. J. Monroe"

In 1993, Monroe took yet another step toward independence, leaving Connecticut, where he lived his entire life, to move to Knoxville to take a job organizing self-advocacy chapters for People First of Tennessee. "I'm on the other side of the desk. I'm a boss," said Monroe, noting that he was now a full-time professional community organizer, no longer simply a volunteer one. "I am still thunder. I make people think."

CHAPTER 7

THE SCREAMING NEON WHEELCHAIR

The story of the disability rights movement could be written about Marilyn Hamilton's impatience. It would start the summer day in 1978 when Hamilton crashed her hang glider nose down into the side of a California mountain. Her spinal cord was bruised and Hamilton became a paraplegic—a very impatient paraplegic.

Hamilton zipped through rehabilitative therapy in three weeks. Most people take at least three months. Then she was impatient with the bulky wheelchair—"a stainless steel dinosaur," she called it—that her physical therapist ordered for her. Hamilton loved sports but the wheelchair was too heavy to get back out on the tennis court. So Hamilton sought out her friends and fellow glider pilots Don Helman and Jim Okamoto. They had begun designing hang gliders from a shed on the farm near Fresno owned by Helman's parents. Build me an ultralight wheelchair, Hamilton asked them, out of the aluminum tubing you put in your gliders.

What they designed was light and sturdy, weighing twenty-six pounds compared to the standard fifty-pound wheelchair. It had a stunning geometry. Instead of being big and boxy like other wheelchairs, Hamilton's sky blue wheelchair was sleek and sporty, with a low-slung back and compact frame that looked as if it belonged to a multispeed racing bicycle. It was such an improvement over traditional chairs that Hamilton, Helman, and Okamoto went into the wheelchair-manufacturing business. They started selling their Quickie wheelchairs as fast as they could turn them out.

From the beginning, Hamilton had hated the "weird" way people acted around her in her first stainless steel wheelchair. "I knew I was the same as always," she says. "I just got around by a different means of transportation." But the gleaming hospital-issue wheelchair scared people, putting up a chromium wall of discomfort between her and the world. Even her doctor addressed himself to her husband, as if she were helpless or not even present. Friends saw her sitting in a wheelchair and their faces would cloud up, putting Hamilton in the odd position of always being perky and bright, the one to cheer them up.

Hamilton's wheelchairs put people—users and those around them—at ease. Instead of chrome, Hamilton's chairs came in a rainbow of hot colors. The customer could personalize a chair in candy apple red, canary yellow, or electric green. Hot pink was added at a user's request. "Screaming neon chairs," Hamilton called them. A Quickie chair was fun, refuting the idea that the user was an invalid. (Quickie's biggest competitor today is Invacare, a name that is an abbreviation for "invalid care.") Quickie chair riders were neither sick nor objects of pity. They just got around a different way. "If you can't stand up," Hamilton likes to say, "stand out."

Hamilton's proud chairs struck a chord with the emerging disability rights movement. For one thing, there were more wheelchair users, up from half a million in 1960 to 1.2 million by 1980, most of whom were no longer living in nursing homes or institutions as they had been just a couple of decades before. This new generation of wheelchair users was newly politicized and wanted maximum independence. They were demanding curb cuts, lifts on buses, and handicapped parking spaces. They had come to expect that they would go to college, take jobs, get married, and sometimes even start families.

Hamilton's brightly colored chairs tapped into this growing sense that there was no shame in being disabled. In a world where the workplace was often closed to a paraplegic and buildings were still inaccessible to a wheelchair, Hamilton's stylish product reassuringly said it was okay, it could even be cool, to be in a wheelchair. Even the double entendre of the wheelchair's name, Quickie ("You need a Quickie," goes one company advertising slogan) was a lighthearted mocking of the pitying "walkies," the rest of the world, who seemed to automatically assume that the loss of the use of one's legs must also mean the end of a sex life. Or that paralysis meant the end of a life worth living.

Hamilton had reinvented the wheelchair. She took a piece of medical equipment and made it fun and sporty. She took the universal symbol of sickness and turned it into a symbol of disability self-pride.

It was Hamilton's uncle who made her understand how a wheelchair represented her liberation. Bill Hamilton was a quadriplegic. When he was a high school student, Bill was thrown from a Model T Ford. His neck snapped on the hard road. Quadriplegics almost never lived in those days between the world wars. Rehabilitative medicine was just developing in a crude form in response to the return of paralyzed war veterans.

The wood-and-wicker wheelchairs then were rigid and rectangular, with high backs. They were too wide to get through most doors, a reflection of the fact that most disabled people then were considered useless members of society. Wheelchairs were made for people who were closeted at home or who lived in institutions. Weighing ninety pounds, Bill's first wheelchair was too heavy to move far by himself. Wheelchairs then were still largely for those rich enough to afford to hire someone to push the cumbersome contrivances. The Hamiltons had the means to hire two attendants for Bill, who assisted him twenty-four hours a day. He went to college and law school in Los Angeles; then he returned home to oversee the expansion of the family orchard, successfully organizing other San Joaquin grape and fruit tree farmers. So, aware of how his family's support had allowed him to succeed as a disabled man, Bill Hamilton also welcomed this niece by marriage into the family fruit brokerage. The trade newspapers wrote about the "crippled" uncle and niece selling fruit out in California. Marilyn would work with Bill during the fruit season and spend several months each year traveling to events on the disabled tennis circuit, where she was an emerging star, thanks in part to her lightweight chair. The exposure the Quickie chairs got in the wheelchair sports world helped her new business thrive.

Wheelchair athletes—a community known for cleverly modifying chairs in search of a competitive edge—were the first to want a copy of Hamilton's featherweight wheelchair. Sales skyrocketed once a folding version of the Quickie was introduced in 1984. Then people wanted the chair not just for sports but for everyday use. Its lightness was liberating. It was light enough for a rider to wheel up to the driver's seat of a car, jump in, and then, unaided, fold the chair, pick it up with ease, and store it in the backseat. Within ten years, Quickie would grow into a $40-million-a-year business and relocate to a 150,000-square-foot facility. Purchased by Sunrise Medical, a large medical equipment company, in 1986, Quickie's lightweight chairs were imitated by all other wheelchair companies.

To appreciate how the revolution in wheelchair design was tied to the revolution in disabled people's self-image, it helps to know some wheelchair history: A man who became a paraplegic in a 1918 mining accident sought out a friend in California, an engineer, and asked him to design a lightweight wheelchair. In 1932, the engineer built one that could be folded and put in the back of a car. It was such an improvement over existing chairs that the two men started a wheelchair manufacturing firm. Together, Herbert Everest, the paraplegic, and Harry Jennings, Sr., his mechanical engineer friend, revolutionized wheelchair design, cutting the weight of a wheelchair from ninety pounds to fifty pounds. Their company, Everest & Jennings, dominated the wheelchair market for the next fifty years.

It is 1991, and Barre Rorabaugh, the new president and chief executive officer of Everest & Jennings, is sitting in his spacious office in Camarillo, California, late on a Friday evening. His wall-to-wall windows look out over the Ventura Freeway, an aquarium of colorful cars whizzing past, headed off for the weekend. E & J has hit on hard times, and Rorabaugh, a corporate turnaround specialist, is talking about how he plans to return the company from the brink of bankruptcy. E & J had lost over $88 million the previous two years and laid off one-third of its local employees. Rorabaugh is retelling the story of the paraplegic who asked an inventor friend to design a lighter chair and how their creation revolutionized the wheelchair and led to the establishment of the hottest wheelchair company in America. Rorabaugh speaks in respectful tones. He could be relating E & J's proud story, but he is talking about Marilyn Hamilton. He is talking about how he will turn around E & J by learning from Hamilton's success: he will listen to consumers; he will seek to dominate the lucrative lightweight market with a new generation of wheelchairs made of even lighter plastic composites. (In 1992, after Rorabaugh brought back E & J from the brink of insolvency, the company was sold and moved to St. Louis for a fresh start.)

E & J lost its edge because the company got smug and stopped paying attention to what people in wheelchairs wanted, says Cliff Crase, editor of *Sports 'n Spokes,* a magazine for wheel-chair athletes. In the late 1970s, the Justice Department brought an antitrust suit, later settled, charging E & J with monopoly practices that set prices of wheelchairs artificially high and squelched competition and innovation from other compa-nies. "People would suggest a change, something like a light-weight chair, and E & J would say, 'Fine, make it yourself,' " says Crase. Even when Quickie came out with its revolutionary chair, it took E & J several years even to enter the lightweight market. By that time, Quickie and other companies were battling for this fastest-growing share of the wheelchair market.

By the 1980s, the company that had made wheelchairs for FDR and Churchill, shahs and sheiks, no longer had strong disabled managers at the top to advise them. E & J missed the rise of a newly independent generation of wheelchair users who, with new jobs and less dependent on welfare, were emerging as a powerful consumer group. In some ways, it was easy to over-look this consumer uprising. Unlike virtually every other prod-uct, wheelchairs are not sold directly to users. Instead, they are marketed through occupational and physical therapists and medical supply dealers who recommend them to disabled clients and customers. But Quickie understood that, to make its mark, it had to reach beyond these usually nondisabled professionals and speak to the growingly self-sufficient wheelchair users. Their product brochures showed their chairs being used by active people, who were pictured at the office, on the basketball court, on the dance floor, and in wedding chapels. The E & J sales material, until recently, kept to the tradition of picturing their chairs in hospital rooms.

Another Hamilton accident, twelve years after the hang-glider crash, may lead to the next liberating design break-through: a lightweight power wheelchair. Broadsided by a driver in November 1990, Hamilton's wrists and legs were broken in her crushed car. Within forty-eight hours, Okamoto had built a streamlined power wheelchair. He simply rigged a motor to one of Hamilton's sportiest lightweight wheelchairs. At first, Hamilton was ashamed to be seen in a power chair. It suggested that her disability was more serious than before, even though her dependence on the power chair was only temporary. But during her three-month convalescence at home, she quickly came to appreciate the freedom it delivered.

There will be great profits for the wheelchair maker who can make an affordable power wheelchair light enough to be lifted. Today's models—which run on an acid battery, like a car, or are electrically charged—weigh hundreds of pounds. They cannot be folded or lifted into the back of a car. They are bulky, look institutional, and maneuver clumsily. They are slow on hills and lack the ability to speed up across the street when the traffic light turns yellow. Manufacturers have been slow to respond to consumer demands, says disability activist and wheelchair aficionado Marylou Breslin, because they fear legal liability if faster, forceful power wheelchairs lead to more accidents. But power-chair users for years have souped up their own by adding a second battery to double the voltage and with other modifications. Seeking to solve the riddle of how to build one that is light, stylish, fast, and powerful but not too expensive, the company now called Motion Designs/Quickie hopes to score with a version of Okamoto's prototype. It also hired Gordon Stout, a Berkeley inventor legendary for a handful of models he made in the 1970s that were designed more after cars than traditional push wheelchairs. California has been the fertile base of wheelchair innovation, due to the state's openness to new ideas, toleration of eccentrics, and clear, sunny weather that makes wheelchair use easy. But also in the hunt is Ohio-based Invacare, now the country's top-ranked wheelchair maker and the leading seller of power wheelchairs. Everest & Jennings, once the market leader (and the originators of the folding wheelchair), has continued to develop its power line, even while it paid a heavy price for failing to acknowledge the lightweight market until too late.

Hamilton's own understanding of the changing world of wheelchair users has paid off handsomely. She lives a good life now, validated by the little "presents" she has bought for herself: the ultrapowered red sports car with a ten-disc compact disc player, a vacation spot big enough for fourteen family members to spend Christmas, and a new house of glass and steel so unconventional that she had to find a commercial builder to construct it. (She and her husband divorced, more due to her emergence as an entrepreneur than for problems resulting from her injury.) Hamilton spends weekends at a soaring stone-and wood-beam condominium on the top of a Sierra mountain ski resort, where she is a familiar figure on the slopes with her specially designed sitting ski device. The condominium with its elevator is wheelchair accessible, unlike the homes of her family members. So she invites everyone to spend weekends and Christmas with her there.

On the way to the resort and back, the road winds past Tollhouse Mountain, the scene of her hang-gliding accident. Its peak rises arrogantly in the distance. But she speaks openly of the accident. For the first five years after the injury, Hamilton was convinced she would walk again. At first, she mastered a way to take "steps." Putting all her weight on a short leg brace, she would plant one foot, then throw the opposite hip to send the other leg swinging forward, repeating the painful process, literally a form of self-torture, for hours during morning physical therapy sessions. Even today, when she dreams, she is not in a wheelchair.

It is not uncommon for paraplegics to believe they will walk again, despite all evidence to the contrary. It is a way to hide from the stigma of disability. There are daily reminders of the shame of not walking—from telethons seeking to cure "crippling" paralysis so that pitiable poster children can take steps

again to inaccessible homes, stores, offices, and buses that admit
only those who can walk. But today, years after her disabling
accident, the woman too impatient ever to take no for an answer
finally accepts the fact that she will never walk again. It is only
right that Marilyn Hamilton, who took the stigma out of using
a wheelchair, should be so at peace.

Assistive Technology

Hamilton's Quickies are proof that, in disabled people's quest
for independence, technology can be the great liberator, by
making physical and even mental limitations largely irrelevant.
A wheelchair is freeing, not confining (the reason many users
hate to be described as "wheelchair-bound" or "confined to a
wheelchair"). It is a device that supplements lost leg muscle
exactly as eyeglasses replace lost vision. The right "assistive
device" can turn passive patients into independent consumers,
able to go to school, work, rear families, and live on their own.

Machines now speak for the voiceless, see for the sightless,
and move and touch for those who cannot move their own
muscles. The late Stanford University professor Cal Pava was
able to resume a career as a highly regarded teacher after brain
surgery to remove a tumor wiped out his memory of how to read.
Instead, he learned to use a Kurzweil Reader, a machine that
scans printed text and reads it aloud with a voice synthesizer.
Technology helped rhythm and blues singer Teddy Pendergrass
work again, too. When an automobile accident left him a quadriplegic, he learned to use similar voice-activated computer technology to compose music.

High school student Stacy Bibb is unable to talk as a result
of cerebral palsy, but he can control his tongue. A wireless
transmitter was fitted into the roof of his mouth, like an ortho-
dontic retainer. With his tongue, Bibb presses buttons on the
retainer, which emit a radio signal that is picked up by a control-

ler box. That way, he writes out messages on a computer, which then speaks for him. He can also turn the television or the room lights on and off with this system. The technology allowed Bibb to communicate with classmates at school and promised a lifetime of unexpected independence. Machines can break down the natural walls of discomfort. Alan Brightman of Apple Computer tells how the world opened up to another young boy who was unable to talk until a $99 voice synthesizer was mounted on his wheelchair. "The other kids had no incentive to get to know him. But with an inexpensive speech synthesizer, he can tell a joke out loud and the whole dynamic changes," said Brightman. Not only did classmates interact with him but teachers expected more of him, too.

Such marvelous breakthroughs are coming at an astoundingly rapid pace. Some devices are simple, others futuristic. Computers have led the revolution. Hundreds of companies, from computer giants to attic inventors, have produced thousands of software and hardware aids that can mitigate the problems posed by even the most severe physical disability. There are computer monitors with magnified, large-type letters; keyboards with oversized keypads; and printers that print in Braille. Someone unable to grip a pen and write can use a computer. If fingers lack the muscles to type, a computer key can be struck with a mouthstick clenched between the teeth or with a headstick strapped to the forehead. There are light-sensitive keyboards, too, which can be stroked, not by a finger but with an infrared beam strapped to the typist's head. The light from the beam, instead of a finger's touch, engages the key.

More sophisticated are several versions of eye-gaze computer systems, in which a user can stroke a key simply by looking at it. The technology, originally created for Israeli and U.S. jet fighter pilots, was a godsend to people with severe disabilities who do not have the muscle control to use a keyboard. An even more sophisticated twist on the eye-gaze system involves implanting tiny electrodes in the scalp that determine where that person is gazing by tracking brain waves. This device was first used by an Oregon doctor with amyotrophic lateral sclerosis (ALS), a degenerative nerve condition better known as Lou Gehrig's disease, who was then able to resume part of his medical practice.

Equally amazing are computers combined with robots. Computer programmer Jeff Doran, a quadriplegic who cannot move even his head, instead uses his voice to control a computerized PRAB Command work station programmed to respond to the sound of his voice. With a few basic voice commands—that take as much time as the keystrokes his colleagues use to operate their computer terminals—Doran can make his computer and robotic arm do virtually anything his coworkers at Boeing in Seattle can do, including pick up a can of soda or take down a ten-pound book from a shelf. Says Walt Weisel of PRAB Command, the Michigan robotics firm that developed the system, "If you or I saw a person in a corner with no legs, we would know automatically to get that person a wheelchair. I want people to see this system as an extention of a broken body. If a person can't move, but can still talk and has a good brain, then this is something we should get for them."

Such technology will revolutionize the workplace, predicts Rachel Cox of the Seattle Resource Center for the Handicapped. "Now it's not surprising to see a black or a woman in a high business position. In the nineties, we hope that it won't be a big deal to see a quadriplegic near the top of a Fortune 500 company," says Cox, who trains disabled workers to use new devices. "And it's technology that will have made it possible."

Some such instruments are highly expensive. Jeff Doran's system cost close to $50,000, which Boeing was willing to pay as a codeveloper of the technology. But the devices with the most promise to create a space-age workplace are those that will be affordable or, even if expensive, are useful to all workers, not just a handful of disabled ones. For example, computer companies are perfecting machines like Doran's that can recognize speech and transcribe dictation. A device invented to meet the needs of severely disabled workers may one day be a fantastic convenience for all. In the workplace of the future, computers that transcribe dictation may make the keyboard, and even typists, obsolete.

With prostheses, too, there are awe-inspiring wonders. New plastics have made artificial legs, feet, and arms stronger, more flexible, and, most important, more comfortable to wear. Today's prosthetic gloves are far more realistic than metal hooks, which can be off-putting, and refined enough to pick up a piece of paper off a desk top. Inventor John Sabolich has created a system that when placed in the sole of a prosthetic foot can pick up the bioelectrical signals from the wearer's remaining muscles and send these impulses to the brain, as if they were coming from the natural foot. It is a trick on the brain, but it enables an amputee's foot to sense when it is stepping on a stone. Chuck Thiemann, who lost his right leg after touching a live electrical wire, uses the Sense-of-Feel (SOF) System to play softball, and he can run and even slide into base. A similar myoelectric arm can pick up signals from a wearer's skin surface and then amplify them 300,000 times to control a prosthetic glove. Right now, such systems are experimental, expensive, and consequently available to a few. But "one does not have to have been a fan of television's 'The Six Million Dollar Man' or 'The Bionic Woman,' " says sociologist Irving Kenneth Zola, "to realize that we are entering an era where almost every human body part and function becomes replaceable, or, at least, assistable by some technical device."

Disabled athletes helped propel such advances, just as they did wheelchair designs. Today there are so many types of prosthetic legs and feet that athletes change them for different activities, just the way other athletes wear different shoes for different sports. Amputee Jim MacLaren, a professional triathlete, used to use one artificial leg for the biking events and then put on another for the running segment. Now a new prosthetic ankle allows him, within seconds, to move the same foot from a walking position to an extended swimming position or to a free-flex position for rowing or skiing. The device was designed by Albert Rappoport, a California prosthetist who lost a leg to cancer, and Mike Ross, who lost both legs in a boating accident. Paraplegic engineer Peter Axelson has taken the concept of a prothesis further to build sports equipment. His monoski is a prosthetic ski. Its hinged, fiberglass seat, custom molded to fit the skier's body, is attached to a ski on a springed aluminum frame. This allows the skier to shift weight with his upper body to ski. Axelson, who has been timed at sixty miles per hour downhill, used his invention to win the gold medal at the first World Disabled Skiing Championships in Sweden. He has also designed a cross-country skiing device and a "dance orthosis."

A False Cure

Faith in technology can play into the hated images of cure and pity that the disability rights movement has sought to erase. No two devices have held the public and the media more in awe than the Functional Electronic Stimulator (FES) and the cochlear implant. FES, which has been featured in breathless reports on CBS's "60 Minutes," ABC's "World of Discovery," and other television shows, promises to let paraplegics stand up and walk again. Cochlear implants, similarly hailed in numerous newspaper features, promise to let the profoundly deaf hear sounds, speech, and music. The realities are often less rosy.

To some, cochlear implants are a miracle. To others, they are an instrument of cultural murder. That such an advanced device can be held in such disparate regard shows the depth of the qualms over assistive technology's power. The clever hearing technology implants a tiny computerized hearing aid into one of the ducts of the cochlea, the spiral-shaped section of the inner ear that contains the auditory nerve endings. The implanted electrodes electrically stimulate the damaged nerves and then send the vibrations to the brain, which interprets the sound to give hearing. Thousands of profoundly deaf adults and children are thankful to have hearing restored with the implant.

But the device is called a form of "genocide" by many deaf people. While hearing people usually think there is something regrettable in deafness, many deaf people abhor the operation as suggesting that deafness is a pathology, something to be corrected or eliminated. It is as threatening as Alexander Graham Bell's eugenicist recommendation to stop the genetically deaf from marrying. Instead, critics of the cochlear implant say, deafness is an identity to be adopted with pride. Tellingly, in England the sign language symbol used for cochlear implant is the same one as "to kill." When the Food and Drug Administration approved the implant for children in 1990, five years after it had been permitted for adults, the National Association of the Deaf condemned it as "invasive surgery upon defenseless children." The advocacy group recommended a ban on the operation in children, so they could grow up and then decide to choose a deaf identity or a hearing one.

Despite all the hype, the cochlear implant is an imperfect operation of limited benefit. The device and surgery are expensive, costing $20,000 to $40,000. Wearers hear an imperfect version of sound, making others' voices sound like the scratchy talk of Donald Duck. Fewer than 1 percent of the 22 million Americans with hearing impairments can benefit from the operation.

FES is part of an expensive long-term research venture to re-create the act of walking. Scientists from Case Western Reserve University and the Department of Veterans Affairs are

seeking to unlock the precise movement sequence of some nineteen interacting leg muscles involved in walking. When some
fifty electrodes are implanted or attached externally to a paraplegic's legs, a computer can be activated to generate an electrical impulse that, in the correct sequence, jolts damaged muscles.
The result is a jerky, torturous version of walking, in which the
test subject holds on to a walker to keep his balance. Despite
progress made on the system, it may never prove practical
beyond the walls of a laboratory. Unlike nature, the artificial
machine overstimulates muscles, leaving users exhausted even
after short distances. Yet FES technology continues to fascinate
a society that equates using a wheelchair with tragedy.

To wheelchair innovator Ralf Hotchkiss, FES is an impractical folly. It unrealistically buys into the Hollywood fantasy
version of spinal cord injury: that with enough determination
and pluck, the person with a spinal cord injury will overcome
paraplegia and one day walk again. Better, argues Hotchkiss,
would be to take the money spent on FES research and study
ways to build better wheelchairs or to replace architectural barriers. These are low-tech fixes and not nearly as sexy to a high-
tech-adoring society as a machine that proposes to make people
stand up and walk, but there is more bang for the buck, Hotchkiss argues, in low-tech solutions for the nation's 450,000 paraplegics, quadriplegics, and those with muscular diseases such as
multiple sclerosis.

Hotchkiss has proven with his own inventions the utility of
simple design. He has invented a wheelchair that can be repro-
duced cheaply with simple tools and materials available in even
the most impoverished Third World country. On a 1980 trip to
Nicaragua, Hotchkiss, a paraplegic as a result of a college motorcycle accident, found there was an acute shortage of wheelchairs
for the Central American nation's war casualties. At a rehabilitation hospital, three or four men shared one broken-down wheelchair. It would cost millions of dollars to set up a wheelchair

factory like Hamilton's Quickie plant, and the new lightweights
that so benefited American wheelchair users would be too expensive and not durable enough for use in poor countries where the
terrain is rugged and there are few sidewalks, much less curb
cuts. So Hotchkiss came up with a sturdy design that could be
replicated in small, local workshops by anyone with the tools to
bang out a dented fender. Each chair costs about $250–$300,
compared to the $1,000 sticker price on comparable factory-
built models.

Hotchkiss, who won a 1989 MacArthur Foundation "genius" award, has traveled from Sri Lanka to Siberia, setting up
workshops in remote corners of the world. Scores of Third World
and American students have enrolled in the Third World wheelchair construction class he now teaches at San Francisco State
University. Many, like Dwight Johnson, a retired IBM engineer,
and his wife, Vivian, then go overseas to spread the Hotchkiss
method.

Reliance on technology can be risky. Machines can close off
worlds to disabled people just as quickly as they can open them.
Not until nearly one hundred years after the telephone's invention, for example, would deaf people begin to overcome the
technology gap it created; in 1964 Robert Weitbrecht, a deaf
American scientist, invented the TDD, or telecommunications
device for the deaf (sometimes also referred to by its original
name, TTY, or teletypewriter). But even then, TDD owners
could talk only to people who also had the machine. They
remained isolated from everyone else. The first relay system was
a short-lived operation. The idea was to create a central operator
who could take a TDD message from one party and then translate it by voice to a second party, or vice versa. A St. Louis
family, working out of their home, set it up in 1969, charging
a flat fee of $2 per month. But the operation was so overwhelmed
by demand that it was forced to shut down within six months.
Today, some thirty states have set up relay networks of their

own, but it will not be until 1993 that, under the Americans with Disabilities Act, such a relay system will be established on a national basis, for the first time guaranteeing people with speech and hearing impairments full access to the telephone, from the ability to call an emergency 911 number to the right to order a pizza.

Technology can threaten once again to isolate deaf people and others with disabilities, warns Deborah Kaplan of the World Institute on Disability. Emerging devices are often incompatible with existing ones, in effect erecting "electronic sidewalks," she says, that close off technology as surely as a sidewalk with no curb cuts limits the access of a wheelchair user. A new design in telephones suddenly made hearing aids incompatible with the new phones, so hearing aids could not pick up the sounds on those new models. It took an act of Congress in 1989 to create "an electronic curb cut," notes technology consultant Jay Brill, to force telephone manufacturers to include both the old and new systems in their phones.

For 13 million people with blindness and low vision, reliance upon technology has created an epidemic of illiteracy. The invention of tape recorders and then computers with voice synthesizers that can read a printed page have been great aids in educating blind students. But the result of reliance on such devices is that few people with visual handicaps bothered to learn Braille. Today, only 12 percent of visually handicapped students read Braille, far below the nearly 50 percent in 1965, according to the American Printing House for the Blind. And there is an acute shortage of teachers trained to teach the system of reading the raised dots that was invented in 1829 by blind Frenchman Louis Braille.

Today, many blind people and educators of the blind consider Braille obsolete. But some blind adults, like Kenneth Silberman, an administrator at the Goddard Space Flight Center in Maryland, are rethinking their failure to learn it. Silberman needed to know how to read to keep up with the increasingly technical field of aerospace engineering. It was impractical to play back a tape recorder to find the information he had dictated to himself. It became impossible to carry off his old trick of memorizing what he needed, as "the work was getting steadily more sophisticated." Learning Braille, he says, allowed him to stay in a technical job rather than quitting work and living on Social Security disability benefits.

Literacy proposals have split the blind community. As usual with such disputes in the disability community, this is not just a fight over education but over rights. The National Federation of the Blind, a strong rights advocacy group whose officials are all blind, is pushing for state laws to require all legally blind students to be taught Braille. Marc Mauer of the Federation says they need to know how to use written words in order to get good jobs and notes that 70 percent of working-age blind adults are unemployed.

Other groups that represent blind people, however, say it is often inappropriate to teach Braille, since 85 percent of legally blind persons have some useful residual vision and can read large type. These groups, like the American Foundation of the Blind, are run largely by people without visual handicaps or, like the American Council of the Blind, by a combination of disabled and nondisabled officials. Susan Spungin of the American Foundation for the Blind speaks of her "amazement" the first time she saw a legally blind child "reading, by sight and not touch, the white Braille dots on the white paper." Mauer, however, notes that some forms of blindness, like retinitis pigmentosa, are progressive, and the student who can read large type today may have no vision tomorrow. Those who refuse to learn Braille, he says, are often ashamed, because of the stigma of being disabled, to admit the extent of their visual limitation. Dick Edlung, a state representative who sponsored a successful mandatory Braille bill in Kansas—one of five states to have one—says the most resistance came from parents. "A lot of parents don't want to have a blind kid," says Edlung.

Yet just as technology once threatened to make Braille obsolete, it may now turn the tide and launch a Braille revival. Inexpensive Braille printers and computer programs that translate print into Braille have made it easier than ever to get a wide variety of texts in Braille, including complex technical or scientific material. In some cities, even the daily newspaper can be translated into Braille by calling a computer bulletin board and downloading articles into one's home computer.

Random Access

The hardest part of the technology puzzle has been simply to get new devices to the people who need them. Making the technological breakthroughs—what would logically be the hard part—has proceeded at a brisk pace. Making those devices available—which should have been the easy step—remains the barrier. "It's cruel," says Dr. Barbara Boardman, who studied assistive devices for the congressional Office of Technology Assessment. "We hold out technology to people as a little shimmering dream and then we don't deliver."

British physicist Stephen Hawking is the shining example of how technology can dramatically improve the lives of people with disabilities. Bob Magee, a retired U.S. Air Force photographer when I first wrote about him was, unfortunately, more the rule.

Both Hawking and Magee were battling amyotrophic lateral sclerosis (ALS). Both men had lost the ability to speak or walk. Hawking's story is fairly well known by now. Widely considered the world's most brilliant theoretical physicist since Albert Einstein, Hawking does his talking—even conducting seminars at Cambridge University—through a computerized voice synthesizer. He picks out words on a computer screen, and an electronic voice "speaks" what he writes. This high-tech wizardry allows

Hawking to continue probing his theories of the universe and black holes, work his peers expect will one day win him a Nobel Prize for physics. Says Hawking in *A Brief History of Time,* his nonfiction surprise best-seller: "This system has made all the difference."

In the United States, Magee of West Valley City, Utah, could not get the computer that had proved so liberating to Hawking. Instead, Magee's days were spent in a nursing home bed. His wife, Claudia, had fashioned a crude device for communicating—a lined, green piece of writing paper, like what an elementary school child uses to practice his letters, with the alphabet written out in large block letters. Claudia would point to each letter until Bob blinked his eyes or gave a jerking shake of his head for "yes," eventually spelling out words and sentences. In this protracted way, Bob could get across a few basic needs and feelings. Often these sessions would end with Claudia and Bob crying in frustration. After one struggle to make himself understood, Bob painstakingly spelled out, "I feel like I'm living in a coffin. I want to die."

Developing a technology is one thing, but for those who need it, affording it is quite another. Hawking could purchase his system because he makes enough money and companies donated the software to the famous man. Claudia Magee priced a computer talking system for her husband that would have allowed him to operate the computer by moving his head to aim an infrared beam at a keyboard. At $4,500, the system was out of reach for the Magees. They had been living comfortably before Bob's illness, diagnosed in 1986, forced him to retire as an industrial photographer for the U.S. Air Force. Claudia quit her job as a company credit manager to take care of Bob. The costs of long-term care quickly ate up the $17,000 nest egg they had put aside for vacations and emergencies. The couple quickly went into debt, with an endless stream of medical bills looming long into the future. "I can deal with the disease. But what I hate most is that Bob can't talk," said Claudia. "I would dearly love to talk to him, but we can't pay for it."

A bigger problem is that assistive technology generally is not covered by insurance. Bob Magee's private insurance reimbursed the first $3,000 of his nursing home stay but would not pay for a computer talker. Drew Batavia, formerly of the National Rehabilitation Hospital in Washington, D.C., says private insurers usually deny claims for such devices out of fear that paying for expensive systems would force them to raise premiums. That could make them less competitive with other insurers.

Access to technology can turn on something as whimsical as what state one lives in or what public funding system one qualifies under. The Department of Veterans Affairs provides some of the most comprehensive coverage of technology but only for those with service-connected disabilities. State vocational rehabilitation programs, another important source of money, are often underfunded. Many school districts provide devices to children but only during class hours. Complains Dr. Howard Shane of Children's Hospital, Boston, "I've got children who can communicate from eight to three, Monday through Friday."

Equally frustrating is working through what Stephen White of the American Speech-Language-Hearing Association calls the "amazing maze" of federal reimbursement programs. Medicare will compensate "medically necessary" expenses, such as devices that replace body parts. Conventional hearing aids are excluded. But a cochlear implant—because it is not worn externally but is a surgically inserted hearing aid and therefore considered a body part replacement—is covered. Even more confusing are Medicaid rules, which vary from state to state. In Massachusetts, for example, Medicaid will pay for one hearing aid. Next door in Vermont, only a hearing aid for a minor is covered. Cross the Massachusetts border south to Connecticut, and Medicaid will pay for hearing aids in both ears until a person is twenty-one, but only for one ear after that. "The rules make no sense," complains Alexandra Enders, an assistive technology policy expert at the University of Montana.

Even for the disabled person with money, finding out what exists is a time-consuming, hit-or-miss exercise. Claudia Magee learned about the computer-synthesized talker only by accident, from another spouse with a similarly disabled husband. "There's no effective center for information," says Judy Heumann of the World Institute on Disability, who points as an ideal to Sweden's fifty-two government-sponsored technical aid centers where disabled citizens can test devices before buying them. Some new resources are springing up around the United States. IBM's Atlanta-based National Support Center for Persons with Disabilities records nineteen thousand queries for information a year. In Berkeley, California, Jacqueline Brand, with help from Apple Computers, set up the Disabled Children's Computer Group, a resource center filled with the latest in assistive devices for parents and their children to try out. Brand, whose original quest was to find technology to allow her multiply-disabled daughter to attend school, later established the Alliance for Technology Access and built 45 other centers around the country.

Ordinary market forces that can spur development of traditional products have tended to hold back most disability technology, which is usually expensive and used by a small number of people. "It's a catch-22," says engineer Walt Woltosz, owner of Words+, who got his start, like many in the adaptive technology business, by trying to invent something for a disabled relative. "The prices are high because the volume is low and the volume is low because the prices are high."

Not all helpful devices are expensive and high-tech. Theaters and conference rooms can be equipped for a few hundred to a few thousand dollars, depending on their size, with an FM, infrared, or audio loop system that transmits sound to a receiver worn by a hard-of-hearing listener. A hearing aid can cost just a few hundred dollars. A lightweight, portable TDD can be purchased for a little over $100. And in 1990, Congress passed a law requiring all new televisions sold in the United States to come equipped with an inexpensive "decoder chip" so that deaf viewers could watch closed-captioned shows and videos. A light that flashes to let a deaf person know when the phone is ringing or someone is knocking at the front door can cost just a few dollars.

Traditionally, the devices that do best tend to have an appeal beyond the market of disabled consumers. The Jacuzzi, with its warm swirling waters, was invented by a man in search of something to relieve his eight-year-old son of the pain of his rheumatoid arthritis. Today the son, Kenneth Jacuzzi, runs the company. He compares the Jacuzzi to curb cuts, which were created for wheelchair riders to cross streets but have become a convenience for bicyclists, mothers with baby carriages, and pedestrians who do not want to negotiate a curb. "We invent technology that we think will help somebody with a disability, but time after time it ends up helping all of us," noted Mary Pat Radabaugh, who before her death to cancer in 1991 ran IBM's technology center. Also among history's examples: the first successful typewriter, patented by Charles Thurber in 1843, was conceived as an aid to the blind.

Consequently, universal design—the idea of making things simple to use by disabled people and nondisabled people alike— is newly in vogue among designers and architects. Lever handles were created to make it easier for a person with a disability, such as arthritis, to open a door, but they are appreciated, too, by those with arms full of groceries or wet hands. Large numerals on a clock or a microwave oven are a boon to people with low vision, or others simply trying to read in the dark. Architects are including design features in houses—from stairless entries to adjustable shelves—so that aging no longer threatens one's ability to live at home.

Often technology developed for the general public—especially what the University of Montana's Enders calls the "yuppie market"—has applications for disabled people. Environmental control systems, built around a computer that can be programmed to turn on or off a home's heating and air-conditioning units, lights, televisions, and other appliances, are particularly convenient to a person with a physical disability who cannot move around a house easily, and just as attractive to a nondisabled person looking for a time-saving device. One such environmental control system, called Butler in a Box, can be programmed to recognize speech and will respond to commands by saying, "Yes, Master." But the voice-recognition characteristic, a novelty for most, is particularly valuable to quadriplegics and others who cannot push buttons.

Sometimes technology does not get used because people are uncomfortable with or scared by machines. Some fear the stigma of being disabled—of being old, dependent, not normal—that can come with using such devices. It is not uncommon for elderly people to refuse wheelchairs and walkers, even if it means never leaving home. Everest & Jennings and Invacare sell a popular line of three-wheeled motor scooters, most of them to elderly people, who fear being devalued once they depend upon a wheelchair. Others are technophobic, again particularly older people from a precomputer generation. Singer Stevie Wonder was one of the first musicians to experiment with electronic keyboards and synthesized sounds, so it is not surprising that he also was one of the very first people, in the early 1980s, to buy a Kurzweil reading machine to scan fan letters, books, and business documents. Ray Charles's singing style is more traditional. He stuck with grand pianos and generally stayed away from electronic gimmickry. It took Wonder to buy Charles his first Kurzweil Reader, as a present for the singer's sixty-first birthday in 1991.

Government, charitable groups, and private businesses have

set up innovative programs to deliver technology. There are federal tax breaks for companies that adapt offices for their disabled employees. Because banks generally refuse to grant loans for assistive technology, states including New York, California, and Maine, and groups such as the United Cerebral Palsy Associations have set up low-interest loan funds for disabled people to use, rent, or buy equipment. Pennsylvania lends assistive devices outright to disabled students. The National Easter Seal Society created an assistive technology grant program for farmers, who face a high rate of disabling farm accidents. Car companies, such as Chrysler Motors, have offered rebates of up to $1,000 to people with disabilities to modify cars and vans. The National Christina Foundation, The Amyotrophic Lateral Sclerosis Society, and other groups donate computers no longer used by businesses to people like Magee who need them. Both IBM and Apple have discounted computer prices to disabled buyers.

Bob Magee got a talking computer a few months before his death. Walt Woltosz, who had set up Hawking's computer, flew from California to Utah with one for Magee. It used an infrared pointer that Magee could aim with his head. "He could talk again," recalls Claudia Magee, and that made him happy. When his muscles continued to weaken and even typing out letters became difficult, he could still play an Airplane Bomber video game that Woltosz had installed in the computer. Claudia would get into his bed and play it with him. "It was a stupid game but it was something he could do better than I could, even in his condition," Claudia remembers sadly. "It was therapeutic. It was marvelous." With the computer, Bob Magee made his peace, saying what he wanted to get across before he died.

Claudia Magee gave the computer to a Utah man whose wife was also dying of Lou Gehrig's disease. They, too, had struggled to find a computer that could help them. When that woman died, Magee sent the device to the ALS Society so that it could be passed on to another family. Her only regret is that she had not known how to get the technology sooner, so that her husband could have used it more.

Since Bob Magee's death in 1989, there has been a new, more militant attitude by disabled people in need of technology. "Most disabled people are beginning to believe they have a right to technology," says Karen Franklin, formerly of RESNA, a technology policy group. "It is no longer a luxury." The newly militant attitude, says Franklin, reflects the emerging rights-based thinking of disabled people. They have come to see barriers—from inaccessible buildings to inaccessible computers—as violations of their right to basic equality.

CHAPTER 8

UP FROM THE NURSING HOME

Jeff Gunderson's voice is choked with worry. He is about to reenter the place he calls "the concentration camp." It is a nursing home, one of two where Gunderson, who has cerebral palsy, was sent from the time he was eighteen until he turned twenty-seven.

"I always said if I had to come back here, I'd rather be six feet under," Gunderson says nervously as his attendant tugs him from the car parked outside the nursing home and lifts him into his wheelchair. Nine years have passed since he has lived here. He has returned to this brown-brick building of his nightmares because he wants to introduce me to his former roommate, another man with cerebral palsy who, he says, is anxious to get out.

Gunderson wound up at this Beloit, Wisconsin, nursing home—where he says he was abused and forgotten—after his mother and father divorced. His mother could not lift her large

son out of bed and care for him. To hire an attendant to come
into the Gunderson home was not covered by private or public
insurance and was prohibitively expensive for the woman who
worked on a canning factory assembly line. But Medicaid does
pay for all of the costs of a nursing home. So Gunderson's
mother, like many other parents of severely disabled sons and
daughters, had little choice: she put her teenage son in a nursing
home.

Now back at the nursing home, Gunderson sees an ambulance that has pulled to the front door. It is a bad omen, he
thinks, reminding him how death was a constant here. The two
nursing homes where Gunderson lived were set up to care for the
elderly, not for the young. Gunderson was required to follow the
same regimen as the generally sickly, elderly people around him.
This made it easier for the nursing home staff. He went to bed
at 7 P.M., the same time as his first roommate, a man in his
eighties. His food was bland, unseasoned, often a form of gruel
made for older residents who could not eat solid food. Gunderson admits he rebelled: "I'd have fits."

At both nursing homes, Gunderson says, the staff tried to
break him. Sometimes aides tied him to his bed. They would
drag him into cold showers as punishment. To make him use the
bathroom on a schedule convenient for the nurses, they would
put ice cubes down his pants. It was a form of torture for
Gunderson, because the cold set off his spastic muscles. On
several occasions, Gunderson says he was given a suppository
before sleep and, since he could not move by himself, he would
spend the night lying in his own feces. (Officials at both homes
say they are unaware of the incidents and that such practices
would have been against their policies.) Until his last years in
this second home, days were spent in bed watching soap operas.
"Many times I wanted to kill myself," he says. "I planned it,
too."

Inside the nursing home, the antiseptic hospital smell is

strong and the hallway lights are bright. Gunderson is panicky. He greets staffers with a cheery "Remember me?" But he ignores the severely disabled young people, who now live on a separate wing, some of whom are excited to see him. Loud music comes from a radio in one darkened room where a man lies curled up in a hospital bed. Gunderson, wheeled down the hall by his attendant, cannot find George, his former roommate. George is gone, he announces; perhaps he no longer lives here.

Quickly outside again, Gunderson relaxes at a nearby restaurant with a hamburger. An elderly man enters, wearing a white cap, white pants, and an emerald green sweater. It is George's father. He comes to the nursing home every day to feed his son. George, it turns out, had been there and Gunderson had spotted him. He was the man with the radio. But Gunderson had not been able to face him. His reasons are vague. "George probably would have thought I would stay there with him," he explains.

Later, on the telephone, George's father, a friendly retired restaurant owner, explains that his son "got hurt at birth." George's mother takes the receiver. Would they like to see their son out of the nursing home, like Gunderson, in his own apartment with an attendant? It is not possible, says the mother. Her son is "absolutely, completely helpless, he has no communication, he needs to be dressed." The staff at the nursing home is very caring, she says. Only she and a few of the aides know George well enough to understand him when he speaks. One nurse has recently devised a board with pictures. George can point to a picture of "water" when he wants to drink or "radio" when he wants his music. A therapist has begun working with him, softly throwing a ball to George and giving him colored blocks to stack. The mother notes, "They have a program with the children, now." George is forty-nine.

Gunderson, now thirty-six, lives in a subsidized, two-bedroom apartment. He works three days a week at a sheltered workshop where he is paid a piece rate to help pack boxes of chili that go to grocery stores. He runs up his phone bill, talking long hours to friends. Bowling trophies—he is in two leagues—are scattered around his large living room. His neighbor comes over to watch football. He shares the apartment with his attendant, Shaun Boyd, who helps him dress, bathe, use the toilet, cook, eat, do housework, and get around town. Boyd has become his closest friend. The two eat out together, take rides in Boyd's secondhand car, or stay up late watching rented movies. "I can go out and do things for myself now," Gunderson says. "I used to be a shy person because of all those years living in a nursing home."

Younger people like Gunderson, between eighteen and sixty-four years old, make up 10 percent of the population of U.S. nursing homes; that translated into about 148,000 people in 1987, according to the U.S. Department of Health and Human Services. In nursing homes they lose "the basic rights that the rest of us take for granted, like choosing where they live, who they live with, what they eat, when to eat, who their friends are or if they are going to have sex," argues Tom Hlavacek of the Wisconsin Coalition for Advocacy. "If it happened to us we would scream holy hell and go to the highest court in the land. We do it to people with disabilities all the time and we feel justified by the fact that they have a disability."

Nursing homes have become the new black holes of isolation and despair for young people with disabilities. Today, twice as many working-age men and women live in nursing homes than in traditional state institutions. Millions of others know they could wind up in a nursing home with the loss of a paycheck or social services or because of some other crisis. This threat makes a mockery of all of the disability rights movement's hard-fought gains of civil rights protections and attitude shifts. Following the passage of the Americans with Disabilities Act, disability activists turned to finding alternatives to nursing homes.

Most disabled people in nursing homes have developmental

disabilities, such as mental retardation and cerebral palsy. Others have muscular dystrophy and similar neuromuscular conditions. But a new class of residents includes young people with spinal cord and head injuries, who likely would have died from their accidents before the medical technology of the last two decades made it possible to save them.

In the 1970s, states started closing and downsizing large institutions after lawsuits and newspaper exposés attacked the hellish conditions at many of these facilities. Often residents were removed from one institution only to be dumped into another—a nursing home—that was equally regimented and inappropriate, and sometimes abusive. The number of people with developmental disabilities in state institutions dropped from 195,000 in 1971 to 88,000 in 1990. But the total of developmentally disabled younger people—from eighteen to sixty-four years old—in nursing homes grew by a third in that same period, according to K. Charlie Lakin of the University of Minnesota.

Some of these younger people with disabilities are there because they or their parents prefer it, but most want to live on their own, says Nancy Hansen-Bennett of United Cerebral Palsy of South Central Wisconsin, the group that helped Gunderson move into his own apartment. Even the most severely disabled person can manage outside a nursing home with attendant help and other support, she says. Power wheelchairs, computers with voice synthesizers, and innovative group homes and work programs allow unexpected independence. And living in the community is always less expensive, Hansen-Bennett says, since nursing homes employ costly nurses and doctors, who are not needed by someone who has a disability but is in good health.

Gunderson spent nine lonely and miserable years in nursing homes. He assumed he would die in one, but in March 1981 a county social worker approached him and asked, "Do you want to be the first person to live on your own under a new program?"

Gunderson's first reaction was fear. He had come to take on faith what doctors, social workers, and family had been telling him— that he would never be able to live outside an institution. "I thought it was impossible," Gunderson recalls, "even though I'd always been screaming, 'Get me out.' "

Even then, those close to him only reinforced his doubts. A social worker at the nursing home contested the move, Gunderson says, arguing with county social service officials that he was better off at the home. When Gunderson sought emotional support, the nursing home's psychologist told him skeptically, "You'll never make anything out of yourself." Most disapproving, however, was Gunderson's mother. In her eyes, her son had always been her dependent child, tragically damaged at birth, and she underestimated his ability to fend for himself. One night at dinner at her home, a few years after Gunderson had moved into his apartment, she had carefully cut his meat into small pieces, then speared each one on a fork to feed to him. Finally, Gunderson explained that he could handle a fork by himself.

Gunderson is one of the first users, and biggest success stories, of Wisconsin's Community Options Program, which gets disabled and elderly people out of nursing homes and into their own apartments and group homes. Some 18,000 disabled people are served by Wisconsin's various community programs, but there are another 5,800 on waiting lists, who either live in institutions or with family members. Wisconsin's program is inspired by "progressive thinking," says Hlavacek, but is fettered by "crummy implementation."

Visits to Gunderson and others in Wisconsin—where there are 4,600 people between eighteen and sixty-four in nursing homes, according to the Wisconsin Council on Developmental Disabilities—make it clear that who stays in a nursing home and who gets out is often a quirky business. It may be a matter of not having a friend or family member to be a strong advocate with the bureaucracy, as in the case of James Lee, a gregarious, intelligent man with severe cerebral palsy that requires him to use a wheelchair. At the skilled nursing home in Milwaukee that had been his residence since 1977, Lee would wake up at dawn but often wait until noon for the nurses at the understaffed facility to get him out of bed.

From the time he was thirteen, Lee lived in state institutions and nursing homes. As one of the few young people at the Milwaukee nursing home, Lee feels out of place. "They play bingo a lot," complains Lee, who watches instead. He cannot remember the last time he slept through the night. Nurses are in and out of the room all night to help his roommate, a sickly man in his eighties. Theft is a problem. Most of Lee's clothes have been stolen, to be replaced by handouts that he knows will disappear, too.

To get out, "I'd move to the moon," says Lee. But he needs an attendant to help him with personal care such as getting in and out of bed, preparing meals, and housecleaning. In 1985, he went on a waiting list for his own apartment, under the program that helped Gunderson. But a large county like Milwaukee, unlike the rural one where Gunderson lives, has hundreds of people seeking to live independently and only a small number of apartments to accommodate them. Once someone gets into one of these apartments, says Maria Ledger, the Milwaukee County official in charge of placements, they rarely leave before they die. State funding has failed to keep up with the demand, and wheelchair-accessible apartments are particularly rare. Lee got lucky when Ledger found him and promised to get him out before his thirty-eighth birthday. But it took persistence—Lee called nearly every day for two years to check on Ledger's progress—and an emergency. When Lee's troubled nursing home was about to shut its doors, Ledger used Lee's impending homelessness to move him to the top of the waiting list. Such emergencies, more than how many years one waits on a list, most determine who gets the scarce placements.

Sometimes it is coldhearted bureaucratic rules that keep people in nursing homes, as in the case of Pamela Erickson, who has no hope of leaving her nursing home until she can get a proper wheelchair. Erickson, with cerebral palsy, is lively and verbal. But her body is so twisted by scoliosis that she needs a customized wheelchair to keep her sitting upright. The special chair would cost about $4,000. Wisconsin Medicaid, however, will not reimburse for a nursing home resident's wheelchair, unless it can be proven that it helps the person work or live on his or her own. No one else can give Erickson money for the chair since, as a Medicaid recipient, she is not allowed to have more than $2,000.

So Erickson spent sixteen years in the home lying on a padded, wooden cart with large wheels. It was her prison. The day I met her at her Milwaukee nursing home, Erickson's cabana cart was left in front of a television set. Most of her friends were visiting a botanical garden, but Erickson's cart was too big to fit in a van. Once five years before someone hired an ambulance, her only means of transportation, to take her to a Milwaukee Brewers game. Her only other trips out of the home have been to a hospital; because she spent day after day without sitting up, Erickson developed intestinal blockages. Medicaid, which denied her the chair she needed, paid for four costly hospitalizations to correct her resulting health problems.

In November 1990, a state hearing examiner ordered Medicaid to pay for Erickson's wheelchair. The decision, according to her attorney, Roy Froemming of the Wisconsin Coalition for Advocacy, gave Erickson "the right to leave the place she lives. She wants to go to church, to go to the store. It's an essential right to a meaningful life." Yet it would take another eight months after Froemming's court victory until the woman received her wheelchair. The state Medicaid bureaucracy had thought little of leaving Erickson without a means of sitting up for sixteen years. It thought nothing of letting the forty-three-year-old woman, even with her rights in hand, waste close to another year of her life while the wheelchair requisition meandered through the bureaucratic process and a state rehabilitation engineer made two widely spaced visits to measure her for the customized chair.

Even disabled people whose families have struggled to keep them at home now face institutionalization as they begin outliving their aging parents. Virginia Helmin, who is fighting cancer, worries about what will happen to her son after she dies. Richard Helmin lives in a simple nine-square-foot room next to his late father's barbershop in Milwaukee. Virginia, who tends to him, lives one floor up. Living at home, Richard can spend time with his girlfriend, who also has cerebral palsy, and can get to a job in a sheltered workshop. There are simple pleasures, too, like his fortieth birthday party, for which his mother hired a belly dancer. "We treated him like a real person and I can't let that go to waste," Virginia Helmin says. "In a nursing home, he'd stagnate."

Her fear is not exaggerated. Consider the case of Jackie, a high school graduate with mild retardation, who reads, writes, can cook, and can take buses around Milwaukee. When her mother died nine years ago she was thrown into a grim and crowded nursing home solely for people with developmental disabilities. At the home, she says, she struggles with theft, violence, and unwanted sexual advances from other residents. She is not allowed to leave the facility because the surrounding neighborhood is considered unsafe. Fearful of retaliation from staff, she asks that her last name not be printed. Her sister, who is fighting for her release, says her sister is losing the skills that once let her live at home. Jackie has been on and off a waiting list for a group home for ten years. "I want my privacy," she whispers in the noisy cafeteria at the home. "I want my freedom. I want to get out of here."

To keep getting people out of nursing homes will require

more money or at least a redistribution of existing funds. Most federal funding is directed to institutions and nursing homes, and that discourages states from setting up community programs, complains Dennis Harkins of Wisconsin's developmental disabilities office. In Wisconsin, two-thirds of such money serves 5,500 residents of nursing homes and institutions, while a third pays for 25,000 people in community programs, he says. Senator John Chafee (R-R.I.) has tried to change this "institutional bias" by proposing legislation that would freeze funding at current levels to institutions with more than fifteen beds, in effect forcing states to spend more on smaller group homes. But Chafee's bill, despite numerous compromises, seems irreversibly stalled, due to forceful opposition from unions fearful of job losses and from vocal parents with children in state facilities who distrust states' ability to provide safe community-based programs.

Recent federal nursing home reform laws are aimed at ending "warehousing" of residents. Facilities are now required to focus on rehabilitation, a tenet of the disability field that is being applied to better the lives of both disabled and elderly residents of nursing homes. Jayn Wittenmyer of the Wisconsin Council on Developmental Disability, a state advisory group, says the changes are double-edged. The reforms assured that Medicaid would subsidize institutional care of younger people, she says, making it "more lucrative" for nursing facilities to set aside beds for young disabled residents. That may make it harder to get them out of nursing homes in the long run. For now, the reforms will bring improvement at some homes for young people, like the Marian Franciscan Home in Milwaukee.

In 1986, the Wheaton Franciscan System, a private Catholic health-care concern, took over the four-hundred-bed nursing home, which had a separate wing for 107 disabled people. The nursing home staff helped Pamela Erickson and thirty others appeal for proper wheelchairs. The previous owner of the home actively discouraged residents from having electric wheelchairs, since that gave them freedom of movement and made it harder for the staff to control them. But, prodded by federal and state audits, the nursing home has begun an expensive and ambitious program to get younger residents out of the home and into work programs. Forty now leave to work in enclaves with other residents to make garbage bags and sheets of fabric softener that are sold in the home.

"We are trying to correct the mistakes of the past," explains Cynthia Sook, an official at the Marian Francisan Home. The 1960s promise of getting people out of large institutions was a good one, she explains, but states like Wisconsin shut down institutions without putting enough money into group homes or supervised living programs. Yet even at an institution like Marian Franciscan, which aspires to do the right thing, officials agree that a nursing home is no place for a young person. "How many of us live with one hundred seven other people?" asks Sook. "We try to make it comfortable for young people, but it's still an institution."

When Gunderson left the nursing home in September 1981—Gunderson reels off the precise date as if it were his birthday—he was moved into a subsidized apartment, given an attendant to help him bathe, eat, and perform other tasks he could not do on his own, and sent to work at the sheltered workshop. He would no longer rely on nursing home staff who ran his life on a schedule convenient to them. He would have more control in the one-to-one relationship with the attendant. (Many activists now prefer the less-common term "personal assistant" to get away from the implications of dependency in the word "attendant.") But Gunderson would have to take the assistant assigned to him, someone in a demanding job that paid minimum wage for less than full-time hours.

An attendant can be a resentful bully, like Bette Davis in *Whatever Happened to Baby Jane,* who served up a dead pet parrot

to Joan Crawford, her sister in a wheelchair, or a saintly Mother
Teresa, who gives cheerful nurture and comfort. Low wages lead
to high turnover and make finding skilled assistants often difficult. Regulation and formal training might improve the quality
of attendant care. But many disabled people prefer an untrained
assistant, since certified attendants or nurses used in the role are
less likely to take direction.

Gunderson went through his share of abusive and bizarre
attendants. He says his first believed that his cerebral palsy was
a manifestation of the devil. This attendant would slip Gunderson from his wheelchair and lie him on his back on the apartment floor to pray over him. Sometimes the attendant would
invite friends over to form a prayer circle around the disabled
man to ask for the release of the "devil" who inhabited his body.
But when Gunderson did not miraculously start walking, the
attendant accused him bitterly of lacking adequate faith. Frightened, Gunderson quit going even to his own church.

His next assistant was more agreeable but had a history of
mental health problems, according to Gunderson and the agency
that hired him. On several occasions, Gunderson says, the second
attendant would decide Gunderson was a tree. He would dress
Gunderson in a green sweater and pour chocolate milk over him,
talking bizarrely about Gunderson's roots needing "nutrients"
to grow. On other days, he decided the disabled man was a boat
to be tied to a dock, and would tie Gunderson to his bed. He
would give Gunderson uncooked meat to eat for dinner. Nevertheless, Gunderson kept quiet about this terrorization. An even
darker terror was to be returned to the nursing home, something
he feared would happen if living in his own apartment did not
work out. "I would put up with anything, just to stay out on my
own," Gunderson says now.

The mistreatment became public knowledge one snowy
winter morning when the second attendant disappeared, leaving
Gunderson outside in biting cold, wearing a flimsy T-shirt and

a pair of pants, unable to move his wheelchair by himself. The attendant hired as an emergency replacement was Shaun Boyd. He would become a reliable and caring attendant and Gunderson's closest friend.

In their federally subsidized two-bedroom apartment—filled with worn furniture—Gunderson and Boyd depend on each other. Boyd attends to Gunderson's needs—from cooking and cleaning to bathing to toileting—with skill and care. He does all this for little pay. He could make more at a fast-food restaurant, and indeed, from time to time he has worked during his off-hours as a janitor at a local steak house. His attendant's salary is for forty-two hours a week, divided into six hours a day seven days a week. Plus he gets a place to live, rent free.

Gunderson and Boyd are kindred souls. With sadness, Boyd talks of never really knowing his mother. He remembers her only from hospitals and nursing homes. By the time he was born, she was already living in a nursing home, weak from multiple sclerosis. Her doctors had told her that having another child was risky. Boyd invokes wispy memories of his mother—of formal Sunday afternoon visiting hours at her bedside, of a woman growing weaker and sicker, surrounded by nurses and clean hospital walls. When he was nine, she died. As a result of these experiences, the trip with Gunderson back to the nursing home with me was almost as traumatic for Boyd as it was for Gunderson.

Gunderson lives on $550 a month from Social Security. He considers the money from his job at a sheltered workshop for disabled adults—he made $1.39 for two weeks of work in one typical paycheck—a joke. He slips cardboard sleeves into plastic bags, the first step to packaging chili cans at the nearby Hormel plant. But there is little work to do and Gunderson spends many hours forced to play alphabet bingo, a child's game that he hates because it is so elementary. This, however, is the only option in his county for someone with a moderate disability, although larger counties in Wisconsin have begun experimenting with supported employment, the idea of putting a disabled person, sometimes aided by a job coach, in a regular job. Until the system changes, Gunderson must stay at the workshop—a job, no matter how dull and useless, is a requirement to living outside an institution. Without the workshop, Gunderson knows he would be back in a nursing home.

"What holds Jim McMahon together is a medical mystery," begins a profile of the quarterback in *Sports Illustrated*. McMahon's chronic tendonitis in his elbow is so painful that not only is throwing a football difficult but combing his long hair, too. "In fact the left hand must help the right move the brush through the postgame tangle. And putting his ponytail up, just reaching behind his head, causes him to grit his teeth," according to the magazine. After one game, the quarterback's elbow was so sore that he had to ask his Philadelphia Eagles roommate, 280-pound tackle Ron Heller, to tie his ponytail into a knot for him. He had to ask backup quarterback Brad Goebel to reach into his "left armpit to administer a dose of roll-on deodorant. McMahon's personal hygiene is a team project, although the Eagles say nothing clears a clubhouse quicker than the sound of McMahon calling out, 'Ron? . . . Brad?' "

In the vocabulary of the disability rights movement, McMahon's teammates were performing personal assistance services. They aided him in the tasks that he could do for himself if his elbow did not hurt. McMahon needed help with a few small activities of daily living but could otherwise do his work, in this case lead his team to victory on a football field.

Most disabled people know that there is often a thin line of luck between independence and institutionalization. Often it hinges on something as simple as having someone around to roll on your deodorant, get you out of bed, or help you eat. Evan Kemp, who left the Equal Employment Opportunity Commission in 1993, depends on personal assistance three hours a day, every day, to help him get out of bed, use the bathroom, wash, dress, cook breakfast, and get into his wheelchair so he can go off to work. Kemp has the money to afford assistance whenever he needs it. But he has "met disabled people in nursing homes who are more capable, brighter, better advocates than I will ever be. There is a fine line between me as chairman of the EEOC and a patient in a nursing home."

Personal assistance services are the new, top-of-the-agenda issue for the disability rights movement. The Americans with Disabilities Act guaranteed that stores and restaurants could not discriminate against people with disabilities and that employers could not refuse to hire someone on the basis of a disability. But what good are such protections for someone who cannot get the help needed to get out of bed in the morning? Activist Judy Heumann says personal assistance is now the movement's "major civil rights issue." After the ADA was passed, ADAPT, the grass-roots protest group, quickly became American Disabled for Attendant Programs Today, junking its original name of American Disabled for Accessible Public Transit. It reaimed its confrontational tactics at the nursing home industry and the federal Department of Health and Human Services, instead of at public transit and the Department of Transportation.

Personal assistants help disabled people with the tasks they cannot do on their own. That includes dressing and undressing, grooming, feeding and bathing, getting in and out of bed, a wheelchair, or a bathtub. For a severely disabled person who cannot breathe on his own, an attendant will clear a respirator's air hose or help someone with bowel and bladder movements and catheterization. Depending on the severity of a person's disability, an assistant might do light cleaning, shop, prepare meals, or, when helping someone with a head injury, mental illness, or mental retardation, balance a checkbook, pay bills, or deal with landlords.

Some 7.7 million Americans need some form of personal

assistance. But although this service is widely regarded as the right thing to do for these people, only 860,000 of them, about 11 percent, received aid through publicly funded programs in 1985, according to one 1990 study. At least 77 percent of those who receive publicly funded personal assistance services are over the age of sixty. Wider access to assistance can keep young and old people out of nursing homes and save states money. For example, it costs Utah $15 a day for the three-hours-a-day attendants who visit Julian Sanchez. But before the young paraplegic moved into his own apartment and began attending college it cost the state $80 a day to keep him in a nursing home.

Despite these savings, states are reluctant to provide such humane assistance. States worry that the savings they currently enjoy from these programs would evaporate if such help is made widely available. Of the 7 million Americans in need of long-term care, only 1.5 million are in nursing homes. The rest live at home. Since three-quarters of caregiving is provided by unpaid relatives, 70 percent of whom are women, states fear that families would come "out of the woodwork" to demand funding for what they already do for free. One study suggests that making attendant services widely available would quickly eat up the savings states now enjoy when they get people out of nursing homes. Yet the experience of a few states with larger programs, like Arizona, suggests that expanded programs can pay for themselves.

Even disability activists clash on how much an extensive system of personal assistance should cost, since it depends on who would be eligible for the service. Estimates range from $500 million a year to serve 50,000 working-age people nationally, to up to $10 billion a year to assist 9 million disabled men and women regardless of age, income, work status, or the severity and type of their disability.

Most states now provide limited attendant services for disabled and elderly people, using money from Medicaid, Social

Security, or federal social service block grant funds. But these programs are purposely kept small, even inadequate, out of fears of the "woodwork" theory. In almost every case, says Simi Litvak of the World Institute on Disability, existing services are too fragmented to foster independence.

In America's often perverse health care universe, however, it is not the most efficient or the most humane system that thrives but the one that makes the most money. In the early 1970s there were a dozen postacute rehabilitation centers for people with brain injuries. But as private insurance began paying for expensive stays, many nursing homes began converting. By 1992, there were 800 of these facilities to treat the survivors of head trauma, usually the result of automobile accidents, assaults, bicycle accidents, and falls. The average stay in one of these centers is fifty-one days, William Graves of the National Institute on Disability and Rehabilitation Research told Congress, at an average cost of $1,069 a day. Yet, doctors and survivors claimed, these centers did little rehab and often excelled only at a "wallet biopsy," the practice of keeping someone as long as their insurance was paying, even if they wanted to go home, and then kicking them out the minute the insurance ran out, even if they wanted to stay. "Steal from the rich and keep it" was the way Dr. Kenneth Hoelscher described the practice of his former employer, the New Medico chain. Another former staffer said her job was to scour local newspapers for stories of car accident and plane crash survivors and then pressure the grieving families to admit their injured relatives. New Medico and other owners denied such charges, but the whole industry is coming under investigation by state and federal law enforcement agencies.

Head injury survivor Sherry Watson says the solution is inexpensive attendant service. Watson, after her accident, lived in an institution where, in addition to her daily stay, physical therapy was charged to her insurance company at $125 an hour, and "cognitive therapy" at $150 an hour. But her biggest improvement came when she joined a health club at $25 a month to redevelop her muscles and paid a tutor $5 an hour to help her learn to read again. The cost of a typical stay in a rehab facility, Watson says, could pay for "years of support" with personal assistance in one's own home.

It is helpful to look at assistance services as falling on a continuum, says Gerben DeJong of Washington's National Rehabilitation Hospital. At one end is the ideal, what DeJong calls the "Independent Living Model." The consumer has control. He can hire, fire, and train attendants. Sometimes a local agency gives an attendant's wages directly to the disabled consumer, who is then in the position of being a true employer in charge of paying the attendant. Assistance is an extension of the social service system. Almost no existing programs fit this ideal model for independent living.

Most fall closer to the other extreme on the continuum, what DeJong calls the "medical model." These most resemble nursing home care. An extension of the health care system, they are designed for a patient with an acute or chronic condition and include supervision by a doctor and a registered nurse. This is often called home health care. The disability rights movement consciously steers clear of the word "care," which suggests that a disabled person is a sick and passive recipient of an attendant's help. Personal assistance, in the eyes of the disability rights movement, is an item of social liberation—just like a lightweight wheelchair or a bus lift—not a form of medical care.

Yet most existing personal service programs send a message that the recipient is a patient, not an independent consumer. Often an assistant's decision or a program's rules substitutes for a disabled person's judgment. One attendant in Montana refused a request to put a bag of Oreo cookies in a disabled woman's shopping cart and then scolded her client for being too fat. This stripped the recipient of her right to self-determination, says Sara Watson, who studied Montana's services for the Washington Business Group on Health, and followed traditional patterns of paternalism by caregivers toward disabled people. More tricky, says Watson, is Montana's rule that prohibits an attendant from acting to help a disabled recipient drink alcohol—from putting a six-pack of beer in a shopping cart to popping the tab on the can. States, Watson says, have a "legitimate concern about legal liability" if a person drinks to the point of danger, but advocates such as Heumann contend that disabled people should have the same right as anyone else to make decisions, even foolish ones about drinking.

An attendant is not a caretaker, advocates argue, but should be a neutral extension of the disabled person. In this way, an attendant is best compared to a piece of assistive technology, like an environmental control system, that simply translates a person's request to turn on the lights; a speech synthesizer that speaks what is typed into a computer; or a robotic arm that can pick up a beer can. Sign-language interpreters are a better model yet. They are guided by a strict code of ethics that demands anonymity and distance. An interpreter must never insert his or her thoughts into a conversation. It is considered bad form for a hearing person to speak to the interpreter or address questions in the third person, instead of speaking and looking directly at the deaf person.

While states try to hold the line on costs, some disabled people are pushing assistance service to a new frontier—their right to be parents. Leigh Campbell and Bill Earl met in a Michigan nursing home in 1978 when they were both fifteen. Both have severe cerebral palsy and use wheelchairs, and Leigh sometimes operates a voice synthesizer to talk. They took advantage of changing attitudes, new laws, and breakthrough technology to go to college, marry, and, in 1988, move into their own apartment, where a state-funded attendant helps them seventeen hours a day. In 1992, Leigh gave birth to a daughter, Natalie. With assistance, Leigh could breast-feed the infant, but she could not pick her up to bathe her or change a diaper. The state, however, prohibited the assistants from handling the child. If Michigan helped the Earls with parenting, state officials reasoned, it would be required to provide similar service to other parents as well. (One irony was that the attendants would have been authorized to handle the child if she had been born disabled.) The couple, both of whom were unemployed, could not afford child care on their own. So county social workers talked of putting their daughter in foster care.

To Bill Earl, this was another example of society devaluing and underestimating people with disabilities, just as it had been to consign him to a nursing home as a teenager. Earl looked forward to seeing Natalie "say her first word, take her first step," he said in a statement submitted to a hearing before state legislators. "Don't take away this family because it is not like your family." To Barbara Faye Waxman, a disabled woman who writes about reproductive rights and disability, the county's eagerness to take away the child was a case of outright prejudice. "The feeling is that there are more deserving able-bodied white middle-class infertile couples in the world," she says. The Earls managed to hold off losing Natalie when friends volunteered to provide round-the-clock child care, while the couple fought the state.

"Home health care can hardly be termed a revolution," notes sociologist Irving Kenneth Zola. "For most of recorded history, the home was the preferred site for the delivery of health services." Disabled people have led the return to home care. It was not until the 1950s, with new technology, that medicine revolved around hospitals and doctors' home visits became a rarity. At the same time, however, people with chronic illness and disability were living longer and had come to understand that the hospital was a cold place and that status as a patient frustrated their efforts to live as normal a life as they knew they could. California started the nation's first In-Home Supportive

Services program in the 1950s to help hundreds of postpolio quadriplegics who realized they could live better, and at less cost, outside a hospital. It was no accident that the beneficiaries of this program, people like Ed Roberts, would later start the disability rights movement with their focus on independent living.

Today, the nursing home reform movement is catching up with the disability rights movement. Nursing facilities mushroomed in size in the 1960s and 1970s, the exact time that institutions for people with mental illness and mental retardation started shutting down. Nursing home construction fed on the billions of dollars provided by Medicare and Medicaid, which were created in 1965. Today, nursing home critics expose the same horrid conditions that led to the deinstitutionalization of people with mental illness and mental retardation: restraints and tying of residents; overuse of drugs; neglect and abuse by aides; institutionalization of people who, with social service support, could live better lives on their own. The trend is toward making nursing homes the institution of last resort, and those who live in them now tend to be the most frail. Leaving an institution, older Americans are saying, is a choice. They are questioning medical models and demanding maximum self-determination. It is one more example of how the disability movement has quietly transformed America's social landscape.

CHAPTER 9

NO LESS WORTHY
A LIFE

T he intensive care unit was the wrong place to put a young man like Larry James McAfee. It was a stopping-off point for patients near death. But McAfee was not dying; he wasn't even sick. Trapped in his hospital bed, he felt as if the weeks were ticking off in slow motion while around him the intensive care unit seemed to whir at hyperspeed. Patients were wheeled in from surgery or wheeled out to the morgue, nurses and doctors hurried through, machines hummed, and lights glared. After three months, in the spring of 1989, McAfee, fed up, called a lawyer with a request. Help me, he said, "I want to die."

Larry McAfee, then thirty-four years old, was a quadriplegic, the result of a motorcycle accident in the mountains of northern Georgia. The muscles that worked McAfee's lungs and air sacs were paralyzed from his injury. So a respirator, which was attached by a tube inserted down his throat, pushed air into his lungs to make him breathe. McAfee's request for the right to die brought Fulton County Superior Court Judge Edward Johnson quickly to Atlanta's Grady Memorial Hospital for an unusual bedside court hearing. Life as a quadriplegic, sustained by a machine and dependent on attendants for everything from eating to coughing, had been "intolerable," McAfee told the judge in the ICU. He spoke in a strained voice—unanimated, almost robotic—trying to be heard over the soft whooshing sound of the air passing through his respirator. He recounted how he had been moved from one far-flung nursing home to another and that he no longer foresaw a life out of a hospital bed. "It is very heartbreaking," McAfee said to the judge. "Everyday when I wake up there is nothing to look forward to."

McAfee, an engineering student, even told the judge how he planned to end his life. The method had come to him while he had been lying in the ICU. He described the device he invented to kill himself in the same matter-of-fact tone he would use to explain any other engineering project. It consisted of a time switch, one relay, and two valves. The simple invention would force the air from the respirator to spill ineffectually into the room instead of into his lungs, without setting off the alarm. A friend would assemble it according to McAfee's instructions. Someone else, with permission from the court, would help McAfee swallow a sedative. Then, before he drifted into a deep sleep, McAfee would clench a mouthstick between his teeth and use it to turn on the timer. It would tick off the last seconds of air pumped into his lungs. Death would come—gently, comfortably—in his drug-induced sleep.

Three weeks later, the judge summoned McAfee's parents and three younger sisters to his chambers. Johnson would allow the young quadriplegic to end his life. They all cried, and tears came to the judge's eyes. McAfee's mother hugged the judge and thanked him for his compassion. "That was the hardest decision of my life," he told Amelia McAfee. "But that young man made the biggest impression on me of any young man in my life."

To disabled people, however, Larry McAfee's story was not a simple right-to-die case. Instead, it was another chilling reminder of how a disabled life was dismissed—by doctors, judges, and the public—as a devalued life. As they viewed it, a judge saw a man with a translucent plastic coil connecting a hole in his throat to a machine and eagerly ruled this a life not worth living. It did not matter that about fifteen thousand Americans living outside of hospitals use respirators. A nondisabled man who asked the state to help him take his life would get suicide-prevention counseling, but McAfee had not been considered rash or even depressed. Instead, a judge had praised him as sensible and brave. It was a bitter insult to the millions of other people with disabilities who were living successfully on their own—including those so severely disabled that they used respirators daily.

From a disability rights point of view, the McAfee decision was better understood as the story of how this country fails miserably to care for severely disabled people. Instead of getting help to live on his own, McAfee was sentenced to indifferent nursing homes and hospitals and stripped of basic decision making about his life. It is not an ignorant system. Rehabilitation therapists have perfected programs for returning injured people to their homes to live and their jobs for work. There is astounding technology—like the wheelchair McAfee could control with his mouth and the portable respirator that fits on its back—to allow for new levels of independence. Nor is the system a stingy one. Over $1.5 million in private insurance, state Medicaid, federal Medicare, and Social Security payments was spent on McAfee in the four and a half years between his accident and the final court decision.

But the generosity was often misspent and misplaced. For example, state Medicaid would pay every penny of McAfee's expenses in a nursing home. Yet it would not pay one cent for what he needed to live at home so that he could go back to work and be a taxpayer instead of simply taking welfare. Social Security and Medicaid are based on out-of-date assumptions that severely disabled people simply need support payments to be attended by family or in a nursing home because they are close to death and can expect little more. This may have been true as recently as Medicaid and Medicare's inception in 1965. Indeed, it has been only in recent decades that someone with an injury like McAfee's had even reasonable odds of survival. Kidney infection and bedsores quickly took the lives of those who lived past their initial injury. Today, doctors save eight thousand people a year who become paralyzed by accidents, from nightmarish highway smashups to mundane slips in the bathtub. There are some 250,000 survivors of spinal cord injuries nationwide.

McAfee was victimized not by a mean-spirited system, just a life-deadening one. Many severely disabled people hold jobs, live in their own homes, marry, and bring up families. Many others, like McAfee, get exhausted trying to cope. Clinical psychologist Carol Gill, a quadriplegic who uses a wheelchair and specializes in counseling disabled clients dealing with depression, calls what McAfee went through "disability burnout." She describes it as the frustration of trying to work through an unresponsive and bureaucratic system of health care that too often promises more than it delivers.

When I met McAfee I found a man angry about his loss of control over his body but more angry still about his loss of control over his life. He was living in a gloomy Alabama nursing home room, his bed separated by a pink curtain from the next bed, which had been home to a succession of elderly men on respirators. McAfee was a large man—he stood six feet, six inches before the accident—propped on his side in a hospital bed. He had no shirt on, and his body was covered by a white blanket. Nurses had not bothered to shave him, and there was

a three-day-old stubble on his face. Out the window next to his
bed, he could see only sky and desolate trees. A stack of un-
opened mail sat on the windowsill, along with a bouquet of
balloons from his mother and a framed picture of an attractive
woman in a nurse's uniform. McAfee spoke in a distant, distracted voice, except when describing the pain of his lowly status
as a disabled man. "You're looked upon as a second-rate citizen,"
he said, the bitterness rising in his voice. "People say, 'You're
using my taxes. You don't deserve to be here. You should hurry
up and leave.' " Nurses and doctors talked about his prognosis
and problems while standing at the bottom of his bed, as if he
were invisible. Attendants pulled his body roughly, at times
dropping him to the floor, and some, he felt, made it clear they
considered caring for him a loathsome chore. "I didn't ask to be
like this at all," McAfee said. "You reach a point where you just
can't take it anymore."

At the time of his accident, the man his family called
"Bubba" was close to completing his engineering degree at
Georgia Tech in Atlanta, while he worked full-time at an engineering firm. He was bright and had an aptitude for math, but
he never applied himself in school, either at the private academy
in rural Sandersville where he finished high school or in college.
He planned to become a mechanical engineer. He had a girlfriend in Atlanta but was not ready for marriage. After the
accident, in his self-pity, he ended their relationship, even
though she had remained supportive.

It is a myth that being disabled means being in bad health.
A person may need a wheelchair for help in moving or a respira-
tor for help in breathing yet live a long and healthy life.
McAfee's health was in danger for the two weeks after the
accident. At Georgia Baptist Hospital, McAfee was stabilized.
Holes were drilled into his skull to attach a brace for traction.
Another hole was opened in his throat to insert the plastic tube
from the respirator. Once his health improved, he was sent to

Atlanta's Shepherd Spinal Center. Quadriplegia means full or partial paralysis of the arms and legs. In rare cases, quadriplegics, like James Shepherd, who founded the Atlanta center after being injured in 1973 while body surfing on a beach in Rio de Janeiro, can even walk with the aid of crutches. "High quads" like McAfee, who have had injuries to the top vertebrae in their spinal column, are completely paralyzed below the neck. Their internal organs—kidneys and liver, for example—still work.

Contrary to common expectation that disabled people become sexless, most men and women with spinal cord injuries report satisfying, and often more adventuresome, sex lives. Many report the physiological sensation of orgasm. They develop secondary erogenous zones—the back, the neck, the breasts. Most men still get erections and many can still father children. Drugs and electrical stimulation methods can help. Many quadriplegic women can get pregnant and bear children.

Another myth is that disabled people are forever depressed. Steve Shindell, the director of psychological services at Shepherd, notes that some studies have found the suicide and divorce rates for quadriplegics are roughly the same as for the population at large, although other studies show higher divorce rates. People whose lives have purpose and inspiration—a spouse, children, or an enjoyable job—are the most motivated to adjust to injury. The "best predictor" of how someone fares, says Shindell, is how well they coped with stress before their injury. Others at Shepherd and the various nursing homes and hospitals where McAfee lived, questioned whether he ever had those coping skills.

Most people with such disabling injuries go through periods of severe depression, but McAfee's was unrelenting. He was difficult, demanding, and sullen. He seemed to want to sabotage any plan to help him and turn against anyone who reached out. There had been bitter rejection for him, for sure. His best friend, who had been riding with him the day of the motorcycle accident, could not handle seeing his friend so disabled and cut off contact, as did McAfee's grandmother and, most devastatingly, the adored grandfather who used to take him hunting. His mother moved to Atlanta for the first six weeks of McAfee's rehabilitation at Shepherd, sleeping either on a rollaway cot in a counselor's room or upright in a chair, with her head on her son's arm and a hand on his mouth in case he needed anything. After that, however, it was hard for the family, several hours away in Sandersville, to make more than infrequent visits. Yet there would be others devoted to him, including a nurse from one of the nursing homes—the one in the picture at McAfee's bedside, a nurse who Amelia McAfee says was in love with her son—who took her two weeks of vacation to be with McAfee when he moved from one nursing home to the next.

At Shepherd, therapists worked to show McAfee that he could live independently. He could do just about anything he had done before, they told him, even though he could no longer move his legs or hands. They taught him to control an electric wheelchair equipped with a "puff-and-sip" switch. If he gave a hard puff on a plastic straw, the chair moved forward. With a sip, it moved backward. One of the first things the Shepherd therapists do is to determine what a person likes to do most, then show him a new way to do it. A painter is taught to hold a paintbrush between his or her teeth. A photographer is shown how to trigger the shutter of a camera by using a puff-and-sip device. There are puff-and-sip kayaks and sailboats. For a hunter, like McAfee, there are rifles, mounted on a lap board, that can be aimed and fired with a puff-and-sip switch. McAfee, however, never showed any interest in taking up hunting again. He went through the rehabilitation program at Shepherd twice, spending fifty-three weeks there. The average stay for a quadriplegic was twenty weeks.

Yet McAfee's future looked bright enough that the spinal injury center even used him in one of its advertising campaigns.

The print ad shows a smiling McAfee working at a computer terminal that was programmed to recognize the sound of his voice so he could control it with verbal commands. At his side was a machine that turned the pages of a book for him. CASE STUDY: LARRY MCAFEE . . . said the ad headline; PROGNOSIS: PROMISING. By the spring of 1986, McAfee was home in his own apartment. He talked of looking for a new job as a computer consultant. His insurance payment from his job at the engineering firm where he had worked before the accident paid for the round-the-clock attendants he needed. He needed medication and had to be turned every three hours to prevent the bedsores that are common with quadriplegics and can lead to life-threatening infections. McAfee, scared and accustomed to the top-quality care he had received at Shepherd, insisted on hiring nurses, although less-skilled and less-expensive attendants would have sufficed. His insurance company paid less than the going rate for private nurses. The result, McAfee claimed, was that the agencies sent him their worst nurses, ones who did not care for him properly. He went through nurses and money quickly.

The year at Shepherd and the expensive care quickly ate up his million-dollar insurance payment. After seventeen months, before McAfee had taken serious steps to return to work, his money ran out and his real nightmare began. Without money, McAfee was dependent—like many quadriplegics—on state Medicaid funding. His parents could not take him into their modest home. "An individual family can't do it for twenty-four hours," explained his mother. "We would have ended up hating him and he would have ended up hating us. We looked at it from every way." Had he been disabled in California, he would have received up to $1,200 a month for attendants so that he could stay at home. Georgia would not pay for such help, although it would pay a skilled nursing home $100 a day to care for him.

Yet here was the McAfee Catch. No nursing home in
Georgia would accept such a severely disabled client for so little
reimbursement. Because he was on a respirator, he required more
attention than the typical nursing home client, an elderly person
who can bathe and eat with little or no assistance. Georgia paid
nursing homes the same daily rate, whether a patient used a
respirator or not. Consequently, Georgia nursing homes refused
the costly clients who depended on respirators.

Other states are more generous. Ohio paid nursing homes
close to $300 a day to care for someone like McAfee, so he was
moved to a nursing home in a small town near Cleveland. It
would be for just a few months, he was assured, until another
facility could be found closer to home and his friends and family,
but McAfee spent fourteen months in Ohio. The promises from
Medicaid officials in Georgia stopped. There was no longer any
talk from optimistic therapists about the possibility of a job. The
twenty-bed ventilator unit was made up almost entirely of geriatric residents. Most, says McAfee, had not been taught how to
speak over the ventilator tube. McAfee tried to show them. He
spent lonely days staring out the window. His roommate was an
elderly man in a coma. Growing more and more frustrated, and
upset about what he thought was poor care, McAfee filed complaints about his treatment with Ohio health officials. Michael
Coury, director of the Aristocrat Berea Skilled Nursing Facility,
says his staff tired of McAfee's grievances and, after talking to
McAfee, felt it was best if he left. McAfee says he was given no
say in what happened next.

The morning after the Super Bowl, in January of 1989,
administrators at Grady Memorial Hospital, Atlanta's large
public hospital, got a 6:30 phone call from Ohio. An ambulance
plane, carrying Larry McAfee, a resident of Georgia, was on its
way to Atlanta. He had been paralyzed in a motorcycle accident,
hospital officials were told, but they were surprised to discover
when he arrived that the accident had occurred not that day but

four years earlier. Georgia Medicaid had given permission to the Ohio nursing home to transfer McAfee but did not warn Grady Hospital. Otherwise, the hospital would not have accepted someone in McAfee's good condition. Once McAfee had been admitted, the hospital by law could not discharge him unless it found another place for him. But the McAfee Catch applied to them as well: no nursing home in Georgia would take a young man on a respirator.

So McAfee sat in the intensive care unit at Grady, growing more and more furious at the way he had lost all control of his life. Because he was in stable health he did not belong in a hospital at all—much less in an intensive care unit. But the ICU was where the hospital put people on respirators. He spent nearly three months on the noisy intensive care ward—when he called the lawyer—and then five more in a step-down section of the intensive care unit. There was no privacy, and only rarely did nurses have time to get him out of bed. When McAfee's parents brought his electric wheelchair to the ward, McAfee says, the staff locked it in a closet. Grady was old, run-down, under-staffed, and the last resort for the poor, the uninsured, and the patients that no one else wanted. "He actually smelled when he was there. They didn't bathe him," complained Amelia McAfee. "They clipped his hair off down to his scalp. They would cut his hair on Thursday and when I came to see him on Saturday the hair was still on the pillow and lying on the floor."

Every day McAfee stayed in the hospital, Grady lost money. Medicare ruled that because he was healthy, it was inappropriate for him to be in a hospital. Therefore, Medicare would not pay the hospital costs. Medicaid would pay, but only if he was in a nursing home. Hank Selinger, a discharge planner at Grady, repeatedly called one hundred nursing homes in search of one that would take a quadriplegic on a respirator. McAfee's hospital bill for seven months came to $175,369, says Grady spokes-woman Beverly Thomas, of which Medicaid would reimburse no more than $3,000 to $8,000. The hospital and state taxpayers picked up the rest.

McAfee's call for legal help went to an agency that assigns volunteer lawyers. The case went to Randall Davis, a young associate in an Atlanta firm. Davis specialized in aviation law, but he knew how to fashion the strongest legal argument for any position. Davis went to Grady to meet McAfee and was appalled to find someone who "shouldn't have been in the depressing atmosphere of the ICU, especially when he was alert." In his brief, Davis played up the tragedy to McAfee's life: he had lost control over his body and found no enjoyment to his life. In short, his life was not worth living.

But Davis had a legal problem. He had to convince the court that to let McAfee turn off his respirator would not be suicide but an act of passive euthanasia, like that practiced daily in hospitals across America. Passive euthanasia occurs when a doctor either withholds or withdraws life-sustaining technology— such as a respirator or feeding tube—from someone in an irreversible coma or a persistent vegetative state who would otherwise die. Medical ethicists, courts, and the American Medical Association sanction passive euthanasia in carefully controlled circumstances, and doctors say the practice is common. More taboo is active euthanasia, in which a doctor deliberately acts to bring about death. In the Netherlands, doctors are allowed to give patients legal injections of drugs, and supporters there say the practice accounts for 2 to 3 percent of all deaths in that country. Some American doctors say it is not uncommon in this country for doctors to help dying patients overdose on drugs, although at the time of McAfee's request the practice was rarely discussed openly and opposed by many medical ethicists and the AMA.

Davis argued that McAfee's respirator was an artificial system of life support. To turn it off, he said, was simply to refuse treatment to prolong his life. McAfee's parents and his three sisters supported his decision to die. The Georgia State Attorney General and even the Catholic archdiocese of Atlanta wrote briefs in support. Nationally, the Catholic Church has been one of the most stalwart opponents of assisted dying, but David Brown, the archdiocese's attorney, compared McAfee's situation to trying to end life support for someone who was "brain-dead."

Davis's argument blurred the line between active and passive euthanasia, since McAfee was otherwise healthy and was in no danger of dying as long as he had his respirator. True, he depended on a machine to breathe. But it was not the respirator itself that required McAfee to be in hospitals and nursing homes. It weighed thirty pounds and was portable. He could go to work with it or travel in an airplane around the world with it. He needed the respirator in much the way he needed an electric wheelchair. Each compensated for a part of his body that no longer functioned. And each represented freedom and independence.

Nevertheless, legal doctrine firmly supports a person's right to refuse medical treatment. Judge Johnson agreed with Davis. To let McAfee turn off his respirator, the judge concluded, would merely be allowing the "injury process to take its natural course." In other words, McAfee would not be committing suicide. He would be dying from the injury of the motorcycle accident of more than four years before. Johnson never considered how the health care system had failed McAfee and even contributed to his wanting to end his life. Instead, Johnson spoke of the tragedy of the "boy who loved sports" and "teased his sisters" before the accident but who, as a disabled man, could no longer find "quality in his existence."

Disability activists in Atlanta reacted with a visceral anger. It was as if McAfee's decision to die—and the sympathetic nods of approval from both church and state—were a direct judgment that their lives were not worth living either. Mark Johnson and Eleanor Smith, two Atlanta-based activists, led demonstrations outside the courtroom. If McAfee could end his life, they asked, didn't that mean the state put a lower value on the life of a disabled person than on the life of a nondisabled one? Why should there be an exception to the ban on state-assisted suicide only because a man was disabled? The activists feared that the court ruling sent a message that disabled people had a duty to die rather than be a burden to their families and society. Because of McAfee's paralysis, the judge's ruling was considered a humane gesture. Yet had McAfee gone to court but not been disabled, a team of psychiatrists would have been dispatched to lift him from his depression and give him suicide-prevention counseling, argued Smith.

In fact, McAfee had sent away social workers and therapists who came to his bedside at the ICU, in part because it was open and public and hardly a comfortable place to be spilling the tale of one's most private misery. But a psychologist did visit him when he sought to die—not to determine if he was depressed but simply to report back to Judge Johnson that McAfee was mentally competent to make a decision to die. Attorney Davis objected that activist Smith was "paternalistic" to suggest McAfee was not clear-thinking enough to make his own decision. "McAfee has a unique personality," said Davis. "He is very independent and he abhors being reliant on others." But what about Smith and other disabled people, even those on respirators, who insisted that life was still rewarding? Replied Davis, "To those, he says, 'I salute you, but it's not for me.' "

One thing that made the McAfee case particularly ominous was that he was seeking an easy suicide, approved and assisted by the state. McAfee argued that as a disabled man he needed someone to help him end his life. But others, including disabled historian Paul Longmore, noted that there were many ways a respirator-dependent quadriplegic could kill himself. McAfee could run his electric wheelchair into a lake and drown or crash it down a flight of stairs. Certainly a man mechanically clever enough to figure out how to clench a mouthstick in his teeth to turn off his respirator could also figure out how to trigger a gun. To die during a drug-induced sleep was a sure out, free of blood and pain. It made suicide inviting. What frightened Longmore was the way the courts were encouraging and applauding McAfee, opening the doors wide to his idea, simply because he was disabled. As a historian, Longmore was disturbed by this echo of past efforts to help disabled people die, often against their will.

In Nazi Germany, doctors marked children and adults with mental retardation, mental illness, epilepsy, chronic illness, and severe disabilities for mass murder. Disabled children, and later disabled adults, were put to death by lethal injection of Luminal, a sedative, or, if that did not work, morphine-scopolamine. Others died in the regime's first experiments with lethal carbon monoxide gas. Some 200,000 disabled men, women, and children would die, according to historian Hugh Gregory Gallagher. "Lebensunwertes Leben"—life unworthy of life—was the concept the Nazi doctors used to justify their practice of direct medical euthanasia. Later the Nazi regime would extend its grim biomedical vision to other undesirables—6 million Jews and other victims of the Holocaust.

The Nazi biomedical campaign came out of the worldwide eugenics movement of the 1920s. As historian and psychiatrist Robert Jay Lifton notes in *The Nazi Doctors,* the early German practitioners of eugenics looked with envy at their American colleagues, who with ease could enforce coercive sterilization, using a simple form of vasectomy first developed at a U.S. penal institution around the turn of the century. By 1920, twenty-five states had laws requiring compulsory sterilization of the "criminally insane" and others considered genetically inferior. German physician Fritz Lenz, a leading advocate of sterilization, complained in 1923 that his country was far behind the United States in experiments with sterilization. Lenz praised America for having laws that prohibited marriage by people with epilepsy and mental retardation and banned interracial marriage. And he bemoaned Germany's lack of eugenics research institutions to compare with those in the United States, where, Lifton notes, work carried on by Charles B. Davenport at Cold Spring Harbor, New York, was funded by the Carnegie Institution.

Unlike in Germany, flirting with the eugenics movement in the United States never resulted in mass extermination, but a few American doctors and scientists did argue for the extermination of people with mental retardation, epilepsy, mental illness, blindness, and "deformations," so that they would not have a chance to perpetuate future generations with their "deficiencies." One of these was Dr. Foster Kennedy, a man with impeccable credentials as professor of neurology at Cornell Medical College and director of the Department of Neurology of Bellevue Hospital. He was also the president of the Euthanasia Society of America, which was created in 1938. Writing in the *American Journal of Psychiatry* in 1942, Kennedy outlined a proposal for killing "defective" children—he referred to them as "defective products" and "Nature's mistakes"—which he proposed was a humane alternative to letting them live. When a "defective" child turned five, Kennedy suggested, the parents or guardians should be allowed to ask a panel of doctors that the child "be relieved of the burden of living." Kennedy compared this to the "solace" given a "stricken horse." If the panel found the child to have "no future nor hope of one," Kennedy wrote, "then I believe it is a merciful and kindly thing to relieve that defective—often tortured and convulsed, grotesque and absurd, useless and foolish, and entirely undesirable—of the agony of living." Kennedy's support of involuntary euthanasia was scorned, particularly as World War II ended and understanding of the roots of the Holocaust spread.

But the idea that it was somehow right or humane to end the lives of disabled people never went away. In 1972, when a

Florida state representative, who was also a doctor, introduced a "death with dignity" bill, he suggested that some 1,500 people in state institutions, 90 percent of the total, "might qualify for elimination." The House passed the bill in principle, but it did not become law. In their 1985 book *Should the Baby Live? The Problem of Handicapped Infants,* ethicists Helga Kuhse and Peter Singer wrote, "We think that some infants with severe disabilities should be killed" and proposed that it be made legal to kill such a child within approximately the first twenty-eight days of life. And in 1991, David Larson, the codirector of the Center for Christian Ethics at Loma Linda University, suggested taking the hearts of disabled children to keep monkeys alive. Asked about the ethics of the Baby Fae case, the first human to receive a heart transplant from a baboon, Larson replied, "If a primate's capability was higher than that of a human—say a severely mentally handicapped child—I think it would be appropriate to support the opposite approach of Baby Fae, a transplant from a child to save the life of a healthy baboon or chimpanzee."

Throughout U.S. history, doctors have routinely starved or ended the lives of infants born with Down syndrome or various birth defects, although those children were in no danger of dying. The practice was given national exposure in 1983, when the Reagan Administration opposed the parents of "Baby Jane Doe," a Long Island infant born with spina bifida. The baby's mother and father chose to withhold medical treatment, agreeing with their doctors that it was more humane for the severely disabled child to die. Surgeon General C. Everett Koop argued that this amounted to involuntary euthanasia. He knew it occurred often. In 1973, two doctors, writing in the *New England Journal of Medicine,* revealed that forty-three infants with various disabilities had been allowed to die in the special care nursery of the Yale–New Haven Hospital "rather than face lives devoid of meaningful humanhood." A California state court in 1979 ruled in favor of the parents of Philip Becker, a thirteen-year-old with

Down syndrome, who wanted to withhold life-saving heart surgery, arguing that his life was not worth living. He was spared
death only because another couple adopted him.

To the disability activists, McAfee's case was an example of
a disabled life devalued. It was a reminder of the many other
cases where an easy right to die was extended to a disabled
person as an act of compassion. In 1983, Elizabeth Bouvia, a
twenty-six-year-old social worker with severe cerebral palsy,
checked into a Los Angeles hospital and asked for painkillers
while she starved herself to death. With the help of an American
Civil Liberties Union attorney, she argued that her severe disability made her want to die and that she had a right to refuse
life-saving treatment. Three mental health professionals who
examined her agreed but ignored the recent emotional crises in
her life. She had lost a child to miscarriage and her marriage had
broken up; her brother had died; she was financially troubled
and had been forced to withdraw from graduate school. A California judge also ignored her depression and concluded that the
hospital should help Bouvia die, given "her helpless and, to her,
intolerable condition." But Bouvia was far from being the helpless woman described by the judge. Instead, as historian Longmore noted, she "is a woman who operated a power wheelchair,
was halfway toward a master's degree, married, made love with
her husband and planned to become a mother. This is a woman
who still could and might do all of those things if she were given
appropriate psychiatric and medical treatment."

Bouvia set the case law that a patient could refuse treatment,
regardless of his or her motives, age, or health. Her struggle got
nationwide press attention. Less well remembered is that Bouvia
never followed through on her death wish. Nor did she get the
support she needed to live independently. A reporter in 1988
found Bouvia in a Los Angeles hospital, living in a tiny, $800-a-
day isolation room and registered as "Jane Doe," still talking of
wanting to die.

David Rivlin was a quadriplegic on a respirator. While surfing at the beach with his girlfriend in 1971, a crashing, foamy wave drove Rivlin headfirst into the sand. The force of the wave broke his neck, leaving Rivlin paralyzed except for some movement in his arms and upper body. He tried to carry on with his life, moving back to Michigan, where he grew up, and enrolling in college. He studied philosophy and lived with an attendant. When he began to lose the limited function of his arms, he moved into a nursing home in Dearborn and fell in love with a woman who worked on the office staff. They were engaged and Rivlin moved into her home in 1980. But the relationship was troubled and short-lived, with Rivlin bitterly blaming the breakup on "the burden of my being a quadriplegic." Both of his parents had died. When his strength continued to deteriorate and he was returned to a nursing home in 1986 he thought about dying.

"The case law is quite clear," concluded Oakland County Circuit Court Judge Hilda Gage, responding to Rivlin's petition in July of 1989. "We are dealing with a competent adult. He has the right to refuse treatment." The thirty-eight-year-old quadriplegic made an appeal through the local newspapers for a doctor who would help him die. "The vent [his respirator] takes away all choice in your life," he told a reporter several days later. "I don't want to live an empty life lying helplessly in a nursing home for another thirty years. Death means to me that I can just rest in peace." Fifteen days after Gage's ruling, Dr. John Finn of the Hospice of Southeastern Michigan gave Rivlin a mixture of Valium and morphine. As Rivlin drifted into unconsciousness, the respirator was shut off. Three close friends, including the woman he had been engaged to, watched. In a half hour, Rivlin was dead.

It was the Rivlin case that had inspired McAfee to seek death, and it was Rivlin's plea for a doctor's help that would inspire Dr. Jack Kevorkian, the Michigan "suicide doctor" who the following summer helped Janet Adkins take her life with the "mercy machine" he had invented. Kevorkian had met Rivlin when the quadriplegic had sought out a doctor to help him die. With $30 of spare parts collected from junkyards and flea markets, Kevorkian built a suicide machine so that someone like Rivlin could pull the plug on himself. It was a more sophisticated version of the suicide machine that McAfee had invented a year before. Kevorkian's had three vials strung to a small metal frame, connected to an electric motor.

Adkins, living in Oregon, heard about Kevorkian and his machine through a newspaper article. The fifty-four-year-old former English teacher had been diagnosed as being in the early stages of Alzheimer's disease, although doctors told her that diagnosis could turn out to be wrong. She remained physically active, beating her son at tennis one week before her death. But she no longer remembered how to keep score. When she first contacted Kevorkian, he encouraged her to continue with medical treatment. But when an experimental drug failed to help, he invited her to Michigan. She and her husband, Ron, were members of the Hemlock Society and talked about "dying with dignity." One friend said Janet Adkins saw ending her life as "a gift to her family, sparing them the burden of taking care of her."

In June of 1990, Kevorkian drove Adkins to a Michigan park with an electrical outlet for campers (no hotel would accept Kevorkian and his "self-execution machine"). In the back of his rusty Volkswagen van, Kevorkian tried three times before he could hook the machine's needle into the small veins in Adkins's arm. When she was ready to die, she thanked Kevorkian. "Have a nice trip," he replied. Then she pressed the button which emptied the harmless saline solution from the first vial into her veins; then the second vial of thiopental sodium, which made her lose consciousness; and then the final vial of potassium chloride, which caused her heart to stop.

Since the 1970s, with advances in life-sustaining technology, Americans have demanded more control over the end of life. There have been notable court challenges over how long to keep comatose patients like Karen Ann Quinlan and Nancy Cruzan on life-support machines. Kevorkian's supporters saw him as a compassionate man, helping people avoid ignominious death. Others saw him as a frightening figure who spouted bizarre ideas about farming organs of dying prison inmates and suggested, with echoes of Nazi Germany, that people with severe disabilities should seek out suicide. Because Michigan was one of the few places that has no law against assisted suicide, a judge later threw out murder charges against Kevorkian. Eight disabled or ill women would die in Michigan with Kevorkian's help before the state's governor signed a law banning assisted suicide in December 1992. Kevorkian vowed not to be deterred and, after some disability activists noted that only women were choosing euthanasia, the pathologist known as "Dr. Death" helped a man die in January 1993. The mixed outrage over Kevorkian, and debate in states like California and Washington over legalizing euthanasia, demonstrate that the controversy over how life should end is becoming as passionate and divisive as the debate over abortion and the beginning of life.

Five Atlanta lawyers, as well as the American Civil Liberties Union, refused the request of disability activist Eleanor Smith to write an amicus curiae brief in opposition to letting McAfee end his life. They demurred, saying they supported an individual's right to choose. McAfee's choice to die was based on the same constitutional right to privacy that was the basis of the right for a woman to choose abortion. Ultimately, the National Legal Center for the Medically Dependent and Disabled, an Indianapolis-based right-to-life law center, wrote the friend-of-the-court appeal to the Georgia Supreme Court. It made a forceful argument "not to join in a misguided campaign to champion Mr. McAfee's right to die" and asked that McAfee get help from a therapist expert in the field of suicide.

The joining of the Indianapolis right-to-life group and the

disability activists was an uneasy marriage of convenience. Legalized abortion is one of the most divisive issues for the disability rights movement, one that the movement has dealt with largely by keeping its distance. Opponents of legalized abortion had seen a natural alliance with disability rights groups, starting with their battles to win medical treatment for infants born with severe disabilities. When the United States intervened in the "Baby Jane Doe" case, it relied on the existing civil rights protection for disabled people. It sued under rules drawn from Section 504 of the Rehabilitation Act, arguing that the hospital, which received federal funds, was illegally discriminating against Baby Jane Doe on the basis of her handicap. Doctors claimed that the girl was so severely disabled that she would never know joy, would live her life bedridden and in constant pain. It was an argument similar to McAfee's. At issue was whether it was right to allow an infant to die if that child had a severe but manageable disability that was not life-threatening. Right-to-life groups called the practice infanticide and took up the fight with vigor. Disability rights groups were divided and fought for "Baby Jane Doe" with less certainty.

To their secret horror, almost every disabled person knows that had his or her condition been congenital, he or she likely would not have survived past the nursery or would not have been born at all. Some, like Evan Kemp, have been told as much by their mothers. California ADAPT activist Lillibeth Navarro calls abortion "this holocaust that is also wiping out our tiny brothers and sisters with disabilities." Of the 1.6 million legal abortions each year in America, about 1 percent of the women have been told the fetus has a defect and 12 percent believe the fetus has been harmed by environmental factors. When told that a fetus has a serious genetic defect, just under 50 percent of women choose abortion.

Proponents of legalized abortion at times have played shamelessly upon parents' fear of giving birth to a child with birth defects—using exaggerated pity talk of "defective children," "a gruesome demand," and "a maimed and distorted human-without-a-future" to defend a woman's option to choose abortion. This is anathema to the disability rights philosophy that disability is not a tragedy and that the quality of a disabled person's life is usually vastly underestimated. "Baby Jane Doe," the girl whose real name was Keri-Lynn, grew up to disprove the dire predictions about her life. After a delay of weeks, her parents, caught in a crossfire of advice by doctors and litigation by the government, changed their minds and allowed medical intervention. *Newsday* reporter Kathleen Kerr visited the family seven years after the girl's birth and found a happy child in a wheelchair, who laughed and played with her parents and friends. "Baby Jane Doe is learning at a level far beyond what doctors testified she would," Kerr wrote, noting that the girl was considered "educable retarded" and took special education classes. Former Surgeon General C. Everett Koop told Kerr that had the girl gotten more active treatment right at birth, "she probably would have been normal today."

Yet leaders prominent in the disability rights movement—and it is a movement with a large percentage of female leaders—often find themselves balancing their anger over selective abortion and their belief in the right to unrestricted childbearing rights. There are basic issues that link the disability rights and abortion rights movements: the control over one's own body and a distrust of leaving such decisions to doctors. Opposition to forced sterilization, for example, was both a feminist and a disability rights issue.

Medical ethicist Adrienne Asch, who is blind, argues the importance of a woman's right to choice. But selective abortion on the basis of disability, she says, is wrong. Most women who abort a fetus diagnosed with a disability like Down syndrome, spina bifida, cystic fibrosis, or muscular dystrophy, she claims, lack knowledge of how the disability rights movement is improving the quality of life for children with these conditions. This reflects society's exaggerations of the tragedy of such disability. Asch draws a distinction between ending a pregnancy and selective abortion. "Aborting because of our own lives says something very different than aborting because we don't like what we find out about the potential life we carry," she argues. To abort on the basis of disability, she says, suggests that a disabled person's life is not worth living. A woman's right to choice is also violated, she argues, when a society expects her to abort a fetus that may be disabled.

The National Right to Life Committee, the nation's most prominent antiabortion group, has tried to play to this schism in the disability rights movement. In 1991 it chose Robert Powell, a paraplegic, as its president. "I am concerned with the theory gaining in popularity that it is better to be dead than to be disabled," Powell said, echoing the concerns of the disability rights movement. "Many of us find it alarming that it is considered acceptable to abort an unborn child just because of disability."

Disability groups, torn among themselves and wary of compromising their effectiveness on other issues by taking sides on abortion, have sidestepped the volatile abortion debate. They will not be able to keep doing so. New research is allowing more and more conditions to be identified through genetic counseling, making more parents face the choice of selective abortion. Recombinant DNA technology now allows scientists to spot genes responsible for inherited conditions such as Duchenne and myotonic muscular dystrophy, cystic fibrosis, Huntington's disease, retinitis pigmentosa, and fragile-X syndrome. These breakthroughs carry uncharted ethical dilemmas. Could an insurance company, for instance, refuse to pay for the health costs of a child born with cystic fibrosis if the parents knew they carried the gene but had a child anyway, or knew their child carried the illness but chose not to abort? Dr. Paul Billings of California Pacific Medical Center says there have already been such cases, including that of a Houston woman who was told that her health maintenance organization would not pay for the birth of her second child with cystic fibrosis. After she objected, the health provider relented. New experiments with gene therapy and the Human Genome Project, a biological moonshot to map all the genes in the human body, may bring breakthroughs to cures but also usher in the day that parents can choose to endow children with genes for good looks, height, or superior intelligence—or choose to avoid even mildly disabling conditions.

By the time Johnson made his ruling, McAfee was in a new nursing home in Alabama. That complicated McAfee's ability to end his life, since the court order applied only to Georgia. That summer, while McAfee was pursuing his court case, a brochure had come across Hank Selinger's desk at Grady advertising a nursing home in Alabaster, Alabama, that was opening a new ventilator wing for clients who used respirators. On August 16, two days after Johnson's bedside hearing, McAfee was transferred to the Briarcliff Nursing Home, half an hour's ride south of Birmingham.

There was pressure for McAfee to end his life quickly. The state attorney general had asked the Georgia Supreme Court to set guidelines for future McAfee cases. It was possible that the higher court would overturn Judge Johnson's decision. Despite saying he still wanted to die, McAfee took no steps to be returned to Georgia. A few days before Thanksgiving, the state supreme court upheld McAfee's right to end his life. But McAfee's slowness to act seemed to prove right his opponents. They had argued that his legal suit did not reflect a sincere death wish but an angry lashing out at the way the health care system had mistreated him. This ambivalence gave a group of people an opportunity to befriend McAfee in an eleventh-hour attempt to save his life.

Pivotal in this effort was Russ Fine, who latched on to

McAfee as his defender and, no matter how sullen McAfee's moods, never let go. Fine was not a disability rights activist, although he was the director of the injury prevention research center at the University of Alabama, studying ways to prevent the kind of accidents that had made McAfee a quadriplegic. Preventable injuries, including vehicular accidents, falls, drownings, and fires, are the biggest cause of death and disablement, notes Fine. However, the most militant disability activists are wary of injury prevention specialists like Fine, since, they argue, to prevent disability is to suggest there is something pejorative about it. "We want more disabled people, not fewer," was the sardonic explanation of the late Timothy Cook, director of the National Disability Law Center, whose point was that prevention is a health issue, not a disability issue. Fine got through to McAfee in part because he did not bring a strong ideology with him. He simply wanted to show McAfee that there could be a better life. Fine made it clear from the beginning that he supported McAfee's right to end his life. But he wanted the disabled man to pursue all his options first. McAfee was openly skeptical and gave Fine little sign of encouragement. He had heard all the promises of independence before—starting at Shepherd—but found they were hollow if the only option was to live in a nursing home or a hospital ICU.

"Larry McAfee is the embodiment of everything that is wrong with the health care delivery and reimbursement system today. It is high tech and low touch," said Fine. "By that I mean we have the technology literally to resurrect the near-dead but not the additional components to address quality of life. The question becomes, Whose needs are we addressing? Are we doing it for our colleagues and professional peers just so we can go to meetings and deliver papers? Do we just want to demonstrate our prowess and expertise in maintaining life in catastrophic illness injuries, where a generation ago our predecessors couldn't do it?"

It was Fine's unconventional manner that eventually led McAfee to trust him. Despite being a health care professional himself, Fine shared McAfee's sneering impatience for the officious nursing home staffers who were constantly citing their rules and demanding that McAfee, like some naughty schoolboy, obey them or be sent back to Grady Hospital. Over the objections of the nursing home staff, Fine brought McAfee the beers and copies of *Playboy* he had been denied. He set up a VCR in McAfee's room and brought an occasional soft-porn movie, and then raised hell when the offended nurses unplugged McAfee's television. "The guy is still a young male," said Fine. "That gets to the quality-of-life issue. They're deciding what he sees. What kind of crap is that?"

Others worked to show McAfee that he could live independently. Engineer Rick Rice hooked up an environmental control system, a remote-control device that McAfee could activate with his voice in order to work the telephone and television in his nursing home room. Kirk Tcherneshoff, a paraplegic who ran the local independent living center, took him in his van on a shopping outing. Gary Edwards, the director of United Cerebral Palsy of Birmingham—who saw McAfee, like his own clients, fighting an indifferent bureaucracy to live independently— added his own vast understanding of how to wade through the social welfare funding system. His assistant, Brenda Carson, figured out ways a quadriplegic could work as an engineer.

McAfee's parents were convinced before their son was that there was a better way. Several months earlier, while sitting in a waiting room to see her son, Amelia McAfee had flipped casually through a medical magazine. A story caught her eye. It was about a Canadian quadriplegic named Walt Lawrence. He and five others—five of them respirator dependent—had left a nursing home and set up Creekview 202, a custom-built apartment suite in Vancouver. Her heart jumped. Maybe it would change her son's mind about dying. At Creekview, each of the

men had his own room with access to a balcony and a view of
mountains. The kitchen was fitted with appliances at wheelchair
level. In the bathroom there was a wheel-in shower and a bath
equipped with a hydraulic lift. A "homemaker"—an attendant—hired by the residents came into the apartment to help
cook and clean. A registered nurse was on duty for two hours
each day. All of the men worked. Two were financial investment
counselors, two were artists, another was a computer analyst.
Lawrence was about to marry and leave.

Amelia McAfee decided to try to build the Larry James
McAfee Apartments, a version of Creekview, in Atlanta. She
hoped it would make Larry want to live. Finding money would
prove frustrating. At a meeting with Governor Joe Frank Harris,
Amelia McAfee explained how Creekview had cost less than half
of the men's nursing home expenses. But the governor said the
state could do little and the McAfees were shown the door. Later
an attempt to raise the money through private donations turned
up only a few hundred dollars. More discouraging still was
McAfee's initial attitude. His mother's idea "will help some
people, but I doubt if it will help me. I've already made up my
mind," he said three months after moving to Alabama. "I'm
tired. I want to get it over with."

But with his parents and the group of activists fighting hard
to change his mind, McAfee began to waver. Particularly crucial
was another machine—a voice-activated computer that cost five
thousand dollars. With it, McAfee could put to work his training as an engineer. Bob Stockwell, a California computer specialist, saw a television news report on McAfee and flew to Alabama
to set up the computer for him. The computer was programmed
to recognize the sound of his voice. McAfee could turn it on and
off and command it to do many tasks just by speaking. With
special software, he could make sharp architectural renderings of
buildings and apartment layouts by drawing on the computer
screen with a sonar beam directed from a band strapped to his

head. He drew by moving his head, and the beam went with it. But when the computer first arrived at the nursing home, nurses would not let McAfee set it up, saying that the institution could not be "liable" for the expensive equipment in case it was stolen. Fine got McAfee's doctor to overrule the nurses and soon McAfee was practicing a few hours a day to the point that he was good enough to show off his skills to a prospective employer.

The computer excited McAfee. For the first time he talked of preferring to live, instead of dying. By February 21, 1990, when he was invited to speak before the Georgia State Senate, McAfee sounded like a full-blown disability rights activist. "Medicaid and Medicare policies that do not work in the best interest of the disabled have caused me and those like me to become prisoners of bureaucracy," said McAfee, from his wheel-chair on the floor of the senate, as Fine held a microphone to his mouth. He had been turned into a "prisoner of fate and bad luck," he said, by "a bureaucracy that will pay for the warehous-ing of the disabled but one that does not address or even consider the quality of our shattered lives."

No matter how good McAfee got on the computer, he still was destined to bounce from one nursing home to another or, worse, to go back to the ICU at Grady. After consulting with Fine and Edwards, McAfee asked for something simple: have Georgia Medicaid take the money it would pay for him to stay in a nursing home and spend it instead on the live-in attendant and other support he needed to move into his own apartment. This was similar to the idea behind the Creekview apartments his mother had read about. In Washington, Allan Bergman of the United Cerebral Palsy Associations drew up a plan for McAfee that would cost $265 a day, compared with the $475 to $650 a day that the Alabama nursing home was billing Medicare to care for McAfee. Once again, McAfee ran into the McAfee Catch. At $265 a day, it was cheaper to let McAfee live at home than in Briarcliff. But Medicare had a limit on how many days it would pay for nursing home care. After April 10, 1990, the Medicare payments to Briarcliff would end. McAfee would be the responsibility of Georgia Medicaid again, and that program still paid a skilled nursing home only $100 a day. Officials at Briarcliff made it clear that they would evict McAfee the minute the higher Medicare rate ended, rather than accept the lower $100-a-day Medicaid rate. Georgia nursing homes also continued to refuse to care for a high-quadriplegic for only $100 a day. Medicaid officials said McAfee might wind up again at Grady, although officials there did not want him. "If I go back to Grady," McAfee vowed, "I will kill myself." His parents, Fine, and Edwards felt he was sincere and saw that there was a new deadline to meet.

It was McAfee's bad luck to be disabled in Georgia. Aaron Johnson, the state commissioner of medical assistance, said it would be "prohibitively expensive" for Georgia to offer home care to people like McAfee. It cost less, he argued, to put someone in a nursing home. But McAfee could not live in a nursing home, because none would take him at Georgia's low reimbursement rate. Complained Amelia McAfee, "Prisoners get better treatment."

When the April 10 deadline arrived, McAfee was caught in a bureaucratic twilight zone. Briarcliff evicted him. Grady Hospital refused to readmit him. No Georgia nursing home would take him. Worse, Georgia Medicaid insisted that McAfee was the responsibility of Grady Hospital, since that was the last place he had lived in Georgia. Either that or the responsibility of Medicaid in Alabama, where McAfee had lived the last eight months. Grady argued he had always been the responsibility of Medicaid in Georgia. Alabama Medicaid agreed. Nor did McAfee want to fall under Alabama's program, since it was one of the few whose reimbursement to nursing homes was even less than Georgia's. McAfee was being handed off like a piece of radioactive waste; the bottom line was that he had no place to live. McAfee's newfound optimism was shattered. Edwards stepped in at the eleventh hour by putting McAfee in a United Cerebral Palsy group home. It was to be a temporary placement, for a week or two while negotiations continued with Georgia Medicaid.

Back in Atlanta, McAfee had new allies. They were the same disability rights activists who had stood outside the courthouse the previous September and angrily denounced his decision to die. On April 10, the day McAfee's Medicaid ran out, Mark Johnson led two dozen protesters to occupy the office of Georgia Medicaid director Aaron Johnson to demand home-care programs for McAfee and others with severe disabilities in the state. (By now there were three other young paraplegics at Grady, two from gunshot wounds, looking for a place to live.) "We're going to disrupt your business until you quit disrupting our lives," Mark Johnson said during a ninety-minute meeting with Aaron Johnson. From the commissioner's office, the protesters made a telephone call to McAfee in Alabama to offer words of support. Ten days later, Mark Johnson would lead a dozen demonstrators in another takeover, this time for six hours in the governor's office.

With negotiations on McAfee's fate dragging out over months, not days, Edwards's organization far outspent its budget on McAfee's housing and round-the-clock attendant care in the group home. His board members grumbled about the fiscal drain. McAfee lost more hope. At one point, visibly and understandably depressed, he was transferred to a psychiatric hospital for several weeks. McAfee's plight got national press attention, and even President Bush asked the Department of Health and Human Services, which administers Medicaid, to put pressure on Georgia.

Not until July did Aaron Johnson relent, and McAfee was able to return home to Georgia. On July 11, McAfee, in his puff-and-sip wheelchair, boarded an ambulance van and was driven to Augusta. Medicaid officials had insisted that he stay at the Medical College of Georgia Hospital for evaluation. But after a month he was moved to a new group home in Augusta, much like the apartment that had been envisioned by Amelia McAfee. There was a round-the-clock attendant, accessible bathrooms and kitchen. There was space for McAfee's computer. Within a year, a few other severely disabled Georgians moved in. Johnson said he hoped the facility would be a model for the nation. Later, Georgia started a new program to give severely disabled people money for attendant care, one that would give recipients broad control that is rare in choosing and hiring attendants. It took over a year, however, for Georgia Medicaid to buy the additional computer equipment that it promised to purchase McAfee and that delayed their helping him find work. But McAfee was freer to get in and out of the house. He took a van to go shopping. He saw his family. His mood bounced up and down, often paralleling occasional respiratory problems. But on the whole, he pronounced himself happy to be alive, living a "good" life that had given him "hope."

CHAPTER 10

CROSSING THE LUCK LINE

The cemetery at Faribault Regional Center, a state hospital for people with mental retardation, offers few clues that this is a place for burying people. I had followed the arrow on the sign, past the residents' neat red-brick households down the side road to the edge of the institution. With ease, I spotted the six-foot-tall white cross that suggested the cemetery was nearby, but it took me several minutes walking back and forth across the small field to realize that coffins were laid under my feet. No headstones jutted out from the ground to dot this graveyard. Instead, each grave was marked by a plain brown stone, a foot long and three inches wide, just big enough for a chiseled number. Each stone was set level with the soil. Once I found one—number 1216, then 1217 and 1218—I knew where to part the overgrown grass to find the others. Some 1,200 men, women, and children had been buried there, with no name, no date of birth or death, not even an epitaph to speak for their

forgotten lives. Another 487 people, those who died at Faribault
before 1924, had also been assigned anonymous digits and laid
to rest at the bottom of an adjacent hill in an inaccessible plot
overgrown with weeds and tall grass.

I had come back to Faribault in southeastern Minnesota to
find Jim, a young man whom I had befriended when I was a
college student. Jim was thirteen when we first met. He spoke
in short staccato sentences, was fascinated by wheels, and usually
kept toy cars stuffed in the pockets of his jeans. He lived at what
was then called the Faribault State Hospital for the Mentally
Retarded. (Until the 1940s, it had been the Faribault State
Hospital for the Feeble-Minded and Epileptic Colony.) Faribault
was Minnesota's first such institution. It opened to care for
"children of weak minds" in 1861. Since then, its red-brick
buildings and squat barracks-style residences have sprawled over
a sylvan 760-acre campus set among maple and pine trees.

When I first met Jim in the early 1970s, Minnesota, like
other states, wanted to empty such large institutions. Jim—he
was Jimmy then—was on a list to move out of Faribault permanently to live with a foster family or in a group home. But before
he left the institution, he needed the experience of living in a
house again, as he had before he was sent to Faribault at age six.
He needed to know what it meant to eat family-style around a
dinner table, instead of in a noisy cafeteria. He needed to sleep
in his own room, instead of in a barracks with three dozen cots
in a row. With eleven friends at nearby Carleton College, I
started a transition program for Jim and others like him at
Faribault. We moved into a rambling, three-story house. We
each "adopted" one kid and, shuttling to Faribault and back in
a turquoise Cadillac with high tail fins, we brought them for
overnight visits.

On my first trip to Faribault, in 1973, staffers had rounded
up a number of residents for us to meet, all on a list to leave for
group homes and foster families. I chose the shy, blond boy who

watched me intently. A few weeks before his fourteenth birthday, Jim made his first visit to our house. For me, it was a
bone-tiring, mind-blurring event. Jim was in perpetual motion,
wild with curiosity and drunk on the excitement of a new place
and new freedom. He dashed up the three flights of the curved
wooden stairs through our Victorian-era house, with me always
a few steps behind trying vainly to catch up. He dove through
doors, into bedrooms, exploring unfamiliar rooms and examin-
ing drawers and desk tops as if they were treasure mines. He
sought out anything that was round—the casters on the bottom
of a bed frame, a hockey puck left on the floor. He did not
communicate. My questions were answered with silence. He
eyed me with suspicion; he made noises. If he spoke, his sentences were never longer than one word. I wondered whether I
had made a mistake. But over the next few weeks, we connected.
Jim's shyness eased and he talked more. I looked forward to our
time together as much as he did. When the year ended, I felt
guilty leaving him (although another student continued to bring
him to campus for the next two years).

At the end of the year, five of our twelve kids had moved into
foster homes or group homes. Jim was not one of them, but he
remained high on the list to leave.

Sixteen years had passed and I had lost track of Jim. Neatly,
the beginning of the disability rights movement could be traced
back to about the time I had last seen him. As I wrote about the
quickening changes in the lives of disabled people, I thought
often about the last time I had seen Jim at our college house. He
had brought an Erector Set to build a go-cart big enough to ride
in. I, along with my housemates, puzzled over the disjointedly
written instructions. Between us—Phi Beta Kappas and magna
cum laudes—we could not figure out which bolts screwed into
what metal plate to keep the cart sturdy. After waiting patiently
for us for well over an hour, Jim tired of our ineptitude. He
threw a small tantrum. We had tried our best, I explained to

him softly. Then I left him on the porch to cool down. When I came back a few minutes later, Jim was sitting on the go-cart he had assembled correctly by himself. He could not read the instructions and he had trouble verbalizing his thoughts. But Jim was mechanically gifted, perhaps a mechanical savant.

To find Jim, who would be thirty by now, I had started with a telephone call to Colleen Wieck in St. Paul. As head of the Minnesota Governor's Planning Council on Developmental Disabilities, Wieck is nationally respected as a champion for the rights of people with retardation. There were three possibilities for Jim, she explained. "The worst-case fear is that he is still at Faribault," she had warned. "The next-worse case, but probably the most likely, is that he is in some large group home setting where no one cares about him. The best thing would be if some really good case manager found him, cared about him, and got him into a small group home or on his own and into a good job."

It took just a few phone calls before I tracked down Jim. It was the "worst case": After sixteen years, Jim was still at Faribault.

Now less than one month after I had located him, I was back at Faribault, walking through the unsettling cemetery and collecting my thoughts in the moments before my reunion with Jim. I had come to Faribault to see if he wanted to get out of the institution and if I could help. I was there to spend a few days with Jim, showing him group homes and job programs that could allow him to work and live independently. He had never seen these things before. His social worker at Faribault had told me on the phone that Jim spoke often of wanting to move "into the community," even if he was not precisely sure what that phrase meant. When I had last seen Jim, there were some twelve hundred people at Faribault. Now there were five hundred. There were long waiting lists to get out. Money was tight, and coveted slots in group homes were scarce. Jim, unlike many of those who had managed to leave, did not have any family members or friends acting as his advocate. Consequently, he had fallen between the cracks in the system and remained at the institution where death still meant an unmarked grave in the cemetery.

At Faribault, a volunteer coordinator led me to a darkened canteen. When I walked in, Jim fixed on me an intense and curious stare. The look was familiar. So too was his smile, broad and easy, when we recognized each other. We sat at a bench, and I pulled out photos from our last time together, when Jim had deftly assembled the Erector Set go-cart. Jim was tanned, with muscular arms from working on a lawn crew. His hair was blond but thinner. He still carried a toy wheel. If anything, though, Jim now looked older than I did, despite the six-year difference in our ages. There were crow's-feet around his eyes, and he squinted hard when he looked at the photographs. He had been fitted with glasses several years before for his advancing near-sightedness, but he had refused to wear them. He seemed smaller than his five feet, six inches, partly because of his thin frame and stooped shoulders.

Over the next three days, I was reminded over and over why I had enjoyed Jim so much and had found him so intriguing. Our first evening together we went to a county fair in nearby Owatonna to watch noisy sprint cars race around a damped-down dirt track. Jim picked his favorite car on the basis of its white wheel rims. We went on some of the carnival rides. On the bumper cars, Jim showed that, somehow, he had learned how to drive. Must bumper car riders like to crash into each other, but Jim got more kicks from avoiding being hit. He expertly eluded me and other riders in his small red car. He took turns sharply and instinctively seemed to know just when to slow down or speed up. His mind was at work on other rides, too. On the Thunder Bolt, Jim casually studied how our small car was suspended from the ride's center frame and how the gears and levers rocked us and swung us around. We went to see *Days of Thunder,*

the Tom Cruise film about a stock-car driver. Jim reveled in the
film, particularly the fast-paced race track scenes.

On our last day together, Jim took me to his storage area,
a small room under the cottage that had been set aside for him
to keep tires, bicycle frames, and wood. From these, he made
sophisticated go-carts patterned after sleek Grand Prix racers
with steering mechanisms and real tires bolted to axles. One of
the counselors in his household had shown Jim an old *National
Geographic* photo of the *Gossamer Condor,* the bicycle-powered
glider that had been flown in 1979. From memory, Jim had
begun constructing a model of it. He made a ten-foot-long
wingspan of light cardboard covered with evenly spaced wire
loops to hold the gauzy wing sail and built a light wooden crate
to hold the bicycle and rider. The storage room was Jim's magi-
cal laboratory. It was a narrow, concrete bunker, dimly lit by
sunlight that pushed through a small ground-level window.
Here, Jim's mind seemed to whir at one hundred miles a minute,
thinking out designs for new cars. I could not follow his plotting. He started laying out pieces of wood on the floor, asking
for my pen to mark where he wanted to cut.

I learned more about how Jim had come to be a ward of the
state. Going through his record file, I discovered that Jim was
born in October 1959, the fifth of nine children, to a struggling
Minneapolis laborer and his wife. Jim's parents had divorced two
years before he was born but continued to live together. According to a sketchy social history written in blue mimeograph ink,
"Reports from the Hennepin County General Hospital suggests
[*sic*] that he was 'abandoned' between age one and two." By the
time Jim was two, it was clear he was hyperactive. At age three,
his mother found him under the kitchen sink, trying to figure
out how to detach the drainpipe. At age four, he began running
away from home. At six he had darted into traffic and been badly
injured by a car.

A few months later, in February 1966, Jim was placed in
Mrs. Ontko's boardinghouse for troubled children in Minneapo-

lis. But Mrs. Ontko and her neighbors were soon complaining that Jim could not be controlled. He ripped the upholstery, the proprietress told social workers, and ran away frequently, only to be returned by police. Testing showed that he had an IQ under 30. A University of Minnesota child psychiatrist examined Jim and concluded: "The final diagnosis was mental deficiency, idiopathic, severe." On September 22, 1966, the board of examiners for the Hennepin County Probate Court held a "hearing on mental deficiency or epilepsy" to decide whether to institutionalize Jim. His mother attended. The examiners determined Jim to be "mentally deficient." By the first week of October—several days short of his seventh birthday—"emergency space" was made available to admit him to Faribault.

The institution was a brutal place for residents labeled severely retarded, like Jim. This was chronicled by University of Minnesota psychologist Travis Thompson, who came to work there in 1968. Thompson asked to work with the toughest residents and was taken to Dakota Building, where the institution kept what it called the "high profounds." "I was confronted with sights, sounds and smells which I had never before experienced and hoped that I would never witness again," the young psychologist later wrote. "Seated in the middle of a large ward area, shackled to a chair, was a young man in his twenties, all of his skin abraded from his knees and blood running down his shins. Along the seventy-foot wall of the ward were seated approximately fifteen men, huddled in fetal positions, with their heads between their knees." Thompson described finding sixty-seven residents in the crowded room, sitting in urine and feces, rocking or walking aimlessly, or running around the walls of the room. Some were naked or nearly naked. Others gnawed their hands or twiddled their fingers in front of their faces. That night, when he got home to his shower, Thompson washed his body for a half hour, trying to get the acrid smell of the ward out of his skin.

Thompson worked to train these "high profounds," using

positive behavior modification techniques that would later be imitated at other institutions. For every task completed, no matter how small, a resident was given a reward. When Thompson began his work, 65 percent of the men on the ward did not use toilets. At the end of a year, 81 percent did. Half did not wear clothing in the beginning, but 91 percent did after a year. Forty percent did not feed themselves at first, but 95 percent could eat with a spoon after twelve months. Many, too, were heavily drugged. Seventy-nine percent, he found, were given daily doses of strong tranquilizers. After a year of Thompson's behavior modification, only 56 percent needed drugs, a total that eventually dropped to 20 percent. Any normal person left in Dakota for six months, Thompson told a reporter at the time, would no longer be normal. "They would fit in with the crowd, rocking and rocking, sitting in their own feces."

Faribault's most famous resident was Bill Sackter, whose story was portrayed by actor Mickey Rooney in the Emmy Award–winning television movie *Bill*. Sackter had been labeled "imbecilic" at the age of seven and sent to the institution, where he would spend forty-four harsh years. He was physically abused and put to hard work pushing food trays. Poor medical care resulted in chronic leg ulcerations that would persist throughout his life. "I was there so long I didn't know I was there" was the way Sackter put it to Barry Morrow, who would later chronicle his life for television. An aide—"the mean one," Sackter would explain—had thrown him down a flight of stairs by his hair, yanking out a bloody clump of his scalp. Sackter thought this injury had something to do with his being "crack-brained," and he wore a hat or an ill-fitting wig to cover the scar. Released to a Minneapolis group home in the late 1960s, Sackter eventually got work scrubbing pots in a country club kitchen. There he met and befriended Morrow, an aspiring young filmmaker whose wife, Bev, was a waitress at the club. Sackter moved with the Morrows to Iowa City and ran Wild Bill's Coffee Shop at the

University of Iowa until his death, at seventy, in 1983. The Minnesota Department of Public Welfare then billed Sackter's estate (which had no money) for $10,000 to reimburse the care he got at Faribault.

When I first volunteered at Faribault in 1973, Jim slept in a large barracks with three dozen closely spaced beds. He had no place to keep private property. The Christmas presents I sent Jim that year were all stolen within a few days. Meals were served in a clamorous cafeteria, a cavernous room with linoleum floors and tile walls that reverberated the shouts and scraping of dinnerware on hard plastic food trays. Flypaper strips hung from the walls. Before every meal, Jim washed his hands in a common bowl of disinfectant and warm water, a procedure to kill the bacteria that cause dysentery, a problem at Faribault and other institutions. Some residents, children as well as adults, were even less fortunate, passing the daylight hours tied to chairs and beds. Some wailed and screamed incessantly. While Jim attended what passed for a school, where he received the most rudimentary education, adults at Faribault generally passed day after day with nothing to do.

By the time I was reunited with Jim in 1990, he was living in a two-story brick building called Osage, the same cottage where he had been sixteen years before, but there were only twelve men on the wing, now called a "household." Jim slept in a small room with three other men. While one bed was less than five feet from his, he had his own posters of sleek Ferraris and a 1960 Chevy Belair on the wall, as well as his own television, which he had purchased with $190 he made from his work on the lawn crew. From 8:30 A.M. until 2 P.M., five days a week, Jim and several other Faribault residents cut grass and trimmed lawns in town or, in winter, cleared snow. Jim's salary: $2.88 an hour, below the minimum wage but higher than what many similarly disabled people earn. Jim was free, during the four hours after work and before dinner, to roam the grounds of the institution. He would take his new blue bike down to the Nature Center or to the woods, or spend his free time in the woodshop, making cars out of wood and junk.

For the most part, the professional staff at Faribault clearly seemed to care for Jim. Ben Weeks, the soft-spoken shop director, had welcomed Jim, instructed him, given him the freedom to experiment with tools and materials, and then exulted over his inventions. But the month before I arrived, the shop had been placed off-campus, ending Jim's use of it. His job coach, Lori Johnson, would occasionally bring Jim for dinner over the weekend. Corinne Fowler, who supervised the Osage cottage, was another admirer of Jim's. Deb Lenway, a cottage counselor, was Jim's "one-on-one," the staffer who took Jim shopping for clothes and wheels and out for dinner on his birthday. She knew Jim better than anyone. Others, too, tried to make Osage as nice a place as possible to live. One night when we came back, a staffer had made Rice Krispies bars, which Jim ate with milk before going to bed.

Yet at the same institution there were constant reminders that residents could be stripped of the respect and dignity automatically given any other adult. A few weeks after my visit, the Rice County district attorney brought criminal abuse charges against four Faribault counselors. Mark Kern, according to charges laid out in a police criminal complaint and an internal social services department report, had abused one man by pouring a chemical cleaner on his genitals and fed chili powder and hot jalapeño peppers to other residents "for kicks." The twenty-five-year-old Kern was also accused of blowing powdered dish detergent—which he jokingly referred to as "nose candy"—through a straw into the nostrils of two other men, who reacted with "uncontrollable sneezing that would last for about thirty minutes," according to the social services department report.

At trial, prosecutor Karen Lewis said Kern had taken an undiluted industrial cleanser, one so corrosive that he had to don heavy rubber gloves to pour it into his hands, and spread it over the genitals of a resident identified as K.S.H. The man had seemed to annoy Kern solely because he was severely retarded and black. Twice, a doctor had noted the burns on K.S.H.'s raw scrotum and his painful walking but had let the matter drop.

The prosecution went disastrously. K.S.H. did not have the ability to communicate what had happened to him, and Kern's close-knit colleagues refused to testify against him although, according to the complaint, Kern had freely bragged of his tortures. It was only by accident that the allegations had become public at all. A nurse at the cottage had retired. At a pub to toast her departure, after liquor had flowed freely, she mentioned that she had seen some terrible things and was glad to be leaving. Her supervisor, among the revelers, passed on her allegations to Faribault's superintendent, who, as required by law, called in the local police to investigate. The state had pushed the issue largely because the sister of one of the alleged victims was a state social worker who knew the system. The nurse who had begun the process with her farewell "confession" was Kern's aunt and seemed reluctant to testify against him in court.

When a jury acquitted Kern, prosecutor Lewis dropped the remaining cases and complained that she had been stymied by a "code of silence" on the Faribault campus. A subsequent investigation by the state ombudsman for mental health and mental retardation found that staffers routinely failed to report abuse, because they either did not take it seriously or feared retaliation from their coworkers. Indifferent institution officials, the report concluded, had been guilty of a "failure . . . to provide a clear message that abuse and neglect of clients is not tolerated."

How, then, could the two types of staffers—some nurturing and professional, the others uncaring and sadistic—exist at the same place? Many, I knew, had valued having a job where they could help people in need. At Faribault, which was unionized, these workers received good salaries, which attracted many skilled staffers and kept turnover at a relatively low level. But Faribault also attracted a large number of others—unskilled workers who received virtually no training when they got hired—for whom this was simply a better-paying job than other options, such as working in one of the town's many fast-food restaurants. Many at Faribault had worked at both.

The ultimate problem, however, was the nature of the institution itself. It had evolved from the model of a prison, not a home, so there was a tacit license to disrespect the "inmates." The bottom line was that Jim was considered a deviant in need of rehabilitation. Everything he did was regulated, from the moment he woke up until he went to sleep at night, a carryover from the behavior-modification techniques Thompson had instituted in the late 1960s. Every morning when Jim woke up a staff person was required to give him the following instruction: "Jim, you are to get dressed, wash your hands and face, brush your teeth, shave, comb your hair, make your bed, and straighten up your room. When you've finished with all of these you are free to do what you want to until 8:30 A.M., when you must be at work." This precise wording was laid out in the "Goal Implementation Form for Problem Behavior" that I found in Jim's file. When he got up he was handed his "token recording sheet" for the day. When he completed a listed task in a "complete" and "compliant" way, such as getting dressed, shaving, or making his bed neatly, he got a smiley face or a check. Those were counted toward tokens that allowed him privileges such as sodas or his beloved free time in the woodshop. When he "misbehaved"—did not do something on time or displayed anger over being required to do the task—he lost his privileges. His goal-implementation form, which was updated yearly, ran for five pages. It regulated everything that he did during the day, from specifying what time he was to wash his hands down to the minute he was expected to check in with his supervisors. If Jim did not check in at 9 A.M., 12:45 P.M., and again at 6:45 P.M., a staffer was ordered to "search immediately" for him and return him to the building.

As a condition for continued use of his storage space, Jim was to keep the basement room neat. An agreement with his counselors specified that he was to sweep the area each week and keep no more than twelve tires and four bike frames there at any one time. At a weekly inspection, a staffer was to find "no dirt or debris on floor." Similar good housekeeping habits were expected in his small bedroom. All of his clothes were to be hung neatly on hangers. There was to be "no dust on shelves or top of wardrobe" and no loose paper left on top of his television cabinet. He was to do these tasks up to fifteen times without fail in order to prove he could master these chores.

Jim kept his storage area tidy, with wood stacked up on wood and go-cart frames leaning against the wall. Jim had even figured out how to cover the basement drain with heavy electrical tape so that after heavy rains water would not back up into the small room and soak his projects. Looking at the small, clean room, I realized I would not fare nearly so well if social workers paraded through my home each week to see that I had dusted precisely and not kept piles of mail and paper lying around.

Even Jim's work productivity was carefully measured: how often he worked a machine properly, set up the materials he needed for work, and notified a supervisor when he had a problem. Jim was a hard worker. "Jim has a strong ethic," Ben Weeks in the workshop told me. "You show him how to do it and he'll do it right every time." According to his file, Jim had an 86 percent "productivity rate." That is, he did every last detail correctly almost all the time.

Yet because Jim's actions were so exactly measured, officials at the institution tended to see his life largely in terms of faults and problems that needed fixing. Jim's abilities—as well as the things that made him an interesting individual—were obscured behind this obsession with the negative. That was clear from reading Jim's file. There, officials at the institution justified why Jim had to live at Faribault and was not ready to live on his own. In short, Jim was deemed a troublemaker. His supervisors wrote that Jim displayed "physically aggressive and destructive behaviors" and that he often "threatened" people verbally. "These behaviors are most prevalent when he does not get something he wants immediately, is not allowed to do something he wants to do, or is required to do something he does not wish to do," said his report. The system of tokens and regulations was designed to break Jim of these behaviors that officials at Faribault considered sociopathic.

Jim's threats, not surprisingly, revolved around cars. His most dire menace was to say, "I'm going to throw rocks at your car" or "I'm going to take the wheels off your car." This was his way of cursing, of venting frustration. In the daily "progress notes" his counselors kept on Jim, I read of one incident a few days before spring when the snow was still piled high in Minnesota. At the evening dinner table, one of Jim's housemates noted that it was going to snow again. Jim "got very upset" and told the housemate to "shut up," the counselor wrote. "He said he didn't like snow, he wanted summer to come. So then I told Jim that he wasn't being very polite, and that I wanted summer to come too." Jim did not like that response and told the counselor that he would "break" his car. That was the kind of seemingly minor irritation that got written up and tracked. Another counselor was more charitable in writing up Jim's maledictions. "Ate breakfast with Jim," says his curt entry. "Threatened to take the wheels off my car. Called it rusty, an accurate statement."

Jim's counselors could proudly tell me how many of these so-called threats he had made. In 1990, there had been nine in March, then fifty-two in April, and only three in May. Nobody could tell me what it was that had bothered

Jim so much in April; nobody had even tried to figure it out.

I had come to Minnesota to show Jim a program called Opportunity Services, which would place him in a job and give him an alternative to living in the institution. Jim's behavior— the aggression, the threats, the destruction of property— sounded pretty serious, but Nancy Gurney, the director of Opportunity Services, just laughed them off. In only a few years, her private nonprofit group had taken hundreds of clients out of Faribault and other state institutions and placed them in jobs. Time and time again, Gurney had picked up a client's file to find the client labeled aggressive, threatening, or worse. Almost always, Gurney assured me, such behaviors disappeared quickly once the person left the institution. "When they walk onto a job site, they see that the other people, who do not have retardation, just do not act that way," said Gurney. "So they stop, too." Jim's threats were a "learned behavior" at Faribault, Gurney said. It was what he had to do to get attention.

Nevertheless, Jim's supervisors at Faribault, starting in the fall of 1989, had begun to chart Jim's incidents of "aggression" and "property destruction." The goal, as laid out in Jim's "monthly maladaptive program progress review," was to cut these incidents down to zero per month for three consecutive months. Before he could be considered a candidate to leave Faribault, officials argued that he had to meet this standard. There had been one particular incident that had led to this intense monitoring of Jim's behavior. In September of 1989, a Faribault social worker backed her black pickup truck out of the parking lot one evening, and the truck's back wheel fell off. Jim was the immediate suspect. After all, of everyone on the Faribault campus, only Jim was considered clever enough to figure out how to loosen the lug nuts of a truck tire. Jim had been angry with the woman, and he had been seen near her car, although no one witnessed him tampering with it. According to Faribault's records when confronted with the evidence, Jim "confessed" and said he wanted to apologize. The penalty was severe. Jim was to make restitution out of his monthly paycheck for damages to the truck. He was to be placed on twenty-four-hour restriction if he was absent without leave, caught stealing, entered an unauthorized area—like the woodshop, where he sometimes went after hours—or threw rocks at anyone's car.

The incident only added to Jim's reputation around campus for his obsession with wheels and his mechanical brilliance. One result was that whenever someone saw what appeared to be new damage to their car, Jim took the rap. Mike Sheady, Jim's social worker at Faribault, told me that a few months earlier Jim had been blamed for scratches found on another staffer's car. But when, after investigation, it became clear that Jim could not have been involved, the complaint was dropped. Similarly, if a workman misplaced a tool, or something could not be found in a workshop, it was often concluded that Jim had stolen it. I asked Sheady if Jim had been caught with any stolen tools. He could not remember any recent incidents but added that it was assumed that Jim kept purloined goods in secret hideaways that he was said to have fashioned in the woods around the institution. There was no report in Jim's file over the last year of his being caught with stolen goods, although on one occasion he was caught trying to get into a locked classroom. I heard a lot about Jim's alleged thefts. But when I found Weeks, the former high school shop teacher said such reports had been exaggerated and that he knew of no case of Jim ever stealing tools.

I did hear one story of how the campus gardener took off his boots, left them at the entrance to the greenhouse, and later found them missing. They showed up on Jim's feet. It struck me as a creative use of "found" shoes, since Jim's own were always in miserable shape, with holes, mismatched, broken laces, and the leather rubbed so raw that it no longer had color. I also came to wonder about what must have been Jim's different notion of property. Clothing had once been communal, and over the years, even now, his possessions were routinely stolen. He now had his locked storage room and a key to his closet in the bedroom. When I sent Jim something—photos from a recent visit, a wheel, or a tool—I would call to see if he had received it. "I've still got it" was Jim's inevitable reply. To this man who had grown up without privacy, property was something temporary and passing.

Nothing underscored the system's negative attitude toward its clients more than all the excuses made for keeping Jim at Faribault. Where would he keep all the tires and wood he collected? A group home, Sheady told me, would not have enough room. ("That's easy to solve," said Gurney. "We can buy him a $100 tool shed from Sears.") Larry Hall, Jim's home-county social worker, explained that state law required that an effort be made to place Jim in the county where his family lived—Hennepin County, which included Minneapolis. But Hennepin County, Hall explained, was not right for Jim. He needed a rural area, someplace where he could ride his bike around freely. In a group house in an urban setting, Hall argued, Jim "could be talked into doing something wrong." There was another reason to keep him away from Minneapolis, Hall explained. Jim's parents feared he was shrewd enough to figure out where they lived. After cutting off contact with Jim, they did not want to find him on their doorstep.

Jim was a ward of the state, and Hall was his legal guardian. Employed by the Hennepin County department of community services, Hall ultimately made decisions for Jim. Hall said he knew of no suitable placements for Jim. I told Hall about Opportunity Services, which could place Jim in rural Minnesota, not too far and not too close to the Twin Cities. I asked Hall to join me when I visited. But when I got to Minneapolis, Hall told me he would not approve of Jim's going into the Opportunity Services program. Now Hall had decided Jim should be in Minneapolis after all. "I'm hoping," he explained, "there can be some kind of reconciliation with the family."

It had been nearly six years since Jim had last seen his mother or siblings. Jim's father had left instructions several years before not to be contacted about Jim. There had been no family Christmases, birthdays, or visits on "family day" at the institution. His mother, I was told, had asked the staff at Faribault not to let Jim call her on the phone. He had last seen her in a brief visit on Thanksgiving Day six years before. Jim, according to Hall, had "trashed" her home in Minneapolis. His offense: he had pulled down the living room drapes. Looking through Jim's file, I realized that a significant event in his life had occurred a few days before the incident. Jim had been recommitted to Faribault. By law, the state had been required to go to court to determine whether Jim should be let out of the institution or placed in a group home. Jim's mother had told a social worker that Jim was "happy and content at Faribault State Hospital and views it as his home." Jim had told the same worker that he "wants to go [to a group home] in about three years."

Today, the only people going into institutions are adults whose parents die or are too old to keep caring for them. Had Jim been born in the 1990s instead of in 1959, he would have stayed with his family and likely would have gone to the same schools as his brothers and sisters. As an adult, he would have moved into a group home or his own apartment and worked with nondisabled people in a job where he got individual attention from a job coach. In Jim's case, he could have worked in a family business. When I looked in the Minneapolis phone book, I found an auto body shop owned by one of his brothers. Jim's mechanical genius seemed to be a family trait. I drove by the low-level brick garage on a busy city street, watched a tow-truck drive in, and wondered how different Jim's life would have been had he been born in a more generous time.

Given his fascination with cars and wheels, Jim would be a natural candidate for a job in a garage. The women who run

Opportunity Services realized this, too. Their program, based out of Red Wing, a pretty Mississippi River town fifty-five miles southeast of the Twin Cities, had a reputation for creatively tailoring jobs to the skills and desires of its clients. That is how Jim got to an auto garage in Red Wing.

Conveniently, it was owned by the husband of Jill Bengs, who ran Opportunity Services' employment program in Red Wing. When we arrived, Tim Bengs was working under a car hoisted on a hydraulic lift, adjusting the brakes on the back wheel drum. Jim watched intently, fingering one of the small plastic car wheels he usually carried with him. In the back room, where Tim Bengs stored rows of black rubber tires, Jim leaned over to stroke them, as if they were pets. He liked the smell and feel of the rubber and the thumping sound the hollow tube made when he hit it. Jim was enough of a tire connoisseur immediately to spot two round, stocky tires as belonging to a race car. We also visited other Opportunity Services job sites: a restaurant where workers washed dishes and prepared food; a high school where they mopped and dusted; a day-care center where they prepared lunch; and a children's clothing factory where they prepared material for seamstresses. Jim seemed most interested in the job where there were many other nondisabled people around.

Our last stop of the day was at a group home. The rambling ranch-style house had a wood-beamed roof and quiet gardens. It felt relaxed and homey. One resident helped the staff cook dinner, another woman sat and watched the woods outside, another man listened to music. Some residents had their own rooms. Jim was impressed by the neatly kept bedrooms, with pictures on the walls and possessions nearby. At one point, Jim put his arm around Joyce Syverson of Opportunity Services and said softly, "I want to live here."

The next day, I told Sheady, Jim's social worker at Faribault, about Jim's thrill at visiting the auto shop. The social worker had one reaction: "Did Jimmy steal anything?"

That type of negative thinking had kept Jim in the institution for many years. But there was a force at play that seemed to guarantee that Jim would one day get out, no matter how unresponsive the bureaucracy. That change, too, was clear to me as I walked through the cemetery of numbered graves.

Seventy yards from the graveyard, I watched workmen sweating to roll out a new silver chain-link fence. The state institution for people with retardation was being turned into a state prison. With crime rising across the country, Minnesota, like other states, had run out of places to incarcerate men and women. A few months earlier, a small group of minimum-security prisoners had been moved into some of the Faribault buildings. The week after my walk through the burial ground, the first group of medium-security inmates would be transferred to the red-brick buildings behind the new fence.

Faribault's population had reached 3,250 in 1958, a time when there was scurrying to build new residences and hire extra staff. Now only five hundred people lived there, so it made sense to fill the emptying buildings with prison inmates. The state had adopted a plan to reduce the number of disabled residents to eighty by the year 2000 and increase the prison population to one thousand. There was a logic, too, in placing criminals and people with retardation side-by-side. Both prisons and state hospitals cut people off from family, friends, and community and constrict their liberties and freedoms. Each seeks to change a person's behavior and personality through isolation, solitude, and regimentation. Both institutions had come out of the same nineteenth-century reformist instinct, notes historian David Rothman, to protect the new American society from deviant people, while at the same time demonstrating the society's generosity in seeking to rehabilitate them. Indeed, under the agreement worked out between the state and Faribault's unions, workers would be offered jobs in the new prison. It was clear that

Jim would leave Faribault sooner or later. It would be easier, I knew, for him to make the transition at thirty-one than at forty-one.

The long-held idea of people with disabilities being deviants is fading only slowly. I wanted to help Jim build on his many strengths to live in the community and work in a job where he would utilize his amazing mechanical skills. But to do so I needed to convince the people in his life to see him in a new and more positive way.

It was this task that brought me back to Minnesota a second time, in October of 1990. At about the time I was reconnecting with Jim, his Aunt Evelyn, inspired by friends with a daughter at Faribault, had sought him out, too. Several weeks before my first trip back to Faribault she had gone there to visit Jim on Family Day. It was the first time since Jim had arrived at the institution in 1966 that anyone from his family had gone to visit him.

I debated calling Evelyn and other members of Jim's family. Jim's family could, after all these years, prefer that he stay out of sight and out of mind in the institution. Even though they had long given up guardianship, their wishes, by state law, could derail any attempt to get Jim into his own apartment. But I knew, most of all, that Jim missed his family. At the end of my first trip I had told Jim that I was leaving to go to Minneapolis, where I would catch my flight back to Washington. "Minneapolis," Jim said in his soft, broken way of speaking. "My mother. Five or six years." I knew what these cryptic fragments meant: his mother lived in Minneapolis and it had been five and a half years since he had visited her.

I decided to contact Evelyn and called her from Washington to invite her to drive to Faribault with me on my return visit. She had thought about her nephew often since seeing him that spring and wished she could do more for him. So early on a clear, brisk Sunday in mid-October, Evelyn was waiting for me on the stoop outside her apartment building just south of downtown Minneapolis. As I drove up, she came down the stairs, a slight woman with pale skin and wavy gray hair.

On the hour-long drive to Faribault, Evelyn told me more about Jim's family history. It was a different, more sympathetic, portrait than I had heard from Jim's social worker. When Jim was young, his father ran a bar and his mother had helped out. But the parents had found their family had grown too big, too fast. There was little money and no child care.

Jim was hyperactive and hard to handle. But his parents had fought to keep him. When social workers had come to take Jim, his parents, too, had been labeled incompetent. In the confusing, belittling swirl of bureaucracy, they had been unable to save their different son. For years, Evelyn recalled, Jim's mother cried at the mention of Jim's name.

Jim's brothers and sisters, I learned from Evelyn, seemed to share Jim's mechanical skills and sometimes even his fascination with wheels, cars, trucks, and all things round. The oldest brother was the mechanic who had recently given up his garage. The oldest sister was a city bus driver. Another brother had studied engineering. The youngest, a brother, was a gifted artist, who, like Jim, had the ability to imagine something in his head and then create it.

Evelyn told me about seeing Jim, who usually carries a wheel or something round, clutching an orange Frisbee. "Jimmy reminded me so much of his Uncle Fortune. You've heard about his Uncle Fortune, of course," she asked. Taken aback when I said I hadn't, she replied, "Oh, Jim's Uncle Fortune. He won a medal in the Olympics. He was a discus thrower."

When I had invited her to ride with me to Faribault, Evelyn was anxious to get some of Jim's siblings to come as well. It would be the first time ever that someone from Jim's immediate family had gone to Faribault to see him. There had been the rare visits by Jim to Minneapolis to see his family, the most recent engineered by Evelyn. Jim, with his peers at Faribault, had gone on an outing to a park in Minneapolis, one week after my reunion with him. Evelyn had pleaded with two of Jim's sisters, Peggy and Julie, to go with her to see him there. When they saw him, the sisters made a fuss over Jim, his large hands, and his friendly manner. Peggy and Julie had not seen Jim in several years. They had been fearful of what they would find. One of the sisters had told a Faribault staffer that day in the park, "We expected him to be a vegetable."

Their confusion was understandable. For much of Jim's life, doctors at Faribault had labeled him "profoundly retarded." The family had been told they could not do anything for him. It was an unfortunate simplification that had kept Jim's siblings from knowing him. It was true that, when he was admitted to Faribault, Jim's IQ had tested out at below 30. But IQ tests are often misleading at best and meaningless at worst. A test of intelligence meant little if the person, like Jim, had trouble verbalizing answers. Jim's inability to respond had been taken as not knowing. By his teens, Jim would be reclassified as "moderately mentally retarded." But even that was a stingy label, given his mechanical brilliance. Today, tests might not label Jim as "retarded" but show him to have a "severe learning disability" or an exaggerated form of dyslexia, says Colleen Wieck, the Minnesota advocate who helped me and befriended Jim. Years of living in an unstimulating institution may have exaggerated Jim's disability. Little was expected of Jim intellectually, and he may have imitated the bad behaviors he saw around him. That was why it was so important to get Jim out of Faribault and into a more natural and challenging environment. At one state institution, I had met a resident who had never been labeled retarded, but she had been sent away in 1941 because she was a wild teenager, constantly in minor trouble. Fifty years later she seemed to have the same retardation as her roommates.

During the course of the October visit with Evelyn and Jim's siblings, Jim's family began to understand that his intelligence was not easily described, and that the loaded label *retarded* sold him short.

Vegetable was the label Jim's family had used. It reminded me of an equally inaccurate and ugly word I had once used: "Zombie." I had never worked with people with retardation before I joined my college friends in the project that led me to Jim. Shortly before moving into the house, however, I had second thoughts. With fears of the demanding academic year ahead, I confessed to a friend uneasily as I headed back to school that September, "I'm worried about coming home after a long day to a house full of Zombies."

My prejudice was the result of ignorance. Like Jim's family, I had no idea what people who had been closeted in institutions would be like. I had only stereotypes and labels to fall back on. I wanted to do a good deed, an act of charity. Soon I would learn that friendship with Jim and the others was rewarding in its own right. The dozen kids who visited us from Faribault were lively, curious, fun, and loving. Each had his or her own talents and distinctive personality. Their delight in their biweekly taste of freedom and family-style living made all of us in Prentice House a little less self-absorbed with our classwork and a lot more relaxed each night.

Evelyn and I drove to Faribault on the day before Jim's thirty-first birthday. When we arrived at Osage at midday, Jim was waiting for us in the bedroom, lying on his bed and watching a football game on his 12" television. The other men in the household watched the same game on the large television in the common room. Jim wore a short-sleeved white shirt, not tucked in, with broad red stripes. He threw on a wrinkled old navy windbreaker, which he buttoned all the way up. Peggy, Julie, and Rob, one of Jim's brothers, were driving separately. Never having been to the institution, they got lost and showed up an hour after Evelyn and I arrived. Jim greeted them eagerly, although with casualness, as if he saw his brother and sisters every week. If he felt any anger at not seeing them in so long, he did not show it. Jim held hands with his sisters and his aunt and slung his arm around his brother's shoulders.

We went to a restaurant for lunch. After the initial nervousness wore off, Peggy and Julie fussed about Jim's chapped lips, sunburnt and lined face, the effects of working outdoors. Jim resembled his siblings, all blond, attractive, and fair-skinned. Back at the institution, Jim sat on his narrow bed, opening the birthday cards from Peggy, Julie, and Rob. He beamed, happy to be the center of his family's love and attention.

The moment that forever changed the family's understanding of Jim came when I suggested that he take us to his basement storage room where he kept his completed projects and works in progress. A high-backed wheelchair of wood, with two bicycle wheels on the back and two small wooden casters on the front, looked clumsy. But Jim maneuvered it smoothly across the concrete floor. Evelyn pulled out her Instamatic camera and flash bulbs to take a picture of it, so that she could show a few friends of hers who used wheelchairs. Julie picked up what looked like a bicycle pedal enclosed in a small wood frame. Jim explained that it was a part to his pedal-powered flying machine. He showed her the cardboard-and-wire wingspan he had assembled and then pointed out the wooden frame for the pilot and his bicycle. He told her he realized the frame was too heavy and that he needed to find a way to make it lighter for it to fly. Jim discussed these things with an almost studied casualness. He kept his right hand tucked in his pocket and pointed with his left, as if he were a college professor speaking from a lectern in the science hall auditorium.

I watched the stunned looks on the faces of Evelyn, Peggy, Julie, and Rob. "Jimmy, can you fix that bicycle?" asked Rob, pointing to a broken one in a corner. Only several weeks before, Jim's siblings had thought him a "vegetable." Now they were trying to figure out if he could work in a bicycle repair shop. It was an entirely correct way to be thinking about him.

It was David Hancox, who ran a Minnesota program to teach parents of children with disabilities how to pressure school boards, health agencies, and other parts of the bureaucracy, who told me about Personal Futures Planning. Families in Minnesota were successfully using futures planning to help people with retardation set long-term goals for themselves. The idea was to bring together a small group of people who cared about Jim— who would advocate for him and could see him positively—to brainstorm with him about how he could fulfill his dreams. The point was to build a group of friends who would make the system work for him.

The team would plan for his future by putting Jim—his wants, his needs, his desires—first. It was for those meetings that I returned in October. There would be a Personal Futures meeting on Monday and Wednesday. In between would be a contrasting third meeting: Jim's annual review, led by personnel at the institution, which focused on his problems to be fixed, not his strengths. "I hate meetings," Jim had told me, referring to these accusatory annual reviews. Personal Futures planning was supposed to be different—friendly and positive. I had even picked a neutral site, off the grounds of the institution, in the oak-paneled conference room of the pretty nineteenth-century Faribault City Hall.

We took our seats around four long conference tables set in a square. Jim sat at the center of one. Our facilitator, Marijo McBride, from the University of Minnesota, explained that our purpose was to help Jim define what was important to him and then strategize ways to help him achieve it. With McBride's help we reconstructed Jim's history, which she wrote on poster paper set on an easel. A stick figure, representing Jim, was drawn in the center. I had invited state and county workers who could help Jim get out of the institution. Among the dozen invitees were the few people from Faribault I felt would be strong advocates for Jim. Instead, Jim's entire social services team showed up. They were defensive and suspicious.

Soon the faultfinding began. Neil Farnsworth, the cottage psychologist, started talking about how Jim had a mean temper. McBride noted that Jim seemed extremely sociable. "When you wear one of his tires around your neck, you don't think of him as very sociable," the psychologist responded. He was speaking figuratively and of no specific incident. Another Faribault staffer said Jim would steal tools or other things needed for his inventions. And the psychologist added that Jim was a "pack rat" unsuited for living in a place of his own. "A gymnasium might last a week," the psychologist pronounced. "He'd fill it."

Throughout this wild faultfinding, Jim appeared not to be listening. He played with a small metal toy car. But after a while he looked up and glowered at Deb Lenway, his Faribault counselor. It had fallen on her to get Jim, always suspicious of a meeting, into her car and bring him to the session. "You're dead, Deb," he muttered angrily under his breath, shooting her a withering glance. "I'm going to break your car."

I was forced to hustle Jim out of the room and back to the institution. "I don't go to meetings anymore," he said petulantly in the car. "I hate meetings. Meetings are boring." I cursed myself, fearful that my efforts to help were about to collapse in hurt, anger, and recrimination. I worried that I had betrayed Jim. But I was particularly fearful that Jim had made a bad first impression on his new case worker.

I had been disappointed that Hall, Jim's social worker of several years, had taken no steps to get Jim out of Faribault. He had denied me access to Jim's records. When I got them I understood why. Jim's individual assessment plan, although required annually by law, had not been done in a number of years. Nor had there been a screening as required before Jim could be considered to go to his own apartment. I realized that

Hall had an expanding caseload and, perhaps because no one was pushing for Jim, it was easy to let Jim's needs drop to the bottom of the pile. I requested a new social worker to be assigned to Jim, and within weeks, Steven Schmit came on the job. I liked him immediately. He was young, energetic, and creative. He was intrigued by my stories of Jim and by what he had read in Jim's file. Unlike Hall, he did not believe that Jim would fail outside the institution. Jim, he told me over the phone, should be out of Faribault. I worried that Jim's outburst, at this first meeting with his new social worker, would alter Schmit's generous thinking about Jim. There was no need for concern. Schmit was experienced enough to understand, just as I had, that Jim was only responding to the unfair criticism that he was hearing.

Things seemed to work out better once I rejoined the group for the last hour of the meeting. McBride had done a good job of keeping things positive. Together the group seemed to take a good first step toward identifying Jim's preferences. Things went even better at our second meeting, which was held two days later in St. Paul so that family members could attend. The distant location reduced the number of negative Faribault staffers, too. Jim smiled broadly when he entered the conference room and saw his aunt and sister Peggy and, at the end of the meeting, his brother Dennis.

I had also asked Irving Martin to be there. He is a self-advocate, active in People First of Minnesota. A large man, with a loud, hearty laugh and genteel manners, Martin had recently been in Washington, where I first met him, to witness President Bush sign the Americans with Disabilities Act. Martin worked at the dietary center of a nursing home, helping to prepare and distribute food. Every day after work he went to Mickey's Diner, which he affectionately called a "high-class greasy spoon," for an afternoon cup of coffee. But what he called the "highlight of my life" was being able to address the congregation at his church, telling them what it meant to have mental retardation.

It was Martin whose common sense and wisdom again changed Jim's family's definition of retardation. At the first meeting, the cottage psychologist had claimed that if Jim were to live outside the institution there was a good chance of his getting into trouble stealing and possibly "ending up in jail." (Jim has heard this so often that he believes it. When he has done something wrong, he will say abjectly, "I'm no good. I'm going to go to jail." Consequently, this kind of talk in front of Jim struck me as emotionally abusive.) At the second meeting, Martin rose to say it was important to let Jim learn from his own mistakes and that he was sure to grow once he left the institution. "I myself am retarded," Martin would say to preface his remarks. "My way of thinking is that you take one step at a time. If he takes one step at a time, with lots of room for mistakes, he'll be okay. There is not one person in this room who has not made mistakes in their life, and why can't he? People learn from their mistakes."

The team now began to talk about Jim leaving Faribault as a given and no longer as a big risk. (There had been no such assumption that Jim was ready to leave Faribault at his annual institutional review the day before. Staffers there had catalogued Jim's shortcomings and stressed how much he needed to change before moving to a group home.) We agreed to accelerate Jim's family contacts, to help him continue to develop his mechanical skills, probably by helping him find work—a bike shop, an auto body shop, and a junkyard all came up as good fits—and to get Jim into a group house or apartment. The group process, despite my initial doubts, had truly worked. Jim seemed to catch the shift in mood, too. He was no longer bored or angry. At one point, McBride asked Jim what he would like in his house. "How about a cat in the house?" Jim said in his slow, soft voice. He, too, had begun to feel empowered.

That night between the two Personal Futures meetings, Jim and I had gone to Owatonna to shop. That meant cruising the

aisles of auto parts shops, tire stores, and farm implement dealers. We looked at car tires, tractor tires, motorcycle tires, and
all-terrain-vehicle tires.

At dinner, Jim mentioned that Robin, a woman who had
lived at Faribault, now resided in Owatonna. The first time I had
heard of Robin was at the initial Personal Futures meeting. She
had been listed as one of Jim's friends—the closest thing he had
to a girlfriend. "Jim, if we can find Robin, would you like to
visit her after dinner?" I asked. "Yes," he said, smiling. A half
hour later we were at the front door of Robin's group house.

It was clearly a "girls' " apartment, a nice four-bedroom
apartment for Robin and her roommates, decorated in pinks and
sky blues, with straw bonnets and dried flowers on the walls.
There were yellow stencils of a woman in a bonnet with a goose
on the wallpaper. The sofa was white with a pink-and-green
floral design. A big television sat against the wall in a small
living room that also doubled as a kitchen and dining area.
When we walked in, I could not figure out if Robin was present.
Four women said hello, but none made any special greeting. Jim
kept close to my side. "Is Robin here?" I asked out loud. One
of the women, with a pleasant, round face, short hair, and pretty
eyes, raised her head and smiled.

Jim and Robin sat on a loveseat while the rest of us watched
a TV movie. Robin placed an orange plastic bowl of popcorn
between her and Jim. At first they made only halting, awk-
wardly shy conversation. But soon Jim was talking away—
talking more and faster, it occurred to me, than I had ever heard
him talk to anyone. From time to time, Robin would excuse
herself to take a trip to her bedroom. She would come back with
something to show Jim: a coffeepot she had bought; a new pair
of shoes from her sister. She showed Jim that she had a key to
her room and explained that nothing was ever stolen from her.
Soon Robin had moved the popcorn bowl from between them.
I sat in front of them, and occasionally I would turn around. Jim
kept an eye trained on me, but from my stolen glances I could

see that, when he thought I was not looking, Jim would timidly run a finger along Robin's knee.

I wondered if the staffers at Faribault would be annoyed with me, but I figured Jim, at thirty-one, was old enough to be "dating," or whatever this was.

After seeing Jim at Faribault and at the Personal Futures meeting, Jim's sisters and brothers had talked excitedly to their mother about their talented brother. She sent word that she wanted Jim to visit for Thanksgiving. Evelyn sent a letter to the institution asking that arrangements be made, as was routinely done, to drive Jim to the Twin Cities.

On Thanksgiving morning, Jim's mother baked two apple pies for her son. Dinner started, but Jim never arrived. Later, staff at the institution apologized to Jim's disappointed family. Evelyn's letter had gotten lost, they said, and they were unaware of the family's desire to see Jim. But I knew that this excuse was untrue. I had made two telephone calls the week before Thanksgiving to make sure the car arrangements were made. I got a bureaucratic shrug. It was in the pipeline, I was told. I did not have the time to march Evelyn's request from person to person to make sure the car pool worked. Evelyn was too polite to do more than write her kindly letter of request.

There was a reunion on Christmas Day. The family video shows Jim sitting quietly in a chair in his sister's living room, beaming with joy, as he watched his boisterous family kidding and exchanging presents. Jim happily soaked it all in, as if his being there for Christmas were a regular occurrence. But the kind of miscommunication and bureaucratic slow pace that had sabotaged a Thanksgiving reunion was delaying efforts to get Jim out of Faribault.

Another year went by, and Jim happily joined his family for a second Christmas, but still he was waiting for a placement out of the institution. It took nineteen months between the October meetings and the time when he finally moved.

My promises of "a few more months" kept spreading out to

still "a few more." Midway in this process I had been at a conference where I heard Gerald Provencal, a Michigan advocate for people with retardation, talk about the double standard of time we apply to people with disabilities. "We're far more tolerant of the passage of their time than we are of our own," he said. Nineteen months might not seem unreasonable for getting a man out of an institution. Yet, as Provencal noted, "the passage of time is something as precious to someone with a disability as it is to us." Just because he had spent a lifetime in an institution did not mean Jim had another year and a half to waste. "If you're in a Club Med, time flies," said Provencal. "If you're in a day room, it is agony."

Even to the end, Jim's status as a disabled man made him a little less worthy, a little less of a priority. People who were pitied were also a little more disposable. Things were going well for Jim. He had advocates; he had friends; he had family. Yet we could not get him out of the disrespectful double standard of time that applied to people caught in the disability system.

But once it was a fact that he was leaving Faribault, Jim suddenly did gain respect. Staff at the institution began to speak of him in a new, positive way. He was retested three months before he moved. Now the man who supposedly needed to stay at Faribault because he was "moderately mentally retarded"— and who had been labeled "profoundly mentally retarded" most of his life—was found to be "mildly mentally retarded." Even that newly generous label seemed to underestimate him. At the discharge planning meeting two weeks before his move, staffers at the institution told newly glowing stories about Jim's capabilities. Residents of the town surrounding the institution would call and ask for Jim by name to mow their lawns. He was so responsible, the lawn crew job coach explained, that Jim would be left at a house with his lawn mower while the rest of the crew went to some other job. When they returned an hour or so later, Jim invariably would be sitting on the stoop, waiting, lawn mower at his side, having done the job to perfection.

Jim left Faribault in May of 1992 and moved to an old farmhouse on ten acres of land in the exurbs of Minneapolis. He shared the small house with two other men but had the entire second floor to himself. He adjusted with ease and happiness, as if he were always meant to live there. Freedom for Jim meant falling asleep at night while listening to his new clock radio— his clothes still on and the overhead light still brightening the room. That had been impossible in a life of three or more roommates. Freedom meant eating lunch with the nondisabled men on the work crew at the state park. Nobody seemed to mind that Jim did his job, riding a small tractor and grading the softball fields, faster than the nondisabled man who had the chore before him. Freedom also meant borrowing a tool from a neighbor, then getting on his bicycle and riding a few blocks to return it. Freedom meant having a barn where he could retreat, at any time of day, to hammer and saw. The cars he built got bigger and more elaborate. But Jim left his flying machine at Faribault, perhaps to aid someone else plotting an escape.

Epilogue
How the Disability Rights Movement Is Changing America

NEW YORK—Women's groups protested the city's plans to install public outdoor toilets, but not include any for women. City officials feared the women's larger toilets would attract junkies needing a place to shoot up and homeless people looking for somewhere to sleep. . . .

No city, of course, would be crazy enough to build public toilets, but just for men. Yet substitute "wheelchair users" for "women" in the paragraph above to understand what New York City did to infuriate disabled activists at the moment that the Americans with Disabilities Act was being implemented nation-wide.

When disabled people protested that they were being un-lawfully excluded from a public service, they got little sympa-thy. Typical was a *Wall Street Journal* editorial that scolded the complainers for putting the narrow self interests of a small number of wheelchair users over the common good of the far greater number of able-bodied people who could use the inaccessible toilets. The *Journal* saw it as an issue of "weighing civil rights against common sense," and came down against the expectation of rights by people in wheelchairs. But to disabled activists, like Frieda Zames of New York's Disabled in Action, the exclusion was as blatant an example of discrimination as if the city had put up toilets and then hung a WHITES ONLY sign on each one. Most galling for Zames was that disabled people were being expected to forfeit, without complaint, their newly won rights to accessibility.

By the time New York unveiled a four-month test of its new toilets in July 1992, the same month that the last title of the ADA went into effect, the city had placed three large wheelchair-accessible toilets next to three regular ones. But side-by-side toilets took up a lot of space, were twice as expensive to build, and disabled users still complained about the unequal compromise that seemed designed to fail: to use their toilets meant going to a nearby city office during business hours to get a special key card (so that officials could keep out the junkies and homeless). In addition, disabled people got second-class toilets, which, unlike the ones for everyone else, were neither heated nor self-cleaning. As a result of complaints by disabled activists, a worker with a mop was posted outside all day long, a quickly ridiculed use of manpower and money that left the future of accessible toilets in doubt after the test run. To Zames the solution was simple: build one toilet that could be used by all. Anything else, she argued, was separate and unequal.

What happens when Congress grants a new group minority rights, but society has little understanding that those rights have been awarded or why they are needed? As the newly recognized minority—disabled people—starts asserting those rights, there are many new breakthroughs for equality. But there are also clashes, misunderstandings, even a backlash. The ADA, which promised integration, will have more impact than any civil rights law since the 1964 act that banned discrimination against blacks, women, and ethnic and religious minorities. But disabled people got their rights without dramatic Freedom Rides, church bombings or "I Have a Dream" speeches to stir the conscience of a guilty nation. African-Americans had changed a nation's attitudes and then won civil rights law. But for disabled Americans the reverse was true. Now disabled people fear that a society that did the right thing—but without the benefit of significant consciousness-raising—has begun to question those rights.

Such doubt is raised not just on seemingly small matters, like the right to use a public toilet. Discord is present, too, on the most pressing social issues like reforming health care. Just a few weeks after the full ADA went into effect and the New York toilets went up, the Bush Administration—citing the disability civil rights law—struck down what was being hailed as the nation's boldest effort to redesign health care. Oregon's Medicaid rationing plan sought to resolve the great hypocrisy of American medicine: those with insurance get the world's best medicine, while the uninsured fourteen percent may get nothing. As part of a plan to provide health coverage to its uninsured residents, Oregon wanted to extend Medicaid to an additional one hundred and twenty thousand uncovered poor people. But to do so would necessitate savings elsewhere in the Medicaid system. Oregon's solution was to ration services. It ranked seven hundred and nine conditions and their treatments on the basis of effectiveness and cost, figured out how much state Medicaid could spend, and then drew a cutoff line at item five hundred eighty seven. Nothing below that would get funded. To put the rationing scheme into effect, Oregon needed formal permission, called a waiver, from federal officials.

There were compelling reasons to support rationing. It was a daring experiment at a time when the federal government seemed too timid to solve the problem of providing health care for some 37 million uninsured Americans. But Oregon's plan came with a cruel twist dictated by an era of fiscal limits: it was offering health coverage to more poor people by cutting back the treatment that other even poorer people already received. Oregon health officials justified this by noting that another kind of rationing already existed. When government said it would pay for the health care of the poorest, but not for that of the slightly less poor, that was, in effect, an implicit method of rationing health care among haves and have nots. Oregon would try to bring some logic to the system by rationing on the basis of what treatment was most certain to improve someone's life, not on the basis of where one fell on the poverty scale. It was in trying to make decisions about what was worthwhile treatment that Oregon's plan ran into problems with treating disabled people fairly.

In early 1992, officials at the Department of Health and Human Services recommended giving the plan a go-ahead and President Bush himself, in his budget plan, had praised the rationing scheme as a "noteworthy" example of state experimentation. But in March, at a brief Oval Office photo opportunity with officers of the National Right to Life Committee, Bush was urged to stop the Oregon program. Bush, who at first seemed unmoved by the antiabortion group's objections, perked up when the group's vice president, Robert Powell, claimed, "If that plan had been in effect when I was born, I'd be dead." The President listened intently as Powell, who uses crutches and a wheelchair, explained how, when he was just five months old, a malignant tumor had attacked his lungs and spinal cord. Doctors said the cancer was incurable, and the infant lived only because his parents found another doctor (one who used a wheelchair, it turned out) who was willing to aggressively treat the "hopeless" case. Oregon, Powell said, would stop paying to treat such incurable cancers. Bush, who had once struggled to find doctors willing to treat his young daughter dying from leukemia, ordered White House legal counsel Boyden Gray to check

Powell's contention that the Oregon plan violated the ADA. The legal opinion that came back supported Powell.

Oregon's rankings, Gray's office concluded, reflected commonly-held prejudices that a disabled life was a lesser one. The classifications had come on the advice of doctors and medical experts. So it was not surprising, for example, that medical treatment for traumatic brain injury fell far below the cutoff. Surviving traumatic head injury was something new, and medicine still has little understanding of how to improve the lives of survivors. But people are now living long after such injury.

In making its list, Oregon also had relied upon a telephone survey to gauge people's attitudes about illness and disability. This, the White House argued, had further polluted the rankings with the public's uninformed stereotypes of a disabled life as a sad and pitiable one. The phone survey, the administration concluded, was tied to a significant reranking of at least one hundred and twenty conditions and their treatments. Medical treatment was not covered for amyotrophic lateral sclerosis, or Lou Gehrig's disease, a particularly frightening illness to most people since the degenerative neuromuscular condition was considered fatal. Yet ALS was not a death sentence for everybody. Scientist Stephen Hawking, after all, has lived long and productively, even though ALS has made his life a far more difficult one. At the very least, each person's case had to be considered separately. To write off everyone with ALS was, in effect, discrimination based on diagnosis. It was to buy into the myth that a disabled life was a tragic one and not worthy of prolonging with medical treatment.

There were other examples where Oregon's list conflicted with the ADA. Although Oregon would pay for a liver transplant in the case of liver failure, it would not pay for the transplant if the patient had a history of alcoholism, no matter if that addiction was five, ten, or twenty years in the past. But the congressional Office of Technology Assessment criticized this rationing of liver transplants, noting that the operation had a similar rate of success whether a person had a past history of alcoholism or not. (No doctor will give a liver transplant to someone currently abusing alcohol, since that would be a waste of a rare liver donation.) The ADA prohibits discrimination against someone on the basis of past alcoholism or drug abuse.

Many of Oregon's decisions had been moved by logic, even if they were flawed with society's automatic devaluing of people on the basis of disability. Saving an extremely premature baby can cost a quarter of a million dollars or more. Prenatal care, which can significantly reduce the chance that a baby will be born prematurely, costs only a few hundred dollars. So Oregon, seeking to emphasize prevention, put crucial prenatal care high on its priority list. But ranked seven hundred eight, next to last, was saving a baby weighing less than eighteen ounces and born before twenty-three weeks gestation. One Oregon official explained to me that the low ranking "is not a problem for our doctors, since they don't try to save babies like that anyway." Indeed, the chances of such a baby surviving are slim, at, by one estimate, about one in ten and even then there is a significant likelihood that the child will grow up disabled. Yet just a few weeks before the Bush Administration's decision, a healthy baby, Zascha Villamar, left a Miami hospital after five months of treatment. She was born after only twenty-two weeks in the womb and she weighed fifteen ounces—a testimony to medicine's ever-growing ability to save younger and smaller babies. Technology and new drugs sometimes could save such premature infants, as long as doctors and governments did not write them off first.

Once Washington told Oregon to redesign its rationing experiment, disabled people and their new civil rights law came under swift and pointed attack. "So now we have the architects of the Americans with Disabilities Act deciding that Oregon's plan, the product of an arduous political consensus within that state, simply doesn't fit the grand design of their legislated benevolence," the *Wall Street Journal* grumbled in an editorial. "The Americans with Disabilities Act is beginning to have the look of Big Brother." The *New York Times,* in an editorial titled "A Bold Medical Plan, Derailed," called the administration's claims of disability bias "unconvincing."

The Oregon decision was a coming-of-age for the ADA. It was an early test that showed the law's vast power to change society and sweep away vestiges of bias. Even most disabled people had not fully realized the enormity of the law's potential. The ADA had been underestimated as just another be-nice-to-the-handicapped law, in part because the two most visible titles of the act required businesses to be accessible to workers and customers. It looked like a law simply to put wheelchair ramps on buildings. Overlooked was the even more significant promise of a third section, which required that all government services, from public toilets to health care, be provided equally. Rights, unlike charity, carried some costs to all. If America was truly committed to providing equality to disabled people, there would be complications and trade-offs, as there had been in the Oregon decision.

The potential for backlash was clear in the gap between the newly militant self-perception of disabled people, and the confused, still stereotypical thinking of the rest of the country. On the eve of the enactment of the ADA, the pitiable poster child and the inspirational "supercrip" remained the defining images of disability. A Louis Harris and Associates survey, released in the fall of 1991, found that 92 percent of Americans said they usually felt admiration when they met people with severe disabilities and 74 percent said they felt pity. Another 47 percent said they reacted with fear "because what happened to the disabled person might happen to them," 16 percent said they felt anger "because disabled people are an inconvenience," and 9 percent said they felt resentment at "the special privileges disabled people receive." But few people, only 18 percent, said they were even aware of the ADA. Americans had missed the new self-definition of disabled people as a group whose primary issues were ones of discrimination and respect, not health, inspiration, and charity. Even to most disabled people, however, the ADA was a revelation. Even while their world was changing, most had internalized the messages of pity and powerlessness that had permeated their lives. The deliverance of rights with the ADA was a license to get angry, instead of politely asking for help and becoming indebted to the kindhearted.

Dr. Richard Edlich had never heard of the ADA until November of 1991 when an official at the University of Virginia, where Edlich teaches medicine, mentioned in passing that the school planned to make its campus accessible in order to comply with the new civil rights law. When asked, Edlich noted that the annual Christmas party was held in an inaccessible location. The university moved it. Then he pointed out that he had been unable to participate in graduation ceremonies since 1987, when he began using a motorized scooter-wheelchair after his multiple sclerosis worsened. The university purchased temporary ramps so that Edlich and other wheelchair riders could join the graduation procession down the Lawn, the majestic quandrangle designed by Thomas Jefferson.

University officials simply followed the law. But the experience radicalized Edlich. In the past, like most disabled people, the plastic surgeon had not wanted to "bother" anyone and thought of his full inclusion as an imposition, not as a right. But after the university welcomed him back to its graduation ceremonies, he decided to attend his nephew's graduation at an elite New York City high school. When the headmaster dismissively said Edlich would have to find someone to carry him up the stairs, Edlich filed a complaint under the newly enacted public accommodations section of the ADA. A Justice Department lawyer flew to New York and the school quickly built a ramp.

Back in Charlottesville, Edlich, energized by the way the world was opening up to him, began a survey of his favorite stores and restaurants, and filed more complaints whenever he found a business out of compliance and unwilling to change. It was not that Edlich was bitter or angry, or stood to make any money off his complaints. He simply began asserting his right to full inclusion. The ADA, the doctor says, "has made life a celebration instead of being filled with apologies and continually saying 'thank you' and 'please help me.' " He had made what he called the "lonely journey" to becoming an activist.

While the cautious were getting militant, the militant were gaining respectability. In Denver, on the day in July that the final title of the ADA went into effect, city officials honored ADAPT. The city erected a plaque to commemorate ADAPT's first protest, in 1978, when nineteen people in wheelchairs sat at an intersection and blocked two city buses for twenty-four hours to demand that wheelchair lifts be added to buses. Only several weeks before ADAPT was hailed in Denver, its members had disrupted a commencement speech by U.S. Health and Human Services Secretary Louis Sullivan, in the type of hostile demonstration that the Bush Administration official had come to expect from contentious ACT-UP protesters demanding more AIDS research. ADAPT insisted on more government spending for personal assistance services and less for nursing homes.

A few months later, in October, ADAPT got the promise of support it wanted after its members took over Bill Clinton's presidential campaign headquarters in San Francisco and refused to leave. Clinton dispatched his top rehabilitation official from Arkansas to negotiate with the demonstrators, and a strong statement was issued in Clinton's name backing the new spending emphasis sought by ADAPT. "I believe that every individual has a right to personal care," Clinton said, and proposed using a national service corps as one way to increase the number of personal assistants. Clinton endorsed the disability movement's insistence on the consumer's "maximum control" over the personal assistance they receive and pledged to reconsider federal regulations and funding that create "a presumption in favor of institutionalized care over home and community-based services." Clinton's promise was a sign of the growing respect that politicians paid to disabled voters and that even the most militant of them were treated with seriousness.

Still, even a strong rights law could not make old barriers fall overnight. The Hockenberry Rule—the idea that the ability of disabled people is always underestimated—did not disappear, as journalist John Hockenberry, himself, would find out when he got evicted from a Broadway theater. He had paid $60 for his ticket and had checked in advance that the theater was accessible. But when he showed up, the theater manager refused to help seat him. "You are a fire hazard, sir," the manager complained. Prior to the ADA, theater owners in most parts of the country were free to make such judgments. This time, Hockenberry filed a bias suit against the theater, citing the public accommodations section of the ADA, which had taken effect just two months before his run-in on Broadway.

For Hockenberry, the experience was a "coming out" of sorts. Like most disabled people, he had put up with such insults and discrimination daily. Even at National Public Radio's offices, there was never an accessible rest room he could use. But like many disabled people, he had tried to ignore such slights and limits by concentrating on personal achievement. "I thought that what defined me was not disability but background and talent," he explained to journalist Mary Johnson. "The biggest joke played on me—and it's my own damn fault— is that I thought that, by accepting no limits, as my geographic reality enlarged, my sense of limits would go down. And just the opposite has happened."

Hockenberry, who that summer was lured to ABC News, could cover some of the biggest stories around the world. But as a disabled man he was still hostage to the underestimation of others. At the theater, said Hockenberry, "that guy just decided I wasn't going in, and everyone then behaved as though it was impossible to get me in. If you spend a lot of time in the Third World and you come back to the United States you realize the obstacles are just guys standing there, telling you it's impossible. And you know it's not." After a lifetime of being told to make it on his own, Hockenberry admitted, he felt a little uncomfortable about making a claim to rights.

Millions of other disabled people were getting angry, too, and like Hockenberry and Edlich were coming to see themselves as a class, united in discrimination and empowered by law. Their expanding ranks would give the disability rights movement soaring power, educate others to their issues, and in the end, create a society more hospitable to all. They are full players now in a civil rights struggle, complete with progress and backlash. But the change in their mind-set is powerful enough to win rights and perhaps eventually convince a nation and the world that people with disabilities want neither pity-ridden paternalism nor overblown admiration. They insist simply on common respect and the opportunity to build bonds to their communities as fully accepted participants in everyday life.

Notes

INTRODUCTION: YOU JUST DON'T UNDERSTAND

5: But in World War I: Irving Kenneth Zola, "The Oration: Ageing and Disability: Toward a Unifying Agenda," *Australian Disability Review* 1, no. 3 (1988).

6: In the mid-1970s: Testimony of Representative Rosa DeLauro (D-Conn.), House Committee on Government Operations, hearing on Americans with head injuries, February 19, 1992.

6: Premature babies born: Mike Snider, "The World's Smallest Baby Soon Turns 2," *USA Today,* May 30, 1991.

6: Today, almost 50 percent: Elisabeth Rosenthal, "As More Infants Live, Choices and Burden Grow," *The New York Times,* September 29, 1991.

6: Today, 32 million Americans: Andrew M. Pope and Alvin R. Tarlov, eds., *Disability in America: Toward a National Agenda for Prevention* (Washington: National Academy Press, 1991), p. 1-1.

6–7: "Disability ranks as": ibid.

7: Some 31 million: Mitchell P. LaPlante, "The Demographics of Disability," in Jane West, ed., *The Americans with Disabilities Act: From Policy to Practice* (New York: Milbank Memorial Fund, 1991).

9: Now, members of the National Council: At the end of 1988, the National Council on the Handicapped changed its name to the National Council on Disability.

CHAPTER ONE: TINY TIMS, SUPERCRIPS, AND THE END OF PITY

18: *Abbott Shines:* Chuck Johnson, "Abbott Shines in Arizona; Rain in Florida," *USA Today,* March 8, 1989.

18: He may have struck: Associated Press, "Abbott Struggles in Debut," *The New York Times,* March 8, 1989.

19: Only a few in the newsroom: Annemarie Cooke and Neil Reisner, "The Last Minority," *Washington Journalism Review,* December 1991; Roxanne Roberts, "Correspondent on Wheels," *Washington Post,* July 23, 1992.

21: On the opinion page: Evan J. Kemp, Jr., "Aiding the Disabled: No Pity, Please," *The New York Times,* September 3, 1981.

23: It would be, he mused: Jerry Lewis, "If I Had Muscular Dystrophy," *Parade,* September 2, 1990.

23: To a reporter: Richard Roeper, "In Waukegan's Alleys with Jerry and His Kids," *Chicago Sun-Times,* October 7, 1991.

23: Yet in his magazine article: Lewis.

23: He wrote, "Let's ask": Robert A. Jones, "Jerry's Kids: It's a Pity But It Works," *Los Angeles Times,* September 4, 1991.

24: Seventy-four percent: *The ICD Survey of Disabled Americans: Bringing Disabled Americans into the Mainstream,* conducted for ICD-International Center for the Disabled, and the National Council on the Handicapped by Louis Harris and Associates, Inc. (March 1986), pp. 9–10.

25: Often the discrimination: Brian Gooney, "Handicapped Child's Access to Zoo Disputed," *The News Tribune* (Woodbridge, N.J.), July 23, 1986.

25: Resentment may have: Associated Press, "Double Amputee

Mistreated While Boarding Pan Am," *Washington Post,* January 15, 1989.

25: Others may feel: Lisa Foderaro, "Glen Ridge Worries It Was Too Forgiving to Athletes," *The New York Times,* June 12, 1989.

25: Because of the girl's retardation: William Glaberson, "Assault Case Renews Debate on Rape Shield Law," *The New York Times,* November 2, 1992; Robert Hanley, "Sex Assault Trial Focuses on Woman's Actions," *The New York Times,* October 31, 1992.

25: In a similar case: John Kifner, "5 Rescuers Held in Death of a Caller," *The New York Times,* June 27, 1990.

26: One such case was that of Tiffany Callo: Jay Mathews, "Tactics Shift in Custody Fight," *Washington Post,* July 5, 1988.

26: The state was willing: "Tiffany Callo and the Disability Movement," *Disability Rag,* March/April 1988.

28: When other costs: Andrew M. Pope and Alvin R. Tarlov, eds., *Disability in America: Toward a National Agenda for Prevention* (Washington, D.C.: National Academy Press, 1991).

29: Edward Yelin: Edward H. Yelin, "The Recent History and Immediate Future of Employment Among Persons with Disabilities," in Jane West, ed., *The Americans with Disabilities Act: From Policy to Practice* (New York: Milbank Memorial Fund, 1991).

30: In the Old Testament: Charles J. Kokaska et al., "Disabled People in the Bible," *Rehabilitation Literature* 45, no. 1–2 (January–February 1984).

30: Many churches now make: Marjorie Hyer, "Methodists Approve Revised Hymnal," *Washington Post,* May 4, 1988.

31: Shakespeare's king: William Shakespeare, *Richard III,* act 1, sc. i.

31: "Lenny, the mentally retarded": Howard Margolis and Arthur Shapiro, "Countering Negative Images of Disability in Classical Literature," *English Journal,* March 1987; see also Robert Bogdan and Douglas Biklen, "Handicapism," *Social Policy* 8 (March/April 1977) and Robert Bogdan et al., "The Disabled: Media's Monster," *Social Policy* 13 (Fall 1982).

31: And journalist Paul Glastris: Paul Glastris, "The Case for

Denial: What the Handicapped Movement Can Learn from a Totally Normal Guy," *The Washington Monthly,* December 1988.

32: Between the 1860s: Robert Bogdan, *Freak Show: Presenting Human Oddities for Amusement and Profit* (Chicago and London: The University of Chicago Press, 1988), pp. 11–12.

32: Other scholars, including: David Gerber, "Volition and Valorization in the Analysis of the 'Careers' of People Exhibited in Freak Shows," *Disability, Handicap & Society* 7, no. 1 (1992).

36: Members of the San Francisco–based: Elizabeth Kastor, "Not So Wild About 'Wanda,' " *Washington Post,* September 13, 1988.

37: Most ridiculous: Leslie Aun, "State Cited for Blocking Path of Blind to Foreign Service," *Federal Times,* February 13, 1989.

38: So society shields itself: Robert F. Murphy, *The Body Silent* (New York: W. W. Norton & Co., 1990), pp. 116–17.

CHAPTER TWO: FROM CHARITY TO INDEPENDENT LIVING

44: UCLA had set up: "Quads on Quadrangles," *Toomey j Gazette,* Spring–Summer 1962.

49: But eight members: Timothy J. Pfaff, "The War of Independence," *California Monthly,* December 1976.

53: There were even: *Toomey j Gazette.*

57: "We're not going": Edward D. Berkowitz, *Disabled Policy: America's Programs for the Handicapped* (Cambridge: Cambridge University Press, 1987), p. 197.

58–59: When the Continental Congress: John Lenihan, "Disabled Americans: A History," *Performance* (former magazine of The President's Committee on Employment of the Handicapped), November–December 1976/January 1977, pp. 11–12.

59: Stephen Hopkins referred: ibid., p. 12.

60: Dix had found: John M. Blum et. al., *The National Experience* (New York: Harcourt, Brace & World, Inc., 1968), p. 258.

59–60: In 1854, Congress: Lenihan, p. 22.

60: Noted historian John Lenihan: ibid.

60: A school for the blind: Richard K. Scotch, *From Good Will to Civil Rights: Transforming Federal Disability Policy* (Philadelphia: Temple University Press, 1984), pp. 15–16.

60: Howe's success: Lenihan, p. 23.

60: This success: ibid., p. 28.

60: The work of Howe: ibid.

60: As historian Lenihan noted: ibid.

61: Mississippi, in 1886, spent: Committee on Veteran Affairs, "Medical Care of Veterans" (Washington, D.C.: U.S. Government Printing Office, 1967), as cited in Lenihan, p. 35.

61: In the North: Lenihan.

61: But, as historian David J. Rothman: David J. Rothman, *The Discovery of the Asylum: Social Order and Disorder in the New Republic,* rev. ed. (Boston: Little, Brown and Company, 1990), p. 237.

62: Historian Hugh Gregory Gallagher notes: Hugh Gregory Gallagher, *FDR's Splendid Deception* (New York: Dodd, Mead & Company, 1985).

62: "He was a 'cured cripple' ": ibid., p. 96

62: Washington was a wheelchair-accessible city: ibid., p. 97.

63: Most important, however: Berkowitz, pp. 202–4.

63: Blind relief laws: Lenihan, pp. 52–53

63: Robert Irwin: ibid., p. 53.

65: When sociologist Richard Scotch: Scotch, pp. 51–52.

65: There had been no hearings: ibid., p. 54.

65: When Ford's presidency ended: ibid., p. 112; Joseph Califano, *Governing America* (New York: Touchstone, 1982), p. 259.

66: Carter and Califano: Califano, p. 261; Berkowitz, p. 216.

66: The HEW secretary: Scotch, pp. 113–15.

67: And then he noted, correctly: "State Rehab Chief Joins the Protest," *San Francisco Examiner,* April 10, 1977.

67: On the thirteenth day: "HEW to Moscone: 'No Shower Heads,' " *San Francisco Examiner,* April 18, 1977.

68: "There will be more sit-ins": Walter Barney, "HEW's Blueprint for Handicapped: 'Separate but Equal Facilities," *San Francisco Examiner,* April 16, 1977.

68: "People with disabilities": ibid.

69: They left singing: Ivan Sharpe, "Winning Was Sweet—and a Little Sad," *San Francisco Examiner,* May 1, 1977.

70: Newspapers widely reported: Berkowitz, p. 222.

71: "It would mean": ibid., p. 221.

71: At the high end: "A Study of Accommodations Provided to Handicapped Employees by Federal Contractors," prepared for the Department of Labor, Employment Standards Administration by Berkeley Planning Associates, June 1982.

71–72: The Supreme Court: Robert Funk, "Disability Rights: From Caste to Class in the Context of Civil Rights," in Alan Gartner and Tom Joe, eds., *Images of the Disabled, Disabling Images* (New York: Praeger, 1986), p. 20.

72: By 1984, sociologist Scotch: Scotch, pp. 164–65.

72: In 1977, according to: Chava Willig Levy, *A People's History of the Independent Living Movement* (Lawrence, Kans.: Research and Training Center on Independent Living, University of Kansas, 1988), p. 19.

72: By 1976, one reporter noted: Pfaff.

72: By 1988, the center reported: Lynn Kidder, "Enabling the Disabled," *Berkeleyan,* June 21–July 18, 1989.

CHAPTER THREE: THE DEAF CELEBRATION OF SEPARATE CULTURE

75: In early February of 1988: Jack R. Gannon, *The Week the World Heard Gallaudet* (Washington, D.C.: Gallaudet University Press, 1989), p. 20.

76: Support for the rally: ibid.

76: On campus: ibid., p. 23.

76: "Many deaf persons had been conditioned": ibid., p. 17.

77: "In 1926, a Black person": ibid., p. 23.

77: "What is your cause?": ibid., p. 25.

77: "You could call this": Molly Sinclair, "1,500 at Gallaudet Urge 'Deaf President Now,' " *Washington Post,* March 2, 1988.

79: Gallaudet's provost got past: Gannon, p. 48.

79: He encouraged the crowd: ibid., p. 50.

80: "If you could sign": Molly Sinclair, "Students Close Gallaudet U.," *Washington Post,* March 8, 1988.

80: Spilman took a hard line: Lena Williams, "College for Deaf Is Shut by Protest over President," *The New York Times,* March 8, 1988.

80: "We don't want to live off": Carlos Sanchez, "Gallaudet Students: 'We Want Ours,' " *Washington Post,* March 8, 1988.

80: "Real life": "The Week That Was—in Photos," *Gallaudet Today,* 18, no. 5 (Summer 1988).

80: "We will not give up": Greg Henderson, "Students Boycott Classes at College for Deaf," United Press International, March 8, 1988.

80: A local law firm: Gannon, p. 95.

80: The protest leaders camped out: ibid., p. 84.

81: Students even planned: ibid., p. 83.

82: And Michigan Representative David Bonior: Molly Sinclair and Eric Pianin, "Protest May Imperil Gallaudet Funding," *Washington Post,* March 9, 1988.

82: Later Jordan would explain: Neal Karlen, "Louder Than Words," *Rolling Stone,* March 23, 1989.

82: That evening at about 7:30: Gannon, p. 96.

84: It was not until 1971: Arden Neisser, *The Other Side of Silence: Sign Language and the Deaf Community in America* (New York: Alfred A. Knopf, New York, 1983), p. 236.

84: Television news first: ibid.

84: By the year of the Gallaudet protest: Molly Sinclair, "The Silent World's Rebellion for Civil Rights, *Washington Post,* March 13, 1988.

84: Many at Gallaudet would see: Sue Schwartz, ed., *Choices in Deafness: A Parents Guide* (Rockville, Md.: Woodbine House, 1987), p. xii.

85: Once again, medicine helped spur: Neisser, pp. 42–43.

85: "Never till I": Karlen.

86: The first deaf resident: Nora Ellen Groce, *Everyone Here Spoke Sign Language: Hereditary Deafness on Martha's Vineyard* (Cambridge, Massachusetts: Harvard University Press, 1985), pp. 23–24.

86: A few villages: ibid., p. 42.

86: The last deaf islander: Oliver Sacks, *Seeing Voices: A Journey into the World of the Deaf* (Berkeley and Los Angeles: University of California Press, 1989), pp. 35–36.

87: In the nineteenth century: Groce, pp. 74–79.

87: Both deaf and hearing islanders: ibid., pp. 79–80.

87: On this island: ibid., pp. 80–94.

87: Deaf people held town positions: ibid., pp. 85–86.

87: Some of the "less educated": ibid., p. 78.

88: The child, Alice Cogswell: Harlan Lane, *When the Mind Hears: A History of the Deaf* (New York: Random House, 1984), p. 155.

88: On the fifty-two day journey back: ibid., p. 206.

89: Together they raised money: ibid., p. 222.

90: George Bernard Shaw praised: ibid., p. 346; Neisser, p. 26.

90: Some Bell biographies: Robert V. Bruce, *Bell: Alexander Graham Bell and the Conquest of Solitude* (Boston: Little, Brown and Company, 1973), p. 120.

90: The Welsh language: Neisser, p. 29.

90: Even the usage of gestures: ibid., p. 30.

90: It was what separated: ibid., p. 22.

91–92: "Speech-reading talent": Leo M. Jacobs, *A Deaf Adult Speaks Out,* (Washington, D.C.: Gallaudet University Press, 3rd ed. revised and expanded 1989), p. 28.

92: Even in the best circumstances: Schwartz, p. 58.

92: "I can consistently understand": Henry Kisor, *What's That Pig Outdoors?: A Memoir of Deafness* (New York: Hill and Wang, 1990), p. xv.

92: A 1972 study by Gallaudet researchers: Sacks, *Seeing Voices,* p. 29.

93: Speaking tends to slow down: ibid., p. 146.

93: In the Southern United States: Carol Padden and Tom

Humphries, *Deaf in America: Voices from a Culture* (Cambridge, Massachusetts: Harvard University Press, 1988), p. 4.

93: It is only now: Shannon Brownlee, "The Signs of Silence," *U.S. News & World Report,* pp. 86–88.

93: Scientists recently discovered: Natalie Angier, "Deaf Babies Use Their Hands to Babble, Researchers Find," *The New York Times,* March 22, 1991.

93: As a result, some researchers: Brownlee.

94: Deaf teachers: Sacks, *Seeing Voices,* p. 28.

94: To avoid the emergence: Alexander Graham Bell, *Memoir Upon the Formation of a Deaf Variety of the Human Race,* 1883, reprinted by the Alexander Graham Bell Association for the Deaf, 1969, p. 45.

95: For that reason: ibid., p. 452.

95: "Sometimes they hold fairs": ibid., pp. 41–42.

96: Bell acknowledged: ibid., p. 42.

96: Deaf adults often lacked: ibid.

96: They were unable: ibid.

96: Deaf students would be located: ibid., pp. 46–47.

96: This would save money: ibid., p. 47.

97: Such "incorrect ideas": ibid., p. 43.

97: "Whatever the cause": ibid.

99: To be "very hard of hearing": Padden and Humphries, pp. 39–42.

100: Mainstreaming, complained David Wolfe: Nicholas C. McBride, "Civil Rights Win for the Deaf," *Christian Science Monitor,* March 15, 1988.

100: Governor Pete Wilson: "Governor Wilson Says 'No' to Deaf Education Bill," DCARA News, November 1991.

101: "But it is time for them": Molly Sinclair, "Gallaudet Euphoria Fades into Reality," *Washington Post,* September 12, 1988.

101: One writer proposed: Tony Papalla, "Gallaudet and Clerc University (No, That's Not a Typo!)," DCARA News, October 1991.

103: "A bardic tradition arose": Sacks, *Seeing Voices,* p. 145.

CHAPTER FOUR: A HIDDEN ARMY FOR CIVIL RIGHTS

105: As Carl told: Julie Rovner, "Promise, Uncertainties Mark Disability-Rights Measure," *Congressional Quarterly,* May 12, 1990.

106: As compared to only 2 percent: *The ICD Survey of Disabled Americans: Bringing Disabled Americans into the Mainstream,* conducted for ICD-International Center for the Disabled, and the National Council on the Handicapped by Louis Harris and Associates, Inc., March 1986, pp. 37–38.

106: And 40 percent: Ibid., pp. 63–65.

106: It was the same poll: Ibid., pp. 49–51.

116: Another 30 percent: "A Study of Accommodations Provided to Handicapped Employees by Federal Contractors," prepared for the Department of Labor, Employment Standards Administration, by Berkeley Planning Associates, June 1982.

117: When a doctor finally: Brooks Jackson, *Honest Graft: Big Money and the American Political Process* (Washington, D.C.: Farragut Publishing Co., 1990), pp. 19–23.

117: At the time: Dennis Farney, "Rep. Coehlo Makes Money, and Waves, for the Democrats," *Wall Street Journal,* June 14, 1983.

117–18: California made him give up: Jackson, pp. 23–24.

118: Even when Coehlo was in position: David Hoffman, "Rep. Coehlo: Democrats' Fund-Raiser Extraordinaire," *Washington Post,* August 26, 1982.

119: After over one hundred days: Steven A. Holmes, "Lobbyist on Civil Rights Wins Despite Hostility," *The New York Times,* December 2, 1991.

119: In 1953: Donnie Radcliffe, *Simply Barbara Bush: A Portrait of America's Candid First Lady* (New York: Warner Books, 1989), pp. 116–21.

119: Bush's son Neil: David Maraniss, "All the President's Kids," *Washington Post Magazine,* January 22, 1989.

119: The youngest Bush son: ibid.

119: He became a spokesman: Kenneth T. Walsh, "Speaking Out," *U.S. News & World Report,* April 15, 1991.

122: Gray, a lanky: Phil McCombs, "The Distant Drum of C. Boyden Gray," *Washington Post,* March 31, 1989.

124: There were 180: *Congressional Record,* S10709, September 7, 1989.

126: There were groups representing: ibid.

129: Patrisha Wright had urged them to do so: The Senate moved quickly and passed the ADA on September 7, 1989, by a 76–8 margin. But the pace slowed when the bill reached the House of Representatives, where four committees had jurisdiction, not one. Bush, who had lobbied for the bill with senators, was more aloof from the battle in the House. Some ADA supporters complained that Bush was seeking to have it both ways—in part not to further anger critics of the bill, particularly the small business lobby. Still, Bush's endorsement of disability rights gave the ADA a winning patina of bipartisanship, which put it on a sure track to passage. The House of Representatives voted 403–20 on May 22, 1990, for the ADA. The House and Senate then passed the final version of the bill on July 12 and July 13.

CHAPTER FIVE: INTEGRATION: OUT OF SHADOWLAND

143: "Historically, the inferior": Funk, p. 7.

143: The result of this history: ibid., p. 8.

147: Approximately, 300,000: K. Charlie Laikin, *An Overview of the Concept and Research on Community Living* (Research and Training Center on Community Living, University of Minnesota, 1988).

151: These workers decreased: *Annual Report to Congress: Supported Employment Activities Under Section 311 (d) of the Rehabilitation Act of 1973, as Amended, 1991,* Rehabilitation Services Administration, Office of Special Education and Rehabilitative Services, U.S. Department of Education, cited in "Report to Congress: Supported Employment a Success," *Futurity: (Minnesota) Governor's Planning Council on Developmental Disabilities,* November 1992.

151: Despite these savings: David Braddock et al., *The State of the States in Developmental Disabilities* (Baltimore: Paul H. Brookes Publishing, 1990), pp. 9, 25.

153: "He went limp": Joseph R. La Plante, "BRI's Punitive Measures Hailed as Last Best Hope, and Decried as Torment," *Sunday Journal* (Providence, R.I.), October 20, 1985.

153: But the Massachusetts Office: Kenneth J. Cooper, "State Suspends Licenses of Program for Autistic," *Boston Globe,* September 27, 1985.

153: Mary Kay Leonard: ibid., and *Sunday Journal,* September 27, 1985.

153: In a settlement: Ric Kahn, "Gains for Pain: Misguided Sympathy for Aversive Therapy," *Boston Phoenix,* January 13, 1987.

153: Israel studied: *Sunday Journal,* September 27, 1985.

153–54: Later, suspecting: ibid.

154: "These aren't people": ibid.

157: The sensation: Linda Himelstein, "Taking Aim at NIH's Scientific Methods: Critics Say Backers of Controversial Shock Therapy Stacked the Deck," *Legal Times,* March 26, 1990.

157: Dr. Duane Alexander: ibid.

157: Three years later: David Armstrong, "BRI at a Critical Juncture," *Boston Herald,* August 10, 1992; David Armstrong, "The 'Shock' Debate: Controversial Electric Therapy for Children with Behavior Problems Draws Praise, Condemnation," *Boston Herald,* March 26, 1992.

158: "We need something": *Boston Herald,* August 10, 1992.

159: Wrote Holmes: *Buck* v. *Bell,* 1927, cited in R. C. Scheerenberger, *A History of Mental Retardation* (Baltimore: Paul H. Brookes Publishing, 1983), p. 191; for a discussion of how Buck was mislabeled as having retardation, see Stephen Jay Gould, *The Flamingo's Smile: Reflections in Natural History* (New York: W. W. Norton & Company, 1985), pp. 306–18

160: Slavery, notes: John M. Blum et al., *The National Experience* (New York: Harcourt, Brace & World, 1968), pp. 211–12.

160: In 1965, Robert Kennedy: John Sibley, "Kennedy Charges Neglect in State Care of Retarded," *The New York Times,* September 10, 1965.

161: The stench of feces: Burton Blatt and Fred Kaplan, *Christmas in Purgatory: A Photographic Essay on Mental Retardation* (Boston: Allyn and Bacon, 1966).

161: This sort of exposé: L. L. Rotegard et al., "State Operated Facilities for People with Mental Retardation," *Mental Retardation* 22, no. 2 (April 1984).

161: Advocates of institutional reform: Scheerenberger, p. 252.

164: The result was a tragedy: Anastasia Toufexis, "From the Asylum to Anarchy," *Time,* October 22, 1990.

166–67: But Timothy, according to his mother: Nat Hentoff, "How Timothy W. Got into School," *Washington Post,* July 2, 1990.

167: But the 1975 law: ibid.

168: But she learned: David Bromberg, "Separate but Equal?," *Suttertown News* (Calif.), September 27–October 4, 1990.

168: Bad publicity: "Disabled Teen Wins Fight to Attend Class Functions," *USA Today,* May 28, 1991.

168–69: Sascha Bittner: ibid.

169: A judge ruled: "Integration Granted in Service Dog Case," *Disability Rights Education and Defense Fund News,* March 1990.

173: Schools spend an estimated: Margaret C. Wang, "Effective School Responses to Student Diversity: Challenges and Prospects, *Issues in Brief,* National Association of State Boards of Education, vol. 11, no. 6 (October 1991), pp. 8–9.

173: "It's like running": Sandy Banks, "Another Fight to Integrate," *Los Angeles Times,* October 27, 1990.

173: Schools spend at least $1,000: Wang, p. 9.

173–74: Some 67 percent . . . of education: Barbara Ayres and Luanna H. Meyer, "Helping Teachers Manage the Inclusive Classroom," *The School Administrator,* February 1992.

174: Forty percent: "Creating Open Communities," Massachusetts Developmental Disabilities Council, January 1990, p. 36.

174: The state-funded: ibid., p. 35.

174: Fifty percent of these are categorized: Virginia Roach, "Special Education: New Questions in an Era of Reform," *Issues in Brief,* National Association of State Boards of Education, vol. 11, no. 6 (October 1991).

174–75: In Connecticut: ibid.

175: In Massachusetts: "Creating Open Communities," *Issues in Brief,* National Association of State Boards of Education, vol. 11, no. 6 (October 1991), p. 36

175: "Many of them": Wang, p. 9.

175: A 1991 report: ibid.

178: Jack Hourcade: Jack J. Hourcade, "Special Olympics: A Review and Critical Analysis," *Therapeutic Recreation Journal,* First Quarter 1989.

180: Only 15 percent take part: Wang, p. 9.

181: Twenty-five percent of people: "Creating Open Communities," p. 46.

CHAPTER SIX: PEOPLE FIRST

193: Reporter Kathleen Megan: Kathleen Megan, "T. J.'s Family," *Northeast* and *Hartford Courant,* November 18, 1990.

193: "They helped him sort through": ibid.

194: "Why should I clean": ibid.

194: Records from Southbury: ibid.

195: "I didn't kiss my mother": ibid.

195: "I wanted to say, 'Why not?' ": ibid.

195: There the start: Scheerenberger, p. 117.

197: As late as 1980: ibid., pp. 188, 193.

199: "What I learned": Victoria Medgyesi, *No More B.S.! A Realistic Survival Guide for Disability Rights Activists* (Clarkston, Washington: People First of Washington, 1992), p. 62.

207: "I didn't know that much about reading": "Interview with David Beem," ARC News of Oregon, Summer 1988.

CHAPTER SEVEN: THE SCREAMING NEON WHEELCHAIR

216: In the late 1970s: Betty Medsger, "The Most Captive Consumers: At the Mercy of the Wheelchair Barons," *The Progressive,* March 1979.

220: The technology allowed Bibb: Nora Zamichow, "Computer

Will Allow Quadriplegic to 'Talk'—and Free Trapped Emotions," *Los Angeles Times,* September 22, 1991.

220: "But with an inexpensive": Peter H. Lewis, "A Great Equalizer for the Disabled," *The New York Times,* November 6, 1988.

221: This device was first used: Michael Rogers, "More Than Wheelchairs," *Newsweek,* April 24, 1989.

221: "And it's technology": ibid.

222: Chuck Thiemann: Mary Glucksman, "Out on a Limb: New Technology Will Help Amputees, Paraplegics, and Fracture Patients Keep Their Feet on the Ground," *Omni,* February 1991.

222: But "one does not have to have been a fan": Irving Kenneth Zola, "The Oration: Ageing and Disability: Toward a Unifying Agenda," *Australian Disability Review* 1, no. 3 (1988).

223: The device was designed: John Pierson, "Prosthetic Ankles Give Users Flexibility," *Wall Street Journal,* August 14, 1991.

224: Tellingly, in England: John Barry, "Silence is Golden?" *Tropic* and *Miami Herald,* September 22, 1991.

224: Fewer than 1 percent: "High-Tech Help for Hearing Loss," *U.S. News & World Report,* May 16, 1988.

226: Many, like Dwight Johnson: Dave Cravotta, "Mobility for the Masses," *Mainstream,* July 1991.

226: But the operation was so overwhelmed: John T. C. Yeh, "What Technological Developments Will Make Telecommunications Relay Services More Effective?" from Stuart N. Brotman, *Extending Telecommunications Service to Americans with Disabilities: A Report on Telecommunications Services Mandated Under the Americans with Disabilities Act of 1990,* The Annenberg Washington Program in Communications Policy Studies of Northwestern University, 1991.

226–27: Today, some thirty states: Mary Johnston, ed., *People with Disabilities Explain It All For You* (Louisville: The Advocado Press, 1992), p. 85.

227: Today, only 12 percent: Karen De Witt, "How Best to Teach the Blind: A Growing Battle Over Braille," *The New York Times,* May 12, 1991.

228: It became impossible: ibid.

228: Learning Braille: ibid.

228: These groups, like the American Foundation of the Blind: ibid.

228: Susan Spungin: "Braille Literacy Makes National News," *AFB News* 26, no. 3 (Fall 1991).

229: "A lot of parents don't want": De Witt.

230: Says Hawking: Stephen Hawking, *A Brief History of Time: From the Big Bang to Black Holes* (New York: Bantam Books, 1988), p. viii.

233: And in 1990, Congress: Johnston, p. 101.

233: Today the son: Kathleen Allen, "Helping Disabled Helps All, Trio Says," *Tucson Citizen,* September 12, 1991.

CHAPTER EIGHT: UP FROM THE NURSING HOME

250: "McMahon's personal hygiene": Richard Hoffer, "A Shot in the Arm," *Sports Illustrated,* December 2, 1991.

251: "There is a fine line": Evan J. Kemp, Jr., testimony before Senate Committee on Labor and Human Resources, July 25, 1991.

252: But although this service: *The Need for Personal Assistance,* World Institute on Disability & Rutgers University Bureau of Economic Research, 1990.

252: At least 77: Simi Litvak, et al., *Attending to America: Personal Assistance for Independent Living* (Oakland: World Institute on Disability, 1987), p. 42.

252: Estimates range: Julie Kosterlitz, "Enablement," *National Journal,* August 31, 1981.

253: "Steal from the rich": From testimony before House Committee on Government Operations, hearing on Americans with head injuries, February 19, 1992.

254: It is helpful: Gerben DeJong et al., "The Independent Living Model of Personal Assistance in National Long-term Care Policy," *Generations,* Winter 1992; Gerben DeJong and Teg

Wenker, "Attendant Care as a Prototype Independent Living Service," *Caring,* November 1983.

254: The disability rights movement consciously: Litvak et al., p. 42.

255: States, Watson says: Sara D. Watson, with Elise Lipoff, *Public Responsibility, Personal Choice: Providing Personal Assistance Services in Montana* (Washington Business Group on Health, 1991).

256: "The feeling is that there are more deserving": Jay Mathews, "Custody Battle: The Disabled Fight to Raise Their Children," *Washington Post,* August 18, 1992.

256: "For most of recorded history": Zola, p. 7.

256–57: California started: Hale Zukas et al. *Descriptive Analysis of the In-Home Supportive Services Program in California,* rev. ed. (Oakland: World Institute on Disability, 1987).

CHAPTER NINE: NO LESS WORTHY A LIFE

260: It did not matter: Jim Seeley of LIFECARE, the largest manufacturer of respirators, estimates that there are some 12,000 to 15,000 respirator users outside of hospitals. Other estimates go as high as 20,000.

263: Many quadriplegic women: Sam Maddox, *Spinal Network* (Boulder: Spinal Network, 1987), pp. 266–76; Ken Kroll and Erica Levy Klein, *Enabling Romance: A Guide to Love, Sex, and Relationships for the Disabled (and the People Who Care About Them)* (New York: Harmony Books, 1992).

271: Others died in the regime's first experiments: Robert J. Lifton, *The Nazi Doctors: Medical Killing and the Psychology of Genocide* (New York: Basic Books, 1986), p. 55.

271: Some 200,000 disabled: Hugh Gregory Gallagher, *By Trust Betrayed: Patients, Physicians, and the License to Kill in the Third Reich* (New York: Henry Holt and Company, 1990), p. xx.

271: "Lebensunwertes Leben": Lifton, p. 21.

271: As historian and psychiatrist: ibid., p. 22.

272: And he bemoaned Germany's lack: ibid., p. 23.

272: Unlike in Germany: ibid.

272: One of these was Dr. Foster Kennedy: Rita L. Marker et al., "Euthanasia: A Historical Overview," *Maryland Journal of Contemporary Legal Issues,* Summer 1991, pp. 275–76.

272: He was also the president: The Euthanasia Society of America later became the Society for the Right to Die, which in 1992 merged with another prominent right-to-die group, Concern for Dying, and was renamed Choice in Dying.

272: Writing in the: Foster Kennedy, "The Problem of Social Control of the Congenital Defective," *American Journal of Psychiatry* 99 (1942).

272: Kennedy compared this: ibid.

272: "If the panel found": ibid.

272–73: In 1972, when a Florida: Evelyn W. Lusthaus, "Involuntary Euthanasia and Current Attempts to Define Persons with Mental Retardation As Less Than Human," *Mental Retardation* 23, no. 3 (June 1985).

273: In their 1985 book: Helga Kuhse and Peter Singer, *Should the Baby Live?: The Problem of Handicapped Infants* (Oxford: Oxford University Press, 1985), preface and p. 173.

273: Asked about the ethics: Deborah Blum, "Which Experiments Are Justifiable?" *Sacramento Bee,* November 26, 1991.

273: In 1973, two doctors: Duff and A. Campbell, "Moral and Ethical Dilemmas in the Special Care Nursery," *New England Journal of Medicine* 289 (1973), pp. 890–94.

274: He was spared death: Lusthaus.

274: A California judge also ignored: *Bouvia* v. *Superior Ct.,* 179 Cal. App. 3d 1127, 225 Cal. Rptr. 297, 1986.

274: "This is a woman who still": Paul Longmore, "Urging the Handicapped to Die," *Los Angeles Times,* April 25, 1986.

274: A reporter in 1988: Myrna Oliver, "Bouvia Still Wants to Die," *Los Angeles Times,* May 23, 1988.

275: But the relationship was troubled: Margot Dougherty, "Tiring of Life Without Freedom, Quadriplegic David Rivlin Chooses to Die Among Friends," *People,* August 7, 1989.

275: "We are dealing": ibid.

275: "Death means to me": ibid.

275: In a half hour: ibid.

276: One friend said Janet Adkins: Bonnie Johnson, "A Vital Woman Chooses Death," *People,* June 25, 1990.

277: Because Michigan was one: Tamar Lewin, "Doctor Cleared of Murdering Woman with Suicide Machine," *The New York Times,* December 14, 1990.

277: Kevorkian vowed: "Death Potion No. 9," *Time,* February 1, 1993.

278: California ADAPT activist: Lillibeth Navarro, "People Don't Want a Child Like Me," *Los Angeles Times,* September 4, 1991.

278: Of the 1.6 million: From a 1990 study by the Alan Guttmacher Institute, a reproductive research and education group affiliated with Planned Parenthood Federation of America Inc., cited in "Abortion's Place in American Life," *National Journal,* May 26, 1990.

278: When told that a fetus: Tim Friend, "Abortion Is Still Leading Defense Against Defects," *USA Today,* August 1, 1989.

278–79: Proponents of legalized abortion: Michelle Fine and Adrienne Asch, "The Question of Disability: No Easy Answers for the Women's Movement," *Reproductive Rights Newsletter,* Fall 1982; Mary Steichen Calderone, "Fetuses' Right Not to Be Born," *The New York Times,* September 16, 1989.

279: Former Surgeon General C. Everett Koop: Kathleen Kerr, "Proving Their Prognosis Wrong," *Newsday,* September 2, 1990.

280: "Aborting because of our own lives": Adrienne Asch, "Real Moral Dilemmas," *Christianity and Crisis,* July 14, 1986.

280: "Many of us": Ronald Smothers, "Abortion Foes Seek Ties with Groups for Disabled," *The New York Times,* June 9, 1991.

287: "We're going to disrupt": Charles Walston, "Disabled Crowd State Offices to Protest Medicaid Policies," *Atlanta Journal and Constitution,* April 11, 1990.

287: Ten days later: Rhonda Cook, "Disabled Protesters Occupy

Governor's Office for 6 Hours," *Atlanta Journal and Constitution,*
April 21, 1990.

CHAPTER TEN: CROSSING THE LUCK LINE

295: "Along the seventy-foot wall of the ward: "Faribault: The
Institutionalized Retarded," *Minneapolis Star,* October 28, 1978.
295: That night, when he got home: ibid.
296: "They would fit in with the crowd": ibid.
298: The twenty-five-year-old Kern: From Rice County District
Court records, and Sam Newlund, "Reports Allege Abuse of
Patients at Faribault," *Minneapolis Star Tribune,* January 19,
1991.
308: Both institutions had come: David J. Rothman, *The Discovery
of the Asylum: Social Order and Disorder in the New Republic,* rev. ed.
(Boston: Little, Brown and Company, 1990).

EPILOGUE: HOW THE DISABILITY RIGHTS MOVEMENT IS CHANG-
ING AMERICA

323: The *Journal* saw it: "Down the Toilet," *Wall Street Journal,*
July 22, 1991.
326–27: But the congressional Office: "Evaluation of the Oregon
Medicaid Proposal," Congress of the United States Office of
Technology Assessment, 1992, pp. 3–30.
327: "The Americans with Disabilities Act": "Washington Prevails," *Wall Street Journal,* August 5, 1992.
328: The *New York Times:* "A Bold Medical Plan, Derailed," *New
York Times,* August 6, 1992.
329: But few people, only 18 percent: *Public Attitudes Toward People
with Disabilities,* conducted for National Organization on Disability by Louis Harris and Associates, Inc., 1991.
330: The city erected a plaque: The 1978 protesters were part of
the Denver-based Atlantis community, which, after several years
of local bus protests, would evolve into the national organization
ADAPT in July 1983.

There would be a setback for ADAPT in February 1993 when Wade Blank, the former Presbyterian minister who had marched with Martin Luther King, Jr., at Selma and who had been ADAPT's visionary founder and co-director drowned in Mexico on a family vacation, as he tried to rescue his son from a strong Pacific Ocean undertow. Blank had reached eight-year-old Lincoln, but the current then swept away father and son.

331: "You are a fire hazard": John Hockenberry, "Limited Seating on Broadway," *The New York Times,* April 13, 1992.

331: Even at National Public Radio: Mary Johnson, "The Prime of John Hockenberry: At Last, He's Mad as Hell," *The Village Voice,* August 4, 1992.

331: "And just the opposite": ibid.

332: "And you know": ibid.

Bibliography

HISTORY

Bogdan, Robert. *Freak Show: Presenting Human Oddities for Amusement and Profit.* Chicago and London: The University of Chicago Press, 1988.

Gallagher, Hugh Gregory. *FDR's Splendid Deception.* New York: Dodd, Mead & Company, 1985.

————. *By Trust Betrayed: Patients, Physicians, and the License to Kill in the Third Reich.* New York: Henry Holt and Company, 1990.

Lenihan, John. "Disabled Americans: A History." *Performance* (former magazine of The President's Committee on Employment of the Handicapped), November–December 1976/January 1977.

Levy, Chava Willig. *A People's History of the Independent Living Movement.* Lawrence, Kans.: Research and Training Center on Independent Living, University of Kansas, 1988.

Lifton, Robert J. *The Nazi Doctors: Medical Killing and the Psychology of Genocide.* New York: Basic Books, 1986.

Rothman, David J. *The Discovery of the Asylum: Social Order and Disorder in the New Republic.* Rev. ed. Boston: Little, Brown and Company, 1990.

Rothman, David J., and Sheila M. Rothman. *The Willowbrook Wars.* New York: Harper & Row, 1984.

Scotch, Richard K. *From Good Will to Civil Rights: Transforming Federal Disability Policy.* Philadelphia: Temple University Press, 1984.

SOCIOLOGY AND LAW

Goffman, Erving. *Stigma: Notes on the Management of Spoiled Identity.* New York: Touchstone, 1963.

Longmore, Paul K. "Elizabeth Bouvia, Assisted Suicide and Social Prejudice." *Issues in Law & Medicine* 3, no. 2 (1987).

Murphy, Robert F. *The Body Silent.* New York: W. W. Norton & Co., 1990.

Phillips, Marilynn J. "Damaged Goods: Oral Narratives of the Experience of Disability in American Culture." *Soc. Sci. Med.* 30, no. 8 (1990).

Sacks, Oliver. *A Leg to Stand On.* New York: Summit Books, 1984.

―――. *The Man Who Mistook His Wife for a Hat and Other Clinical Tales.* New York: Summit Books, 1985.

―――. *Awakenings.* New York: Harper Perennial, 1990.

POLICY

Berkowitz, Edward D. *Disabled Policy: America's Programs for the Handicapped.* Cambridge: Cambridge University Press, 1987.

Gartner, Alan, and Tom Joe, eds. *Images of the Disabled, Disabling Images.* New York: Praeger, 1986.

Johnson, Mary, ed. *People with Disabilities Explain It All for You.* Louisville: The Advocado Press, 1992.

Maddox, Sam. *Spinal Network.* Boulder: Spinal Network, 1987.

Ogletree et al. *Americans with Disabilities Act: Employee Rights & Employer Obligations.* New York: Matthew Bender, 1992.

Pope, Andrew M., and Alvin R. Tarlov, eds. *Disability in America: Toward a National Agenda for Prevention.* Washington, D.C.: National Academy Press, 1991.

West, Jane, ed. *The Americans with Disabilities Act: From Policy to Practice.* New York: Milbank Memorial Fund, 1991.

Zola, Irving Kenneth. "The Oration: Ageing and Disability: Toward a Unifying Agenda." *Australian Disability Review* 1, no. 3 (1988).

FICTION AND POETRY

Miller, Vassar, ed. *Despite This Flesh: The Disabled in Stories and Poems.* Austin: University of Texas Press, 1985.

Stewart, Jean. *The Body's Memory.* New York: St. Martin's Press, 1989.

Zola, Irving Kenneth, ed. *Ordinary Lives: Voices of Disability & Disease.* Cambridge, Massachusetts: Applewood Books, 1982.

MEMOIRS

Beisser, Arnold. *Flying Without Wings: Personal Reflections on Being Disabled.* New York: Doubleday, 1989.

Callahan, John. *Don't Worry, He Won't Get Far on Foot.* New York: Vintage Books, 1990.

Dickenson, Mollie. *Thumbs Up: The Jim Brady Story.* New York: William Morrow and Company, 1987.

Finger, Anne. *Past Due: A Story of Disability, Pregnancy and Birth.* Seattle: Seal Press, 1990.

Kovic, Ron. *Born on the Fourth of July.* New York: Pocket Books, 1976.

Mathews, Jay. *A Mother's Touch: The Tiffany Callo Story.* New York: Henry Holt and Company, 1992.

Milam, Lorenzo Wilson. *The Cripple Liberation Front Marching Band Blues.* San Diego: Mho & Mho Works, 1984.

Puller, Lewis B., Jr. *Fortunate Son: The Autobiography of Lewis B. Puller, Jr.* New York: Grove/Weidenfeld, 1991.

Thompson, Karen, and Julie Andrzejewski. *Why Can't Sharon Kowalski Come Home?* San Francisco: Spinsters/Aunt Lute, 1988.

Zola, Irving Kenneth. *Missing Pieces.* Philadelphia: Temple University Press, 1982.

DEAF

Bell, Alexander Graham. *Memoir Upon the Formation of a Deaf Variety of the Human Race.* 1883, reprinted by the Alexander Graham Bell Association for the Deaf, 1969.

Gannon, Jack R. *The Week the World Heard Gallaudet.* Washington, D.C.: Gallaudet University Press, 1989.

Groce, Nora Ellen. *Everyone Here Spoke Sign Language: Hereditary Deafness on Martha's Vineyard.* Cambridge, Massachusetts: Harvard University Press, 1985.

Jacobs, Leo M. *A Deaf Adult Speaks Out.* 3rd ed., revised and expanded. Washington, D.C.: Gallaudet University Press, 1989.

Kisor, Henry. *What's That Pig Outdoors?: A Memoir of Deafness.* New York: Hill and Wang, 1990.

Lane, Harlan. *When the Mind Hears: A History of the Deaf.* New York: Random House, 1984.

————. *The Mask of Benevolence: Disabling the Deaf Community.* New York: Alfred A. Knopf, 1992.

Moore, Matthew S., and Linda Levitan. *For Hearing People Only: Answers to Some of the Most Commonly Asked Questions About the Deaf Community, Its Culture, and the "Deaf Reality".* Rochester: Deaf Life Press, 1992.

Neisser, Arden. *The Other Side of Silence: Sign Language and the Deaf Community in America.* New York: Alfred A. Knopf, 1983.

Padden, Carol, and Tom Humphries. *Deaf in America: Voices from a Culture.* Cambridge, Massachusetts: Harvard University Press, 1988.

Sacks, Oliver. *Seeing Voices: A Journey into the World of the Deaf.* Berkeley and Los Angeles: University of California Press, 1989.

Wright, David. *Deafness: A Personal Account.* London: Farber and Farber, 1990.

DEVELOPMENTAL DISABILITY

Blatt, Burton, and Fred Kaplan. *Christmas in Purgatory: A Photographic Essay on Mental Retardation.* Boston: Allyn and Bacon, 1966.
Mount, Beth, and Kay Zwernik. *It's Never Too Early, It's Never Too Late: A Booklet About Personal Futures Planning.* Minnesota Governor's Planning Council on Developmental Disabilities, 1989.
Perske, Robert. *Unequal Justice?: What Can Happen When Persons with Retardation or Other Developmental Disabilities Encounter the Criminal Justice System.* Nashville: Abingdon Press, 1991.
Scheerenberger, R. C. *A History of Mental Retardation.* Baltimore: Paul H. Brookes Publishing, 1983.

AUTISM

Grandin, Temple. *Emergence: Labeled Autistic.* Novato, California: Arena Press, 1986.
Hart, Charles. *Without Reason: A Family Copes with Two Generations of Autism.* New York: Harper & Row, 1989.
Williams, Donna. *Nobody Nowhere: The Extraordinary Autobiography of an Autistic.* New York: Times Books, 1992.

DOCUMENTS

National Council on the Handicapped. "Toward Independence: An Assessment of Federal Laws and Programs Affecting Persons with Disabilities—with Legislative Recommendations." 1986.
———. "On the Threshold of Independence." January 1988.
United States Commission on Civil Rights. "Accommodating the Spectrum of Individual Abilities." September 1983.

POLLS

The ICD Survey of Disabled Americans: Bringing Disabled Americans into the Mainstream. Conducted for ICD-International Center for the Disabled, and the National Council on the Handicapped by Louis Harris and Associates, Inc., March 1986.

The ICD Survey II: Employing Disabled Americans. Conducted for
ICD-International Center for the Disabled, the National Council
on the Handicapped, and the President's Committee on Employment of the Handicapped by Louis Harris and Associates, Inc.,
March 1987.

Public Attitudes Toward People with Disabilities. Conducted for National Organization on Disability by Louis Harris and Associates, Inc., 1991.

Index

ABOUT THE AUTHOR

JOSEPH P. SHAPIRO writes about social policy issues for *U.S. News & World Report.* He used an Alicia Patterson Foundation fellowship to study the disability rights movement. His prize-winning stories on disability subjects have appeared in *U.S. News & World Report, The Washington Post, The Progressive, The Disability Rag,* and numerous other publications.